Adirondack Mountain Club

Catskills Trails

Fourth Edition
Forest Preserve Series (4th ed.), Volume 6

Editors, Carol and David White

Adirondack Mountain Club, Inc.
Lake George, New York

Copyright © 2013 by Adirondack Mountain Club, Inc.
All rights reserved
Cover photograph Sunset Rock, by Hardie Truesdale
Other photographs by James Appleyard, James Bullard, Bill Chriswell, Joan Dean, Joanne Hihn, Ann Hough, David Hough, Mark Meschinelli, Mark Schaefer, Moonray Schepart, Hardie Truesdale, Henning Vahlenkamp, Tony Versandi, Alan Via, and David White

Maps by Therese S. Brosseau
Overview map by Forest Glen Enterprises; redesigned by Therese S. Brosseau
Hiking boots illustration by Colette Piasecki-Masters
Design by Ann Hough
First edition 1988. Second edition 1994. Third edition 2005. Fourth edition 2013.

Published by the Adirondack Mountain Club, Inc.
814 Goggins Road, Lake George, NY 12845-4117
www.adk.org

The Adirondack Mountain Club is dedicated to the protection and responsible recreational use of the New York State Forest Preserve and other parks, wild lands, and waters, vital to our members and chapters. The Club, founded in 1922, is a member-directed organization committed to public service and stewardship. ADK employs a balanced approach to outdoor recreation, advocacy, environmental education, and natural resource conservation.

ADK encourages the involvement of all people in its mission and activities; its goal is to be a community that is comfortable, inviting, and accessible.

Library of Congress Cataloging-in-Publication Data

Adirondack Mountain Club Catskill trails / editors, Carol and David White. -- Fourth edition
  pages cm. -- (Forest preserve series ; volume 6)
Includes bibliographical references and index.
  ISBN 978-0-9896073-0-8 (guidebook alone : alk. paper) -- ISBN 978-0-9896073-1-5 (catskill trails guide & map pack : alk. paper) 1. Hiking--New York (State)--Catskill Mountains--Guidebooks. 2. Trails--New York (State)--Catskill Mountains--Guidebooks. 3. Catskill Mountains (N.Y.)--Guidebooks. I. White, Carol, 1940- II. White, David, 1944-
  GV199.42.N652C3717 2013
  796.5209747'38--dc23
                              2013001352

ISBN 978-0-9896073-0-8   Printed in the United States of America
25 24 23 22 21 20 19 18 17 16 15 14 13   1 2 3 4 5 6 7 8 9 10

Dedication

We dedicate this guidebook to the resilient and compassionate people of the Catskill Forest Preserve, who in the aftermath of Tropical Storm Irene literally moved mountains to give help to their regional neighbors. Thanks to Herculean efforts of countless volunteers, civic and charitable organizations, and dedicated professionals, the region not only rebounded but came to know the true meaning of love thy neighbor.

Let us also remember the forest ranger. Since 1885, when the ranger force was created with the establishment of the Forest Preserve, rangers have protected both the forests of the state and the people who use them. It has been a job well done.

Every hiker meets a forest ranger sooner or later, and it is a memorable encounter. Helpful information may be exchanged in a friendly conversation on the trail. Or the ranger may be acting as an educator, speaking to your organization on a topic of common concern. Perhaps the ranger descends out of the sky from a helicopter to provide assistance to an injured hiker. The ranger may be on patrol, fighting a fire, catching up on paperwork, or providing essential information to guidebook editors about changes in the forests and trails.

In all cases, the hiker has come to expect a helpful attitude, a quiet professional competence, and a sense of dedication from the person wearing the forest ranger shoulder patch.

—*Carol and David White*

WE WELCOME YOUR COMMENTS

Use of information in this book is at the sole discretion and risk of the hiker. ADK, and its authors and editors, makes every effort to keep our guidebooks up-to-date; however, trail conditions are always changing.

In addition to reviewing the material in this book, hikers should assess their ability, physical condition, and preparation, as well as likely weather conditions, before a trip. For more information on preparation, equipment, and how to address emergencies, see the introduction.

If you note a discrepancy in this book or wish to forward a suggestion, we welcome your comments. Please cite book title, year of most recent copyright and printing (see copyright page), trail, page number, and date of your observation. Thanks for your help!

Please address your comments to:
Publications
Adirondack Mountain Club
814 Goggins Road
Lake George, NY 12845-4117
518-668-4447
pubs@adk.org

24-HOUR EMERGENCY CONTACTS
In-town and roadside: **911**
See page 23 for information on contacting regional DEC rangers and other emergency personnel.

Contents

Overview Map	7
Preface	9
Introduction	11
Black Dome Valley–Northern Escarpment Section	27
Palenville, North-South Lake Section	45
Platte Clove Section	67
Stony Clove Section	87
Lexington to Shandaken Section	101
Woodstock-Shandaken Section	115
Peekamoose Section	131
Big Indian–Pine Hill to Denning Section	145
Prattsville to Arkville Section	169
Arkville to Seager Section	177
Delaware Wild Forest Section	193
Beaver Kill–Willowemoc Creek Section	215
Extended and Challenging Opportunities	231
Appendices	235
I. Glossary of Terms	235
II. Catskill 100 Highest Peaks List	237
III. State Campgrounds and Day Use Areas in the Catskill Park	241
About the Editors	242
Adirondack Mountain Club	243
Index	245

ROUTE GUIDES AND MAPS

Big Hollow Rd. Route Guide and Map 29
Palenville, North-South Lake Route Guide and Map 47
Platte Clove Map and Route Guide 68
Stony Clove Route Guide and Map 89
Lexington to Shandaken Route Guide 102
Spruceton Rd. Route Guide 102
Lexington to Shandaken and Spruceton Rd. Map 104
Woodstock-Shandaken Route Guide and Map 116
Peekamoose Rd. Route Guide and Map 132
Big Indian–Pine Hill to Denning Route Guide and Map 147
Prattsville to Arkville Route Guide and Map 170
Arkville to Seager Route Guide and Map 178
Kelly Hollow Ski Trail Map 191
Margaretville–NY 206 Route Guide 195
Beaver Kill Rd.–Quaker Clearing Route Guide 195
Margaretville–NY 206, Beaver Kill Rd., and Livingston Manor to Claryville Map 216
Livingston Manor to Claryville Route Guide 218
Frick Pond Loop Map 226

Note: This guidebook is specially designed to be used with the National Geographic Trails Illustrated Map 755 of the Catskill Park. This guidebook can also be used with the New York–New Jersey Trail Conference's six-part topographic map set of the trails of the Catskill Forest Preserve. Maps may be purchased from ADK.

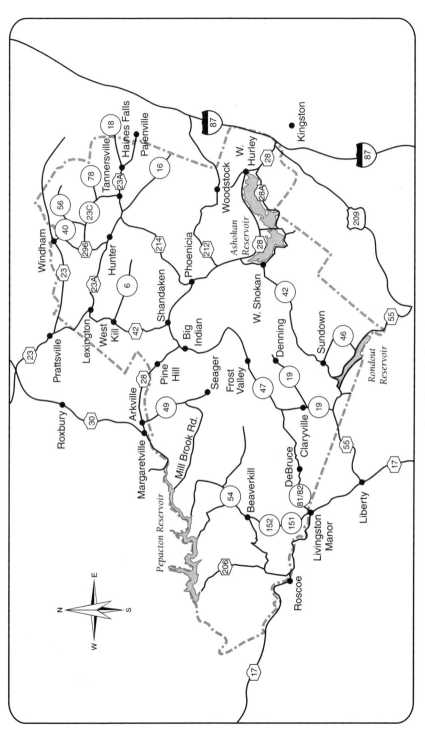

Catskill Park Overview

Contents 7

View from Sugarloaf. Hardie Truesdale

Preface

The first two editions of Catskill Trails were written by Bruce Wadsworth and the Schenectady Chapter of the Adirondack Mountain Club. Much assistance was provided by personnel of the New York State Department of Environmental Conservation (DEC), especially Bill Rudge.

From October 2001 to June 2003, we measured 350 miles of Catskill Forest Preserve trails by surveying wheel to achieve precise accuracy for the third edition. The guidebook is updated more regularly than DEC updates its trail signs, so is the more reliable source of distance information.

The measuring process brought about a review of each trail description in this guidebook. The book was substantially rewritten to offer more detail along the trails. The editors, having written ADK's *Catskill Day Hikes for All Seasons*, are alert to the task of seeing the trails with fresh eyes and writing about them as clearly and accurately as possible.

This fourth edition is coordinated with Trails Illustrated Map 755, which includes the entire Catskill Park on two sides of one map. Trails or sections of trails are numbered on the map to match this edition. The trails in the book are renumbered and re-sequenced to be more useful. Lower-numbered trails are on the eastern side of the map and higher-numbered trails are on the western side. Trailless peaks are assigned a number, even though those numbers are not pictured on the map. Longer trails such as the Escarpment Trail and the Devil's Path, which are in multiple sections, are placed in sequence for easier comprehension; they are also recapped in the opposite direction. Trails are also divided to assist the day-trip hiker in planning the day's itinerary. Each trail description lists the map coordinates of both Map 755 and the tenth edition of the New York–New Jersey Trail Conference maps.

We especially appreciate the meticulous attention and diligent communication provided by Lisa Metzger to make this edition even more useful to the hiker and as error-free as is humanly possible.

—*Carol and David White*
Clinton, New York

May 16, 2013

North-South Lakes and Hudson Valley from North Point. David White

Introduction

The Adirondack Mountain Club Forest Preserve Series

The Forest Preserve Series of guides to Adirondack and Catskill trails covers hiking opportunities on the approximately 2.5 million acres of Forest Preserve (public) land within the Adirondack Park and nearly 300,000 acres in the Catskill Park. The Adirondack Mountain Club (ADK) published its first guidebook, covering the High Peaks and parts of the Northville-Placid Trail, in 1934. In the early 1980s, coinciding with the decade-long centennial celebration of the enactment of the Forest Preserve legislation in 1885, ADK set out to achieve its long-time goal of completing a series of guides that would cover the two parks. This series now includes the following guidebooks:

1 Adirondack Mountain Club High Peaks Trails
2 Adirondack Mountain Club Eastern Trails
3 Adirondack Mountain Club Central Trails
4 Adirondack Mountain Club Western Trails
5 Adirondack Mountain Club Northville–Placid Trail
6 Adirondack Mountain Club Catskill Trails

The public lands that constitute the Forest Preserve are unique among all other wild public lands in the United States because they enjoy constitutional protection against sale or development. The story of this unique protection begins in the 1800s and continues today as groups such as ADK strive to guard it. This responsibility also rests with the public, who are expected not to degrade the Forest Preserve in any way while enjoying its wonders. The Forest Preserve Series of trail guides seeks not only to show hikers, skiers, and snowshoers where to enjoy their activities, but also to offer guidelines whereby users can minimize their impact on the land.

THE CATSKILLS

Aboard the *Half Moon* in September 1609, Hendrick Hudson must have been impressed as he watched the sun fall behind the mountains to the west. His vantage point on the Hudson River gave a commanding view. Gazing upward, he admired what Henry Rowe Schoolcraft called Ontiora, the "Mountains of the Sky." To the Dutch, they became the Katts Kills, but nobody is quite sure why. In Dutch, the word kill means "stream." A Dutch ship, christened *The Kat*, voyaged up the Hudson shortly before the term appeared. Some believe a creek was named after Jacob Cats, a well-known poet, magistrate, and keeper of the Great Seal of Holland during that period.

For a time, the mountains were known as the Blue (Blew) Mountains. John Burroughs thought it would be more fitting to call them the Birch Mountains, since this tree is so common there. They were once the Hooge Landt van Esopus, the Lothian Hills, the Blauwbergen, or the Katzbergs. Today, they are the Catskill Mountains, although geologically they are not mountains but an eroded plateau. Over millions of years, erosion gouged out the characteristic cloves and notches; the remaining plateau forms structures that outwardly resemble mountains. True mountain ranges have tilted or folded rock, whereas the almost horizontal rock layers in the Catskills are proof that the uplift was uniform. Catskill ranges and valleys generally run southeast to northwest.

The Great Wall of Manitou, as it was called by Native Americans, forms the eastern scarp of the region, rising 1600 feet above the Hudson Valley. The slopes peter out to hills in the west, so the Catskills are said to be mountains with only one side. Catskill historian Alf Evers asked an old man where the Catskills began. The answer was, you keep on going until "there are two stones for every dirt." Evers quotes his son, Christopher, as saying, "They used to say that for six days the Lord labored at creating the Earth and on the seventh he threw rocks at the Catskills."

Catskill trails tend to be firm and dry. Catskill shale and sandstones readily accept water between or in their layers, resulting in underground aquifers rather than the lakes lying on the impervious rocks of the Adirondacks and throughout New England. Adirondack and New England mountain ranges, running southwest to northeast, were affected far more significantly by glaciation than were the Catskills. Consequently there are few naturally formed lakes in the Catskills, and relatively few other glacial formations. The glacial melt-waters did cause rapid erosion of the shale layers, forming the many waterfalls seen today throughout the Catskill vales wherever more resistant sandstone or siltstone layers slowed the process.

Native Americans feared the land on the Great Wall of Manitou, behind which the evil spirit Mitchie Manitou lurked to defend against human spirits. The region reminded the Dutch and Palatine Germans of the deep, forbidding forests of Europe. They, too, avoided going into it. Colonial land survey records show that 20 percent of the original Catskill forest was hemlock—dark hemlock whose shadows hid the wildcats that screamed in the night. Behind that steep wall lived the Devil himself, evidenced by names like the Devil's Path, Devil's Kitchen, Devil's Pulpit, Devil's Tombstone, and Hell Falls. Transforming old legends from Europe, blending in Indian stories and weaving their own tales, colonists developed a deep fear of these mountains.

The Dutch sought the rich bottomlands around the steeper slopes. The Palatine Germans left the Hudson and settled the Schoharie Valley in the west. When the English changed New Amsterdam to New York, a century after Hudson had explored the great river, they were after tall timbers for the masts of the king's navy ships. A prosperous Kingston merchant, Johannis Hardenbergh, managed to be granted a 1.5-million-acre land patent in 1708. It essentially included the whole of the Catskill Mountains. Years of legal battles chipped off pieces as the Livingstons, Cornelius Cool, the Hurleys, and others gouged out their fiefdoms. Homesteaders were enticed to rent the deeper valleys. The hated Colonial Whig absentee landlords found that English promises of free land made Tories of many of their Dutch tenants during the American Revolution. The Mohawk Chief Joseph Brant was quite selective in whom he ordered his tribesmen to kill or capture.

Once the American Revolution ended, the attack on the Catskills by outside interests began in earnest. The targets were trees. Landlords reserved trees above a certain diameter for their own use. Landlords required tenants to transport specific amounts of lumber to mills as part of their yearly obligations. One species of tree, *Tsuga canadensis*, the Eastern hemlock, became more prized than all others. Tannin was needed for tanning leather, and the hemlock's bark had a rich supply. By 1816, when Colonel William Edwards came to the Catskills, there were at least seventy-five tanneries in the mountains.

These small tanneries wounded, but did not slay, the forest. Colonel Edwards, backed by New York City money, established in Hunter on the Schoharieskill a tannery of such scope that it soon not only drove the small tanners out of business, but also changed the character of the Catskills forever. Colonel Pratt did the same thing a few years later, in Prattsville. Whole hemlock groves disappeared, letting in the sunlight and drying out the earth to foster conditions more appropriate for birch, oak, and maple. Acids from the tanneries polluted the streams, but there was prosperity until the hemlock was gone. Over a century later, there is again pressure to cut these great slopes, now protected in the Forest Preserve, even though 85 percent of the forests within the Catskill Park are on private lands.

The nineteenth century brought the world to the Catskills. Several forces simultaneously converged to make the Catskills famous. In 1819, Washington Irving wrote *The Sketchbook of Geoffrey Crayon, Gent.*, and the world was introduced to Rip Van Winkle. That delightful character from the Village of Falling Waters (Palenville) went off to South Mountain and, after bowling a bit with the ghosts of Henry Hudson's crew, slept for twenty years.

Then there was Thomas Cole. There had been other painters of the Catskills before Cole—notably Van Berganin in the 1730s, P. Lodet in the 1790s, John Vanderlyn in the early 1800s—but it was about Cole that John Trumbull, the recognized leader in American art in this period, said, "This youth has done what I have all my life attempted in vain!" Cole, a romantic realist, was the first person in what came to be known as the Hudson River School of landscape painting.

Steamboats now brought vacationers upriver from New York City. Railroads began to penetrate the valleys. Grand hotels such as the Overlook Mountain House, Catskill Mountain House, Hotel Kaaterskill, Grand Hotel, Tremper House, and Rexmere hosted the elite of the United States and Europe.

The Forest Preserve was created on May 15, 1885, to protect the state's water resources. The Catskill portion of the preserve included "all the lands now owned or which may hereafter be acquired by the State of New York" in Greene, Sullivan, and Ulster counties. Delaware County was added to the list in 1888. The Catskill Park was created in 1904. Its boundaries encompassed the Forest Preserve land and some of the private lands in the four counties named above.

Then came World War I, automobiles, airplanes, and new vacation meccas around the world. Like Rip Van Winkle, the Catskills slept (except for the Sullivan County resorts such as Grossinger's and the Concord, which are outside the Catskill Park). The best of the mountains was protected by the Forest Preserve, but little else developed in an organized manner until the Catskill Center for Conservation and Development formed in 1969, followed by the creation of the Temporary State Commission to Study the Catskills by the state legislature in 1971. The commission was charged to study over 6000 square miles of Catskills in the counties of Greene, Delaware, Otsego, Schoharie, Sullivan, and Ulster, plus the townships of Berne, Coeymans, Knox, New Scotland, Rensselaerville, and Westerlo in Albany County.

The commission reported its findings in 1975, and the Catskill Park State Land Master Plan was released in 1985. The implementation of unit management plans by DEC has resulted in many new trails. The great resources and cultural heritage of the Catskill region are once again receiving the critical attention needed to preserve them for the future.

The year 2004 marked the one hundredth anniversary of the Catskill Park, which embraces over 700,000 acres, of which almost 300,000 acres are state-owned land known as the Catskill Preserve.

USING THIS GUIDEBOOK
The trails described in this book are, for the most part, within the Blue Line of the Catskill Park. Principal highways in the region are NY 30, NY 23 and 23A, NY 28, NY 42, NY 212, and NY 214. Interstate 87 in the east, Interstate 88 in the west, Interstate 86/NY 17 in the south, and NY 32 in the north are used by motorists to reach the region. (See map p. 7.)

An extensive network of roads into the larger valleys and cloves makes day trips feasible for most Catskill outings. This book is designed to accommodate the day-tripper. The organization of the book is built around major valleys and their road networks. Each section has one or more Route Guides for roads that lead to trailheads; sections also have a map to be used with the Route Guide to assist with locating the trailheads. Since one of the most difficult problems in the Catskills is determining trailhead access, this system will greatly simplify planning for hikers.

Like all the volumes in the Adirondack Mountain Club's Forest Preserve Series, this book is intended to be both a reference tool for planning trips and a field guide to carry on the trail. All introductory material should be read carefully; it contains important information regarding current camping and hiking regulations as well as numerous suggestions for safe and proper travel on foot. The introductions to each of the sections will give hikers an idea of the varied opportunities available to them.

NEW YORK CITY WATER SUPPLY LANDS

New York City owns and manages, through the NYC Department of Environmental Protection (DEP), more than 64,000 acres of land and reservoirs within the Catskill Park. The majority of this land is open for public recreation.

Generally, DEP has two types of public access: lands where hiking, fishing, hunting, and trapping are allowed with a DEP Access Permit (marked with "Recreation by Permit" signs); and lands that are open without the need for a permit (marked by "Public Access Area" signs). DEP lands that are open to the public are indicated on the National Geographic Trails Illustrated Map 755, Catskill Park.

More information about recreational uses of NYC-owned land and how to obtain a DEP Access Permit can be found at www.nyc.gov/html/dep (select "Watershed Protection") or by calling 800-575-LAND.

ABBREVIATIONS AND CONVENTIONS

In each book in the Forest Preserve Series, R and L, with periods omitted, are used for right and left. The R and L banks of a stream are determined by looking downstream. Likewise, the R fork of a stream is on the R when one faces downstream. N, S, E, and W, again without periods, are used for north, south, east, and west. Compass bearings are given in degrees. N is 0 degrees, E is 90 degrees, S is 180 degrees, and W is 270 degrees. The following abbreviations are used in the text and on the maps:

ADK	Adirondack Mountain Club
DEC	New York State Department of Environmental Conservation
PBM	Permanent Bench Mark
USGS	United States Geological Survey
CR	County Route
ft	feet
jct.	junction
km	kilometer or kilometers
m	meter or meters
mi	mile or miles
yd	yard or yards

MAPS

Every guidebook in this series matches trail information provided on National Geographic Trails Illustrated maps covering the Catskill and Adirondack Parks. This book also includes map coordinates for the New York–New Jersey Trail Conference Catskill Trails map set.

The National Geographic maps are large-format, two-sided, folding, waterproof maps. They were created in partnership with ADK. Together the guides and maps are vital hiking tools, the latter also serving as road maps within the

Introduction 15

LEAVE NO TRACE

ADK supports the seven principles of the Leave No Trace program:

1. Plan Ahead and Prepare
Know the regulations and special considerations for the area you'll visit.
Prepare for extreme weather, hazards, and emergencies.
Travel in groups of less than ten people to minimize impacts.

2. Travel and Camp on Durable Surfaces
Hike in the middle of the trail; stay off of vegetation.
Camp in designated sites where possible.
In other areas, don't camp within 150 feet of water or a trail.

3. Dispose of Waste Properly
Pack out all trash (including toilet paper), leftover food, and litter.
Use existing privies, or dig a cat hole five to six inches deep, then cover hole.
Wash yourself and dishes at least 150 feet from water.

4. Leave What You Find
Leave rocks, plants, and other natural objects as you find them.
Let photos, drawings, or journals help to capture your memories.
Do not build structures or furniture or dig trenches.

5. Minimize Campfire Impacts
Use a portable stove to avoid the lasting impact of a campfire.
Where fires are permitted, use existing fire rings and only collect downed wood.
Burn all fires to ash, put out campfires completely, then hide traces of fire.

6. Respect Wildlife
Observe wildlife from a distance.
Avoid wildlife during mating, nesting, and other sensitive times.
Control pets at all times, and clean up after them.

7. Be Considerate of Other Visitors
Respect other visitors and protect the quality of their experience.
Let natural sounds prevail; avoid loud sounds and voices.
Be courteous and yield to other users on the trail.

For further information on Leave No Trace principles log on to www.lnt.org.

Catskill and Adirondack Parks. The following list identifies each map and the Forest Preserve Series guide to which it corresponds. All are available from ADK.

ADK Guide	Trails Illustrated Map
Catskill Trails	755 Catskill Park
Adirondack High Peaks Trails	742 Lake Placid/High Peaks
	746 Saranac/Paul Smiths
Adirondack Eastern Trails	743 Lake George/Great Sacandaga
Adirondack Central Trails	744 Northville/Raquette Lake
Adirondack Western Trails	745 Old Forge/Oswegatchie
	746 Saranac/Paul Smiths
Northville–Placid Trail	744 Northville/Raquette Lake
	742 Lake Placid/High Peaks

These maps are letter-number coded, with letters running up and down the right and left borders, and numbers running horizontally along the top and bottom. Each trail's coordinate appears with the corresponding description in this book (sample coordinate: A4), and each trail is numbered on the map and in the book. These numbers are not used on any signs on the trails.

All of the maps discussed in the preceding are available from ADK. Other maps, guidebooks, and information also can be obtained from ADK's Member Services Center in Lake George and the High Peaks Information Center on ADK's Heart Lake Property near Lake Placid.

TRAILLESS PEAKS

Trailless peaks are included in this guide and a few of them have old woods roads or informal paths to follow. Hikers should not expect these to be in as good condition as the maintained trails. Most of the trailless peaks are pure bushwhacks and although frequently used approaches are described, good map navigation skills and thorough planning are essential. Sometimes there are herd paths, which may or may not lead to the desired destination.

Reaching the summit of a trailless peak presents a different kind of challenge than following a marked trail to a mountain summit. It is always a good idea to purchase the larger-scale USGS 7.5-minute series topographic maps for off-trail use. The greater topographic detail of these maps can add a significant degree of safety and enjoyment to bushwhack outings.

The hiker must be able to read a map, use a compass, and possess that all-too-rare commodity, common sense. When you are picking your way through cripplebush, trying to set a steady course, and swatting blackflies all at the same time, there can be considerable psychological strain. It always seems you've walked farther than you actually have, so when a checkpoint isn't hit at the estimated time, it's easy to second guess yourself. A significant mental error, an injury, a sudden change in the weather, or any unforeseen event can result in an unexpected night in the woods.

CELL PHONES
Cell phones should not be relied upon in case of emergency. Despite several highly publicized stories, their use in the backcountry is limited by terrain, distance from communication towers, and other factors. Those who carry them should, out of consideration for their fellow hikers, use them only when necessary—and should have alternative plans for handling emergencies in case they do not operate.

Consequently, while off-trail hiking is probably the most satisfying outdoor adventure, one should ease into it. Learn from experienced people, have planned escape routes in mind, and be sure someone at home knows where you are hiking and what to do to get help if you don't return by a given time.

Trail access points and general routes of ascent for those trailless Catskill mountains over 3500 ft in elevation are given in this guidebook. Estimated distances and specific routes have intentionally not been given. If you cannot determine a good line of ascent and make a fair estimate of the distance, you are not ready for off-trail hiking. Being able to set your own course and then demonstrate that you can successfully reach your destination is one of the primary satisfactions of bushwhack experiences.

The Catskill 3500 Club has placed canisters on the summits of those trailless peaks over 3500 ft in elevation. The canisters mark the true summits and contain notebooks for the recording of ascents.

Select your party members carefully. The group should be small to reduce impact on the land. Be sure each individual is up to the challenges of the outing. Stick together on the mountain. Carry extra clothing and food. Determine your ascent and descent routes and write in compass bearings in the comfort of home rather than at the top of a windswept mountain in the rain.

TRAIL SIGNS AND MARKERS
Marked and maintained DEC trails normally have trail signs at the trailhead and at major junctions. Mileage in this guidebook may differ from DEC mileage on trail signs; this guidebook is updated more frequently than the signs and should be considered more reliable.

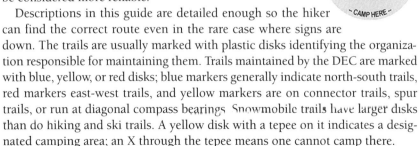

Descriptions in this guide are detailed enough so the hiker can find the correct route even in the rare case where signs are down. The trails are usually marked with plastic disks identifying the organization responsible for maintaining them. Trails maintained by the DEC are marked with blue, yellow, or red disks; blue markers generally indicate north-south trails, red markers east-west trails, and yellow markers are on connector trails, spur trails, or run at diagonal compass bearings. Snowmobile trails have larger disks than do hiking and ski trails. A yellow disk with a tepee on it indicates a designated camping area; an X through the tepee means one cannot camp there.

The amount of use makes some trails easier to follow than others. Each hiker must remain alert for changes of direction. Group leaders have a responsibility not to let inexperienced members of the party travel by themselves. A trail that seems obvious to a more experienced person may not be obvious at all to an inexperienced member of the group. All hikers should carry a map and compass and know at least the basics of their use. A compass can be an indispensable aid in the unlikely event that you lose your way.

All trails described in this guide are on public land or on public rights-of-way that cross private land. There may be "posted" signs at some points; these are usually there to remind hikers that they are on private land over which the owner has kindly granted permission for hikers to pass. In most cases, leaving the trail, camping, fishing, and hunting are not permitted on these lands.

DISTANCE AND TIME

Trails in this guidebook have been measured with a professional surveyor's wheel. Distances are expressed to the nearest tenth, and in some cases hundredth, of a mile. Shorter distances are expressed as yards, and the number of yards has usually been derived from a wheel measurement in the field. In cases where there is disagreement between a trail sign and the guide's stated distance, the latter can be assumed correct. DEC has been informed of these discrepancies.

At the start of each section of this guide, there is a list of trails in the region, the mileage unique to the trail, and the page on which the trail description begins. All mileages given in the trail description are cumulative, the beginning of the trail being the 0.0-mile point. A distance summary is given at the end of each description, with a total distance expressed in kilometers as well as in miles. If a trail has climbed significantly over its course, its total ascent in both feet and meters is provided.

To the inexperienced hiker, distances are likely to seem longer on the trail, depending on the weight of the pack, the time of day, and the frequency and degree of ascents and descents. He or she will quickly learn that there is a significant difference between "sidewalk miles" and "trail miles."

No attempt has been made to estimate travel time for these trails. A conservative rule to follow in estimating time is to allow an hour for every one and one-half miles, plus one half hour for each one thousand feet of ascent, letting experience indicate how close the individual hiker is to this standard. Most day-hikers will probably go a little faster than this, but backpackers will probably find they go somewhat slower. Some quickening of pace usually occurs when descending, though this may not be true on steep descents.

WINTER HIKING

Many Catskill trails have steep, rocky ascents and ledges. Great care is needed. Instep or full crampons should always be in your pack after first frost. There are also newer products such as STABILicers™ and MICROspikes® that may suffice. (Catskill 3500 Club hikes require full crampons.) Ski poles are another useful piece of winter equipment. Always have a good flashlight. Get an early start be-

> **TRAIL MARKERS**
> It should go without saying that one should never remove any sign or marker. Hikers noticing damaged, missing, or incorrect signs should report this fact to DEC, Region 3 Headquarters, 21 S. Putt Corners Rd., New Paltz, NY 12561 for Sullivan or Ulster counties; or DEC, Region 4 Sub-office, 65561 State Highway 10, Suite 1, Stamford, NY 12167 for Delaware and Greene counties.

cause nightfall comes early.

Sudden weather changes can rapidly create hypothermic conditions, most common between 30 and 50 degrees, for the unprepared. Cotton clothing should never be worn in winter because when wet it clings to the body, does not dry, and is cold. Wool, if wet, remains warm. Best is polypropylene, capilene, or polar fleece clothing that wicks away sweat and is quick-drying. Wind protection such as breathable GORE-TEX™ should be carried. A down vest is a good, warm, intermediate layer, but remember that if down becomes wet it is useless.

Energy output is higher and heat control becomes a major concern while winter hiking. Drink plenty of water and eat high-energy food regularly. Snowshoes and boots add greatly to the weight lifted with each step. Daylight hours are shortened, so good planning is essential. The price for error is much higher in winter than in summer. Go on trips with experienced winter hikers before heading your own party.

Your vehicle should be in good operating condition. Many Catskill trailheads are at isolated places where a breakdown is no joke in winter. Be sure you have a full tank of gas, a shovel, and a well-charged battery. A sleeping bag and extra food are also good things to have available.

Excellent books are available on winter hiking and camping. ADK's *Winterwise: A Backpacker's Guide* by John Dunn is a good starting point. The mountains are great in the winter, but you must know what you are doing.

DAY HIKING AND WILDERNESS CAMPING

It is not the purpose of this series to teach one how to hike or camp. The information below should, however, serve to make hikers aware of the differences and peculiarities of the Catskills while giving strong emphasis to currently recommended procedures for reducing environmental damage—particularly in heavily used areas. Users who intend to hike or camp for the first time are urged to consult a current book on the subject, attend one of the many workshops or training sessions available, or at least join a group led by someone with experience.

There are no huts in the Catskills for public use, such as are common in the White Mountains of New Hampshire. There are many lean-tos at convenient locations along trails and also many possibilities for tenting. The regulations regarding tenting and the use of lean-tos are simple and unrestrictive compared to those of other popular backpacking areas in this country and Canada. It is important that every backpacker know and obey the restrictions that do exist, because they are designed to promote the long-term enjoyment and protection of the resource.

Listed below are some of the most important Forest Preserve regulations, many of which pertain to day-hikers as well. These can also be found at www.dec.ny.gov. Complete regulations are available from the DEC and are posted at most trail access points.

- Except where marked by a "Camp Here" disk, camping is prohibited within 150 feet of roads, trails, lakes, ponds, streams, or other bodies of water.
- Groups of ten or more campers or stays of more than three days in one place require a permit from the New York State forest ranger responsible for the area.
- Lean-tos are available in many areas on a first-come, first-served basis. Lean-tos cannot be used exclusively and must be shared with other campers.
- Use pit privies provided near popular camping areas and trailheads. If none are available, dispose of human waste by digging a hole six to eight inches deep at least 150 feet from water or campsites. Cover with leaves and soil.
- Do not use soap to wash yourself, clothing, or dishes within 150 feet of water.
- Fires should be built in existing fire pits or fireplaces if provided. Use only dead and down wood for fires. Cutting standing trees is prohibited. Extinguish all fires with water and stir ashes until they are cold to the touch. Do not build fires in areas marked by a "No Fires" disk or sign. Camp stoves are safer, more efficient, and cleaner.
- At all times, only emergency fires are permitted above 3500 feet in the Catskills.
- Carry out what you carry in. Use Leave No Trace practices (see p. 16).
- Keep your pet under control. Restrain it on a leash when others approach. Collect and bury droppings away from water, trails, and campsites. Keep your pet away from drinking water sources.
- Observe and enjoy wildlife and plants but leave them undisturbed.
- Removing plants, rocks, fossils, or artifacts from state land without a permit is illegal.
- Do not feed any wild animals.
- Store food properly to keep it away from animals—particularly bears.
- Except in an emergency or between December 21 and March 21, camping is prohibited above an elevation of 3500 feet in the Catskills.
- The use of bicycles in Wilderness Areas is prohibited.

LEAN-TOS
Lean-tos are available on a first-come, first-served basis up to the capacity of the shelter—usually about eight persons. Thus a small party cannot claim exclusive use of a shelter and must allow late arrivals equal use. Most lean-tos have a fireplace in front (sometimes with a primitive grill) and sanitary facilities. Most are located near some source of water, but each camper must use his or her own judgment as to whether or not the water supply needs purification before drinking. It is in poor taste to carve or write one's initials in a shelter. Please try to

keep these rustic shelters in good condition and appearance.

Because reservations cannot be made for any of these shelters, it is best to carry a tent or other alternate shelter. Many shelters away from the standard routes, however, are seldom used, and a small party can often find a shelter open in the more remote areas.

The following regulations apply specifically to lean-tos, in addition to the general camping regulations listed above:

- No plastic may be used to close off the front of a shelter.
- No nails or other permanent fastener may be used to affix a tarp in a lean-to, but it is permissible to use rope to tie canvas or nylon tarps across the front.
- No tent may be pitched inside a lean-to.

GROUPS

Any group of ten or more persons or smaller groups intending to camp at one location three nights or longer must obtain a permit before camping on state land. A permit is also required for group events, including day hikes, involving more than twenty people. This system is designed to prevent overuse of certain critical sites and also to encourage groups to split into smaller parties.

Permits can be obtained from the New York State forest ranger closest to the actual starting point of one's proposed trip. The local forest ranger can be contacted by writing directly; if in doubt about whom to contact, send a letter to the DEC Lands and Forests Division Office address for the county in which your trip will take place (refer to DEC addresses in "Trail Markers" section, p. 20). They will forward the letter to the proper ranger, but write early enough to allow a response before your trip date.

One can also make the initial contact with the forest ranger by telephone. Note that forest rangers' schedules during the busy summer season are often unpredictable. Forest rangers are listed in the white pages of local phone books under "New York, State of; Environmental Conservation, Department of; Forest Ranger." Bear in mind when calling that most rangers operate out of their private homes; observe the normal courtesy used when calling a private residence. Contact by letter is much preferred. Camping with a large group requires careful planning with a lead time of several weeks to ensure a happy, safe outing.

EMERGENCY PROCEDURES

Emergency calls should be directed to 911, according to the New York State Department of Environmental Conservation (DEC). The 911 dispatchers can contact the appropriate DEC forest ranger or other emergency personnel.

Alternatively, emergency calls can be directed as follows:
DEC Region 3 (Ulster and Sullivan counties): 845-256-3000 during normal business hours.
DEC Region 4 (Delaware and Greene counties): 607-652-5076/5063 and 518-357-2161, respectively, during normal business hours.
DEC twenty-four hour dispatch number: 877-457-5680.

Alternatively, on weekends and after hours call the New York State Police in Ulster County (Kingston, 845-338-1702), Sullivan County (Liberty, 845-292-6600), Greene County (Catskill-Cairo, 518-622-8600), or Delaware County (Margaretville, 845-586-2681). Or call the Sheriff's Department in Delhi at 607-746-2336.

Note: Queries, information, and concerns can also be directed to the pertinent DEC numbers cited above.

FOREST SAFETY

The routes described in this guidebook vary from wide, well-marked DEC trails to narrow, unmarked footpaths that have become established through long use. With normal alertness and careful preparation the hiker should have few problems in land navigation. Nevertheless, careful map study and route planning are fundamental necessities. Hikers should never expect immediate help should an emergency occur. This is particularly true in winter, when fewer people are on the trails and weather is a more significant factor.

In addition to a map, all hikers should carry a compass and know at least the basics of its use. In some descriptions, the Forest Preserve Series uses compass bearings to differentiate trails at a junction or to indicate the direction of travel above timberline. More important, a compass can be an indispensable aid in the event that you lose your way.

Winter trips, especially, must be carefully planned. Travel over ice on ski and snowshoe trips must be done with caution. The possibility of freezing rain, snow, and cold temperatures should be considered from early September until late May. True winter conditions can commence as early as November and last well into April, particularly at higher altitudes. It is highly recommended that hikers travel in parties of at least four people, be outfitted properly, rest when the need arises, and drink plenty of water. Leave trip plans with someone at home and then keep to your itinerary. For more information on winter travel, refer to the ADK publication *Winterwise* by John Dunn.

BIG GAME SEASONS IN THE CATSKILLS ARE AS FOLLOWS:
Early Archery Season (deer and bear): October 1 through the day preceding regular deer and bear season.

Regular Season (deer and bear): Third Saturday in November and lasting for twenty-three days.

Late Archery and Muzzle-loading Season: First day after the close of the regular season, running for nine days.

Hikers should also be alert during turkey season. Spring: From half-hour before sunrise until noon, May 1 through May 31. Fall: October 1 through the day before the start of regular big-game season.

On occasion, special situations require DEC to modify the usual dates of hunting seasons.

For further information, consult the DEC website at www.dec.ny.gov or call the Game Management Section in the DEC Division of Fish and Wildlife, at 518-402-8883.

DRINKING WATER

Unfortunately, as in many other mountain areas, many Catskill water sources have become contaminated with a parasite known as *Giardia lamblia*. This intestinal parasite causes a disease known as giardiasis—often called "beaver fever." It can be spread by any warm-blooded mammal when infected feces wash into the water; beavers are prime agents in transferring this parasite because they spend so much of their time in and near water. Hikers themselves have also become primary agents in spreading this disease because some individuals appear to be unaffected carriers of the disease, and other recently infected individuals may inadvertently spread the parasite before their symptoms become apparent.

Prevention: Follow the guidelines for the disposal of human excrement as stated above. Equally important, make sure that every member of your group is aware of the problem and follows the guidelines as well. The health of a fellow hiker may depend on your consideration.

Water Treatment: No water source can be guaranteed to be safe. Boil all water for two to three minutes, utilize an iodine-based chemical purifier (available at camping supply stores and some drug and department stores), or use a commercial filter designed specifically for giardiasis prevention. If after returning from a trip you experience recurrent intestinal problems, consult your physician and explain your potential problem.

BEAR CANISTERS

Bears in many wilderness areas have figured out the long-popular campers' technique of hanging food from a rope strung between two trees. Thus authorities are now recommending—in some cases strongly encouraging—the use of bear-resistant food-storage canisters.

These can be obtained from many outdoor retailers, borrowed from many ADK chapters, or rented or purchased from the Member Services Center at ADK's Lake George headquarters. The canisters also protect food from many smaller forest creatures.

The DEC's current management goal with respect to bears is to educate campers about proper food storage. Bears unable to get food from campers will, it is hoped, return to their natural diet. Thus campers play an important role in helping to restore the natural balance between bears and humans. Losing one's food to a bear should be recognized as a critical failure in achieving this goal.

HUNTING SEASONS

Unlike the national park system, public lands within the Adirondack and Catskill state parks are open to sport hunting. There are separate rules and seasons for each type of hunting (small game, waterfowl, and big game), but it is the big-game season, i.e., deer and bear, that is most likely to concern hikers. Confrontations can occur when hikers and hunters are inconsiderate of the needs and rights of each other. Problems can be greatly reduced by careful planning.

It is advisable to avoid heavily hunted areas during big-game seasons. Because it is difficult to carry a deer or bear carcass long distances or over steep terrain, hikers will find few hunters more than a mile from a roadway or in rugged mountain country. Lower slopes of beech, maple, and hemlock have much more hunting pressure than cripplebush, spruce, and balsam fir on upper slopes. Try to avoid the opening and closing day of regular deer season. For safety, wear a bright-colored outer garment; orange is recommended.

ADK does not promote hunting as one of its organized activities, but it does recognize that sport hunting, when carried out in compliance with the game laws administered by the DEC, is a legitimate sporting activity.

BEAR SAFETY

Most wild animals in the Adirondacks and Catskills are little more than a minor nuisance around the campsite. Generally, the larger the animal the more timid it is in the presence of humans. Some animals are emboldened by the aroma of food, however, and bears, the most intimidating of these, quickly habituate to human food sources.

The following tips will reduce the likelihood of an encounter with a bear.
- Never keep food in your tent or lean-to.
- Use bear-resistant canisters available from ADK.
- Alternatively, hang food at least fifteen feet off the ground from a rope strung between two trees that are at least fifteen feet apart and one hundred feet from the campsite. (Hangs using a branch have a high failure rate.) Using dark-colored rope tied off five or more feet above the ground makes it less likely that a foraging bear will see the line or find it while sniffing along the ground.
- Wrap aromatic foods well.
- Plan carefully to keep trash and leftovers to a minimum. Wrap in sealed containers such as large Ziploc bags, and hang or place in canister.
- Hang your pack, along with clothing worn during cooking.
- Keep a garbage-free fire pit away from your camping area.
- Should a bear appear, do not provoke it by throwing objects or approaching it. Bang pots, blow a whistle, shout, or otherwise try to drive it off with sharp noises. Should this fail, leave the scene.
- Report bear encounters to a forest ranger.

RABIES ALERT
Rabies infestation has been moving north through New York State. Although it is most often associated with raccoons, any warm-blooded mammal can be a carrier.
Although direct contact with a rabid animal in the forest is not likely, some precautions are advisable:
- Do not feed or pet any wild animals, under any circumstances.
- Particularly avoid any wild animals that seem to be behaving strangely.
- If bitten by a wild animal, seek medical attention immediately.

INSECT-BORNE DISEASES
Although not unique to the Adirondacks and Catskills, two insects found in these areas carry potentially lethal diseases. Deer ticks can spread Lyme disease, and mosquitos can transmit West Nile virus. These are issues of particular concern in the Catskills.

In both instances, protection is advisable. Wear long pants and long-sleeved shirts and apply an insect repellent with the recommended percentage of N, N-diethyl-meta-toluamide (commonly known as DEET). On returning home, thoroughly inspect yourself and wash yourself and your clothing immediately. Seek immediate attention if any early symptoms (rash, long-term fatigue, headache, fever) arise.

Black Dome Valley–Northern Escarpment Section

The great horseshoe of mountains and ridges surrounding Black Dome Valley offers the hiker a large variety of options for day trips or backpack outings. The Blackhead Range on the S side of the horseshoe includes the third, fourth, and fifth highest mountains in the Catskills (Blackhead, Black Dome, and Thomas Cole, from E to W), all over 3900 ft. Windham High Peak on the N side of the horseshoe is over 3500 ft in elevation, and the Burnt Knob–Acra Point ridge tops 3100 ft along the Escarpment Trail that comprises the N and E part of the great horseshoe.

The N half of the Escarpment Trail, completed in 1967, is described in this section from Dutcher Notch to NY 23, E of the village of Windham. (This is also part of the Long Path.) All access routes to the Escarpment Trail and the Blackhead Range are included in the trail descriptions.

This area of the Catskills offers magnificent vistas E over the Hudson River Valley, N to Albany, and S to Slide Mt. and to the six Devil's Path peaks. Climbs range from 1000 ft ascents to escarpment overlooks to the 1780 ft ascent to the summit of Black Dome. The terrain here offers everything from long, level grades along the escarpment ridge to near-vertical scrambles up the rugged ledges of the Blackhead Range.

❈ Trails in winter: Full crampons are essential on the Blackhead Range. Many sections in this high range require good wind clothing. Windham High Peak is an easy winter climb and a good one for novices. Blackhead Mt. from the Black Dome Range Trail provides excellent views, but is more demanding.

The following areas should be attempted only by experienced winter hikers: (1) The Escarpment Trail N of the Blackhead Mt. summit jct., which has very steep sections on icy north-facing trail; (2) the Black Dome Mt. Trail on the E side of Black Dome, which has very steep sections and sharp drops; (3) the Blackhead (or Black Dome) Range Trail W of the Caudal; 1 mi up the ridge from Barnum Rd. toward Camel's Hump is an extremely steep, short, and icy pitch to the top of a cliff.

Following is a list of suggested hikes in the region.

SHORT HIKES

Burnt Knob: 2.7 mi (4.3 km) round-trip. A pleasant ascent via the Acra Point/Burnt Knob Access Trail to the northern Escarpment Trail, ascending the knob to 3000 ft; a spur path L goes to a cliff top with a sweeping view of the Blackhead Range and northern escarpment. Add a comparable excellent viewing spot, 0.3 mi up the other side, R, from the approach trail jct.

Elm Ridge Trail: 1.8 mi (2.9 km) round-trip. A gradual ascent of 250 ft on an interesting flat-rock trail to imposing cliffs (the rock is very slippery if wet). The Elm Ridge Lean-to is atop this scenic terrain. Also hike 1.25 mi to Batavia Kill Lean-to from end of Big Hollow Rd.

MODERATE HIKES

Windham High Peak from NY 23: 7 mi (11.2 km) round-trip. Generally moderate grades lead to a summit providing excellent views of the region. Hike E across the 0.15 mi summit, descending slightly, to the best views from a broad, open ledge.

Acra Point Loop: 5.1 mi (8.2 km). This loop includes a short part (0.6 mi) of the Black Dome Mt. Trail to the Batavia Kill Trail; climb to the Escarpment Trail and hike L to the Acra Point/Burnt Knob Access Trail, which descends back to the Big Hollow Rd. parking area. This trek offers views of the Hudson Valley and a close view to the Blackhead Range.

Black Dome Mt. Trail: 5.2 mi (8.3 km) round-trip. This trip, though short, requires stiff climbing. Two excellent views of the region are from Black Dome Mt.

HARDER HIKES

Blackhead Mt., Northern Escarpment, and Windham High Peak: 11.6 mi (18.6 km). This trip requires spotting a second vehicle or a road walk of 4 mi. From the end of Big Hollow Rd., climb via the Black Dome Range Trail to the Blackhead Mt. Spur Trail. Ascend to the summit of Blackhead Mt., then N on the Escarpment Trail over Windham High Peak to the Elm Ridge Trail and Peck Rd. This is a rigorous hike with many rewarding views.

Black Dome Range Trail from Barnum Rd. to Big Hollow Rd.: 6.3 mi (10.1 km). This trip requires spotting a second vehicle or a road walk of 5.7 mi. Though a relatively short hike, the cumulative vertical ascent and descent makes this a challenging but very interesting trip. Add another quarter-mile up Blackhead to open rocks with sweeping views S, W, and N.

	Trail Described	Total Miles (one way)		Page
1	Black Dome Mt. Trail	2.6	(4.2 km)	29
2	Blackhead Mt. Spur Trail	0.7	(1.1 km)	31
3	Black Dome Range Trail	3.7	(5.9 km)	31
4	Elm Ridge Trail	0.9	(1.4 km)	33
5	Acra Point/Burnt Knob Access Trail	1.0	(1.6 km)	34
6	Batavia Kill Trail	0.9	(1.4 km)	34
7	Dutcher Notch Trail	1.9	(3.0 km)	35
8	Colgate Lake Trail to Dutcher Notch	4.3	(6.9 km)	36

9 N-S Northern Escarpment Trail
      (NY 23 to Dutcher Notch)   12.6   (20.2 km)   38
9 S- N Northern Escarpment Trail
      (Dutcher Notch to NY 23)   12.6   (20.2 km)   42

Route Guide to Big Hollow Rd. (CR 56) (see map p. 30)

Mileage W to E	Description	Mileage E to W
0.0	Windham High Peak trailhead parking area, jct. Cross Rd and NY 23, 17 mi W of I-87 (NYS Thruway); continue W from this point.	8.5
1.2	Turn L on CR 65 for Maplecrest.	7.3
2	Turn L, just before bridge, onto CR 65A.	6.5
2.3	It becomes CR 40, which continues to Maplecrest.	6.2
4.2	Maplecrest. Turn L on CR 56 to Big Hollow Rd. trailhead.	4.3
	If going to Barnum Rd., turn R 0.5 mi.	5.7
	Batavia Kill Day Use Area; lake	2.8
6	Peck Rd. Turn L 0.8 mi for Elm Ridge trailhead.	2.5
8.45	Acra Point Access Trail on L	0.05
8.5	DEC parking area on R	0.0

1 Black Dome Mt. Trail

Trails Illustrated Map 755: M17 / Map 141, NE Catskills: O3, trail BD

Black Dome Mt., the third highest mountain in the Catskills, is a frequent destination of hikers from both Big Hollow Rd. and Elmer Barnum Rd. In this guide, the E end of what is called the Blackhead or Black Dome Range Trail is described as the Black Dome Mt. Trail, to assist hikers starting from Big Hollow Rd.

▶Trailhead: The trailhead is near the parking area at the E end of Big Hollow Rd. (CR 56). Walk the gravel road to a jct. 0.05 mi E of the parking area. A DEC signpost is found at the trailhead (0.0 mi).◀

Red DEC trail markers lead SE 150 ft to a trail register. The trail crosses Batavia Kill on a bridge at 0.1 mi and continues E to a second bridge crossing at 0.5 mi. The jct. with the Batavia Kill Trail (trail 6) is at 0.6 mi. (The yellow-marked Batavia Kill Trail leads 0.65 mi to a lean-to and another 0.25 mi to the Escarpment Trail [trail 9].)

The red-marked Black Dome Mt. Trail climbs a gradual grade to a small brook crossing at 0.8 mi, and at 1 mi reaches a wide rocky stream (often dry). The slope becomes moderate. At 1.4 mi, a spur path leads L to a spring. At 1.6 mi, switchbacks ascend the steep slope to the Blackhead Mt. Spur Trail jct. at 2 mi in Lockwood Gap, the col between Blackhead and Black Dome mts. (This yellow-marked spur trail [trail 2] leads L 0.3 mi to excellent views and 0.7 mi to the wooded

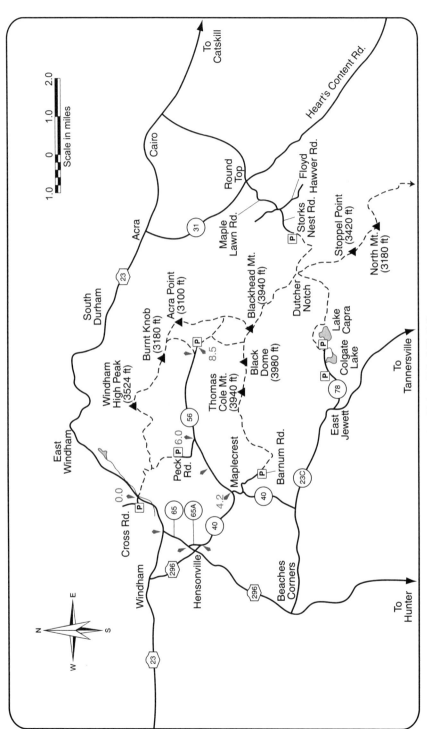

Blackhead Mt. summit.)
Turn R at this jct. and continue W on the red-marked trail, which climbs steeply up Black Dome Mt. At 2.2 mi, it swings L under a ledge, then circles R to the top of the ledge. A spur trail leads R to a magnificent viewing point from which the Helderbergs, the Hudson Valley, Blackhead Mt., Kaaterskill High Peak, and the Devil's Path can be seen in a wide sweep.

The trail is moderately steep from here, becoming a gradual grade near the summit, which is at 2.6 mi. A short spur path L leads to a large rock ledge with an extensive southern vista. All the peaks on the Devil's Path lie before you: Indian Head, Twin, Sugarloaf, Plateau, Hunter, and West Kill mts. Farther S are Cornell, Wittenberg, Slide, and Table mts.

🌂 Distances: To Batavia Kill Trail jct., 0.6 mi; to spring spur, 1.4 mi; to Blackhead Mt. Spur Trail jct., 2 mi; to ledge lookout spur, 2.2 mi; to Black Dome summit, 2.6 mi (4.2 km). Ascent, 1780 ft (543 m). Elevation, 3980 ft (1213 m).

2 Blackhead Mt. Spur Trail

Trails Illustrated Map 755: L17 / Map 141, NE Catskills: O3, trail BM

▶Trailhead: The Blackhead Mt. Spur Trail originates at Lockwood Gap at the 2 mi point of the Black Dome Mt. Trail (trail 1). It ascends to the summit of Blackhead Mt.◀

The trail climbs E from the Black Dome Mt. Trail jct. (0.0 mi), marked with yellow DEC trail markers. The moderate upgrade soon reaches the DEC 3500 ft elevation sign.

At 0.2 mi, steps are cut into the slope at the base of a short, loose rock slide. The grade continues to steepen. Sweeping 180-degree views from the open rock on the trail at 0.25 mi reward the hiker. Entering a forest of conifers on gradual grades at 0.3 mi, the trail progressively levels out across the long wooded ridge, almost 0.4 mi to the summit from the viewing area. Blueberries abound in open places. The trail intersects the blue-marked Escarpment Trail (trail 9) at 0.7 mi.

🌂 Distances: To views, 0.25 mi; to summit jct., 0.7 mi (1.1 km). Ascent from col, 500 ft (152 m). Summit elevation, 3940 ft (1201 m).

3 Black Dome Range Trail

Trails Illustrated Map 755: L17 / Map 141, NE Catskills: N3, trail BD

The Black Dome Range of Camel's Hump, Thomas Cole Mt., and Black Dome Mt. offers the hiker a fine variety of terrain, forest, and views. The trail described below begins in Maplecrest at the end of Barnum Rd. and terminates at the summit of Black Dome Mt. Refer to the Black Dome Mt. Trail (trail 1) and the Blackhead Mt. Spur Trail (trail 2) for point-to-point trips. Carry plenty of water.

▶Trailhead: The trailhead is at the end of Barnum Rd. (see p. 30), 0.9 mi E of Maplecrest Rd. (CR 40).◀

Red DEC trail markers lead SE up the gradual grade of an old woods road to a trail register at 0.4 mi. The route turns sharply NE from the register, leaving the old road. The state Forest Preserve boundary is reached at 0.6 mi. Steady climbing moderates as the trail switchbacks to the bottom of a cliff. A short, extremely steep pitch up massive boulders rewards the hiker with an excellent view S and W to Devil's Path peaks at 1 mi.

The grade is a moderate ascent to the Caudal at 1.3 mi, where the terrain levels for a short distance. (In anatomy, a caudal part is found near the tail. It has been suggested that this knob represents the tail of the camel.) After descending a short pitch, the route is gradual to 1.8 mi, where it swings R and ascends Camel's Hump on moderate grades.

Passing between two boulders, the trail reaches the top of Camel's Hump at 2 mi. Elevation is 3500 ft. Thomas Cole Mt. is visible nearby to the E from a spur path, R. Stoppel Point and Kaaterskill High Peak are seen to the SE; viewing is best when leaves are off the trees. A spur path L has views when leaves are off N to Windham High Peak, to the Windham ski slopes, and down to Black Dome Valley.

After a slight descent, the trail becomes level on flat rock in an interesting open meadow with flat bedrock. Thomas Cole Mt. is in full view. At 2.45 mi, the trail begins climbing; look for a side path R for views S and W. The route gains about 500 ft in elevation from the meadow to the summit of Thomas Cole Mt.

The flat ridge trail passes just below the true summit; a yellow-marked spur trail leads to a treed-in lookout S at 2.9 mi, better in winter. Summit elevation is 3940 ft. Onteora Mt. and Parker Mt. are across the valley; Devil's Path peaks are in the distance. Thomas Cole Mt. is named for the painter who established the Hudson River School of painting in the nineteenth century.

The trail soon descends at a moderate rate, with occasional steep pitches. The col (3550 ft) between Thomas Cole and Black Dome is quickly reached at 3.3 mi. This is a beautiful spot in winter, with good viewing S. Moderately steep climbing leads to the summit spur path of Black Dome Mt. at 3.7 mi, with excellent viewing from a large, flat rock shelf. Summit elevation is 3980 ft.

This is a perfect lunch spot. Views can be seen from 150 degrees to 260 degrees, including the Hudson Valley, Kaaterskill High Peak, Indian Head, Twin, Sugarloaf, Plateau, Stony Clove Notch, Cornell, Wittenberg, Slide, Table, West Kill, and Rusk.

The trail beyond descends steeply to Big Hollow Rd. (see trail 1), or leads to the Blackhead Mt. Spur Trail (trail 2), with more sweeping views just a quarter-mile up.

🥾 Distances: To state land, 0.6 mi; to cliff-top view, 1 mi; to Camel's Hump, 2 mi; to Thomas Cole Mt. summit, 2.9 mi; to Black Dome Mt. summit, 3.7 mi (5.9 km). Total ascent from parking area, 2290 ft (698 m). Elevations: Thomas Cole Mt., 3940 ft (1201 m); Black Dome Mt., 3980 ft (1213 m).

Blackhead Range from Burnt Knob. Tony Versandi

4 Elm Ridge Trail

Trails Illustrated Map 755: M16 / Map 141, NE Catskills: N3, trail ER

The Elm Ridge Trail connects to the Escarpment Trail (trail 9) from Peck Rd. (see Route Guide to Big Hollow Rd., p. 29).

▶Trailhead: This short trail leaves the parking area at the end of Peck Rd. (0.8 mi from Big Hollow Rd. [CR 56]). It is marked with both yellow DEC trail markers and cross-country ski trail markers. A trail register is found 100 ft along the trail.◀

Heading N, the route is a nearly level, old woods road that has standing water in wet seasons. The trail ascends interesting flat rock, which is very slippery if wet. Stone walls are on both sides of the trail at 0.4. A pipe spring (not obvious) is L at 0.6 mi. The trail passes picturesque cliffs.

The jct. with the Escarpment Trail (trail 9) is reached at 0.9 mi. (Turning R, a side trail R in 0.1 mi leads 100 yd to the Elm Ridge Lean-to.)

🐾 Distances: To stone walls, 0.4 mi; to spring, 0.6 mi; to Escarpment Trail jct., 0.9 mi (1.4 km).

5 Acra Point/Burnt Knob Access Trail

Trails Illustrated Map 755: M17 / Map 141, NE Catskills: O3, trail BD

Acra Point. Joanne Hihn

The Acra Point/Burnt Knob Access Trail provides a connection with the Escarpment Trail (trail 9) and thus permits a variety of loop options for day hikes in the region. This trail is sometimes included as a section of the Black Dome Range Trail. Since it connects with the Escarpment Trail on the opposite side of the valley from the Blackhead Range, this guide's trail designation is considered less confusing.

▶Trailhead: The trail begins on the N side of Big Hollow Rd. (0.0 mi), 0.1 mi W of the parking area at the end of the road.◀

The trail follows red DEC trail markers into woods, and in 80 ft crosses a bridge over Batavia Kill to a trail register. A small tributary is crossed (avoid path straight ahead at register); the crossing on rocks can be difficult in high water. The route then follows the E side of the tributary through very attractive forest and crosses it again on rocks at 0.35 mi.

Leaving the creek, the trail now climbs steadily, bearing NW at 0.8 mi and becoming gradual. The grade becomes nearly level to a jct. with the Escarpment Trail at 1 mi. (A fine overlook S below Burnt Knob is 0.35 mi W. Acra Point is 0.7 mi E, but excellent viewing is 0.3 mi E from a large ledge a bit off-trail to the R.)

※ Distances: To first tributary crossing, 100 ft; to last crossing of tributary, 0.35 mi; to Escarpment Trail, 1 mi (1.6 km).

6 Batavia Kill Trail

Trails Illustrated Map 755: M17 / Map 141, NE Catskills: O3, trail BK

The Batavia Kill Trail provides access to the Escarpment Trail (trail 9), enabling the hiker to have several options for day hikes. It gains 500 ft in elevation before reaching the Escarpment Trail.

▶Trailhead: The trail originates at a jct. (0.0 mi) with the Black Dome Mt. Trail (trail 1), 0.6 mi from the Big Hollow Rd. parking area.◀

From the jct., the yellow-marked trail crosses the Batavia Kill and heads SSE along the S stream bank. The gradual upgrade route is often in view of the stream. The trail makes a swing to the E before it reaches the Batavia Kill Lean-to at 0.65 mi. Beyond the lean-to, the grade is gradual on switchbacks and reaches the jct. with the Escarpment Trail at 0.9 mi.

☸ Distances: To Batavia Kill Lean-to, 0.65 mi; to Escarpment Trail (trail 9), 0.9 mi (1.4 km). Total distance from Big Hollow Rd., 1.5 mi (2.4 km).

7 Dutcher Notch Trail

Trails Illustrated Map 755: L18 / Map 141, NE Catskills: P3, trail DU

The Dutcher Notch Trail offers a little-used route to the Escarpment Trail (trails 9 and 10) from below the escarpment in Round Top. Its gradual but steady grade makes an excellent woods walk, and a strenuous all-day outing can be made by taking the Escarpment Trail S to Stoppel Point or N to Arizona or Blackhead mts.

▶Trailhead: Access to the trailhead is off NY 32, along Heart's Content Rd. (CR 31), the road to Round Top and Purling. Follow Heart's Content Rd. 4 mi to Maple Lawn Rd. Turn L and travel 1.1 mi to Floyd Hawver Rd. Turn L and then immediately R at the DEC signpost at Storks Nest Rd. Travel 0.4 mi along Storks Nest Rd. to a small parking area on the L side of the road, now dirt. Just beyond, the road enters private property, where vehicles are not allowed.◀

The yellow-marked DEC trail heads SW past a large house, entering woods at 0.1 mi. It follows a woods road gradually upgrade to a trail register and small bridge across a brook at 0.3 mi. Now a little steeper than before, the route becomes rockier as the eroded cuts in the road deepen. Often the trail is on a bank with much better footing.

State land markers, first seen at 0.8 mi, are followed by a large swing to the NW at 1 mi. A grassy lane replaces the rocky passage as elevation increases. The trail slabs the slope, which drops off on the R with good views far down into the open woods. In summer, only occasional glimpses of the broad Hudson Valley can be seen through leaves of the trees, but a winter climb on snowshoes or skis would present marvelous views from this terrain.

A well-tended, shallow spring is located at 1.6 mi, on the L side of the trail at the base of a large rock outcrop. The trail passes scenic mossy ledges and an attractive grove of hemlocks before reaching the Escarpment Trail at Dutcher Notch at 1.9 mi. This large, flat area has fire rings, but a DEC sign notes that camping must be at least 150 ft from the trail.

(The Escarpment Trail [trail 10] continues S 1.2 mi to Milt's Lookout and 2.3 mi to Stoppel Point [E side]. The Escarpment Trail [trail 9] proceeds N with many views along the route to the wooded summit of Blackhead Mt. at 2.8 mi; the views from Blackhead are 0.35 mi W on the yellow-marked Blackhead Mt. Spur Trail [trail 2]. The yellow-marked Colgate Lake Trail [trail 8] heads W from the jct. of the Dutcher Notch Trail and the Escarpment Trail for 4.3 mi to a DEC trailhead near Colgate Lake, E of the hamlet of East Jewett.)

☸ Distances: To state land, 0.8 mi; to spring, 1.6 mi; to Escarpment Trail jct., 1.9 mi (3 km).

Colgate Lake. Henning Vahlenkamp

8 Colgate Lake Trail to Dutcher Notch

Trails Illustrated Map 755: L18 / Map 141, NE Catskills: O4, trail CL

The trail is nearly level most of the way to Dutcher Notch, where the route intersects the Escarpment Trail (trails 9 and 10). The old woods road continues down to Storks Nest Rd. in Round Top as the Dutcher Notch Trail (trail 7). During a pleasant walk along this trail, the hiker will see interesting evidence of the historical past of the Catskills.

This trail was the shortest way for nineteenth-century farmers of the Jewett Valley to get to market in the village of Catskill. Colgate Lake is named for Robert Colgate, of the Colgate Palmolive–Peet Co., who once owned much of the land the trail passes over. The trail now skirts Lake Capra, which is on private land.

▶ Trailhead: Trailhead access is off CR 78, E of the hamlet of East Jewett. Drive 1.7 mi E from East Jewett to the third DEC parking area on the L side of the road. The yellow-marked DEC trail starts at the L side of the parking area and follows the edge of a field. Dutcher Notch can be seen to the R in the distance with the Blackhead Range to the N ◀

At 0.2 mi, the grassy trail enters a birch and maple forest where a trail register is located. The trail swings NE from its original N direction at 0.5 mi and begins a

36 *Catskill Trails*

loop around the Camp Harriman property. A sign "Trail" at 1 mi alerts the hiker to a sharp turn L. Occasional wet, rocky footing improves markedly after the trail passes into the Forest Preserve at 1.25 mi.

The trail crosses an inlet stream of Lake Capra at 1.3 mi on a bridge. The way then leads up a pitch, crosses a woods road, and pitches up again, turning L onto a second woods road. At 1.5 mi the trail turns R at berry bushes near a meadow, and at 1.9 mi crosses another bridge.

The trail swings S at 2.4 mi, completing the loop around Lake Capra, paralleling at a distance the shore of a beaver meadow. It passes through a grove of new hemlock and pine; look for a side path L to a view of the escarpment over the meadow. The trail turns L out of the woods at 2.6 mi and crosses East Kill on a good bridge. Look for large crayfish in the pools.

Joining the old East Jewett–Catskill road along the river in an attractive section with large evergreen trees, the route bears R at an old arch bridge at 2.8 mi to skirt a section flooded by beaver activity. Iron implements used for past lumbering operations can be seen here. The East Kill is crossed again on rocks at 3 mi, where the trail swings L and soon passes an old wrecked car.

The trail crosses a small stream and rejoins the old route, turning R at 3.1 mi at an extensive meadow filled with blueberry bushes. Arizona and Blackhead mts. loom above. A sign says, "No camping within 150 ft of trail," near a fire ring.

At 3.2 mi, listen for falling water. Passing over a large water bar across the trail, look for an old path in the woods, R, heading to the waterfall. It's the site of an old foundation and scenic double waterfall creating a fairly deep pool (the rock is slippery).

The trail climbs on easy grades. At a fork, the marked trail bears L where an old road continues straight. Passing a cascading tributary at 3.7 mi, the trail becomes a lovely walk up the gradually rising northern escarpment, amidst interesting terrain. Approaching the notch, the landscape closes in on the trail, surrounded by scenic rocky ledges and overhangs.

The grade moderates before reaching the four-way jct. with the Escarpment Trail at 4.3 mi. The trail continues straight ahead, as the Dutcher Notch Trail (trail 7). There is a mostly reliable spring 0.3 mi farther down that trail. The notch jct. has a large clearing, which DEC has posted with signs prohibiting camping within 150 ft of the trail. Stoppel Point (E side) is 2.3 mi S on the Escarpment Trail (trail 10) and Blackhead Mt. is 2.8 mi N on the Escarpment Trail (trail 9) from this jct.

On return, hikers can enjoy a swim and picnic at Colgate Lake, newly dammed and landscaped, on CR 78, 0.1 mi closer to East Jewett from the trailhead. A DEC sign marks a parking area in a large clearing W of the outlet stream, where informal campsites are allowed on an embankment and in the woods.

🗮 Distances: To Lake Capra inlet stream, 1.3 mi; to footbridge, 1.9 mi; to bridge over East Kill, 2.6 mi; to meadow with mountain views, 3.1 mi; to jct. with Escarpment Trail in Dutcher Notch, 4.3 mi (6.9 km).

Dutcher Notch Trail to Stoppel Point. Mark Schaefer

9 N-S Northern Escarpment Trail, NY 23 to Dutcher Notch

Trails Illustrated Map 755: M16 / Map 141, NE Catskills: N3, trail ES

The NW section of the Escarpment Trail climbs Windham High Peak from NY 23 and continues over Burnt Knob, Acra Point, and Blackhead Mt before descending to Dutcher Notch. The last Sunday of July, there is an annual trail run over this entire section and part of trail 10 to the North-South Lake picnic ground. Several access trails offer options for a traverse: A point-to-point trip of 7.1 mi with additional overlooks is possible by spotting a second vehicle at the end of Big Hollow Rd., using the Acra Point/Burnt Knob Access Trail (trail 5), and also a 10.2 mi trip by continuing past the Acra Point/Burnt Knob Access Trail jct. to the Batavia Kill Trail (trail 6), descending to that parking area. Continuing over Blackhead Mt. and descending the Black Dome Mt. Trail (trail 1) to the same parking area makes a good two-day backpack or a 12.2 mi day trip.

▶Trailhead: A DEC sign marks the trailhead parking area, 3 mi E of Windham on NY 23 at a jct. with Cross Rd., which heads N.◀

The trail (0.0 mi) is across NY 23 and heads SE following blue DEC trail markers. A bridge crosses a stream to a flat, grassy route past old stone walls and apple trees to a trail register at 0.1 mi. A boardwalk was constructed because beavers had flooded the area. In 2010, several bike trails were constructed E of the register.

After passing through a gap in a stone wall and switchbacking through it again, the trail ascends gradually through sometimes wet sections to recently constructed switchbacks, adding 0.2 mi through attractive forest; note older-growth hemlocks. The trail turns R onto an old woods road that climbs moderately to the Elm Ridge Trail (trail 4) jct. at 1.3 mi. (The Elm Ridge Trail leads 0.9 mi S to Peck Rd.; a pipe spring is 0.25 mi down the Elm Ridge Trail.)

Continuing on the blue trail, a side trail R at 1.4 mi leads 100 yd to the Elm Ridge Lean-to. Varying grades, never really difficult, climb through many fine stands of large spruce and red pine, each section more marvelously dark and dense. The trail crosses sections of split logs (exercise care on uneven, slippery surfaces) over a wet area at 2 mi and emerges again into open deciduous woods.

After one steep pitch up, the terrain becomes nearly level; nice views of the Blackhead Range are available when leaves are off the trees. Swinging R, the trail crosses a stream and ascends moderately up rocky terrain; views are seen as the trail ascends more steeply. After a final steep pitch up, the climb moderates somewhat and then becomes gradual to a DEC 3500 ft elevation sign at 3.4 mi. The trail levels at the summit ridge of Windham High Peak.

R is a fine view of the Blackhead Range. A spur trail across offers a view N. Continue 0.15 mi across the true summit, marked with a geodetic survey marker, with a view N. Descend slightly to an open rock shelf with magnificent views N to Albany and E over the Hudson Valley.

From Windham High Peak's lookout ledge, the trail begins a long steady downgrade to a col at 4.4 mi before the trail climbs around another knob and again drops into a dip. Two other side trails R at 5 mi offer excellent views S and W. At 5.4 mi the trail reaches a path L to a cliff top that offers expansive viewing N, E, and W to Windham High Peak. Beyond, the trail climbs briefly (smooth rock is slippery!) to level terrain below the summit of 3180 ft Burnt Knob. At 6 mi, a short spur trail, R, leads to an open rock cliff top with excellent views to the Blackhead Range and the northern escarpment.

The Escarpment Trail descends to the jct. of the Acra Point/Burnt Knob Access Trail (trail 5) at 6.3 mi. (The red-marked Acra Point/Burnt Knob Access Trail runs 1 mi down to the end of Big Hollow Rd. A good stream is 0.7 mi from the jct.)

A switchback provides gradual grades up to a side trail R at 6.6 mi, which presents outstanding views of the Blackhead Range and Burnt Knob from several rock ledges. Smaller viewing ledges, including Acra Point, provide views E and N from here to the Batavia Kill Trail (trail 6) jct. at 9 mi. (The yellow-marked Batavia Kill Trail descends 0.25 mi to Batavia Kill Lean-to, where water is found at the source of the Batavia Kill. It continues to Big Hollow Rd., a total of 1.5 mi from the jct.)

The trail gains 1100 ft of elevation in the next 0.9 mi to the summit of Blackhead Mt., at first ascending very gradually through a shady hemlock grove and then steepening through a pretty birch woods. At Yellow Jacket Lookout at 9.4 mi, vistas as far N as Albany are possible. Sections above here are extremely steep, and in winter full crampons are essential. The trail reaches the three-way jct. at

Burnt Knob Escarpment Trail lookout. Tony Versandi

3940-ft Blackhead Mt. summit, fourth highest peak in the Catskills summit, at 9.8 mi. (The yellow-marked trail heading W from the jct., the Blackhead Mt. Spur Trail [trail 2], reaches open terrain in 0.35 mi, with sweeping 180-degree views to the S, W, and N. It descends a total of 0.7 mi to the col between Black-

head Mt. and Black Dome Mt. [Lockwood Gap]. It's well worth the round-trip to the outstanding views.)

The Escarpment Trail continues S and in 110 yd passes an open rock area where the words "Camp Steel" are written on the ledge. Views are good when leaves are off. The trail begins a steep descent, passing a 3500 ft sign at 10.5 mi.

The trail ascends briefly to a height of land, Arizona Mt., at 11.3 mi. Several overlooks to the Hudson Valley and views toward Blackhead Mt. await the hiker on the descent. At 12.2 mi, a side trail cuts sharply back to the L for 50 yd to an outstanding lookout point from which Lake Capra is seen far below. Devil's Path peaks and Stoppel Point are also visible.

The route descends very steeply to Dutcher Notch at 12.6 mi. (The Colgate Lake Trail [trail 8] descends gradually S and W for 4.3 mi to a DEC parking area at the end of CR 78 in East Jewett. The Dutcher Notch Trail [trail 7] descends N to a trailhead in Round Top in 1.9 mi. A spring is located 0.3 mi down the Dutcher Notch Trail on a gradual grade. The Escarpment Trail [as trail 10] continues another 11.6 mi to its southern trailhead at Schutt Rd. outside the toll gate of North-South Lake Public Campground.)

🐾 Distances: To Elm Ridge Trail jct., 1.3 mi; to Elm Ridge Lean-to, 1.4 mi; to bog bridging, 2 mi; to 3500 ft elevation sign, 3.4 mi; to Windham High Peak summit, 3.5 mi (5.6 km). (Ascent to Windham High Peak, 1784 ft [544 m]. Elevation, 3524 ft [1074 m].) To Acra Point/Burnt Knob Access Trail, 6.3 mi; to Batavia Kill Trail, 9 mi; to summit of Blackhead, 9.8 mi; to Dutcher Notch, 12.6 (20.2 km).

9 S-N Northern Escarpment Trail, Dutcher Notch to NY 23

Trails Illustrated Map 755: L18-M16 / Map 141, NE Catskills: O4, trail ES

Refer to the Palenville, North-South Lake Section for a description of the first 11.6 mi of the trail from Schutt Rd. near North-South Lake Campground to Dutcher Notch (trail 10).

▶Trailhead: Refer to paragraphs above for access trails to Dutcher Notch (trails 7 and 8).◀

From the jct. of trails 7, 8, and 9 (0.0 mi), the trail soon climbs steeply NW out of Dutcher Notch and the hiker will work until reaching a side trail at 0.4 mi to an outstanding lookout to Lake Capra. Several more overlooks to the Hudson Valley and views toward Blackhead Mt. await the hiker on the ascent to Arizona Mt. at 1.3 mi, 3400 ft elevation.

The 3500 ft sign is at 2.1 mi, and the trail now begins steep grades toward Blackhead, with more open views and blueberries in season. A rock ledge with views E has the words "Camp Steel." At 2.8 mi the trail reaches a three-way jct. at the 3940-ft summit of Blackhead Mt. The blue-marked trail turns below the summit rock at the jct. (The yellow-marked trail [trail 2] heads W, descending 0.7 mi to Lockwood Gap, passing open ledges in 0.35 mi with magnificent 100-degree views; a side trip to the views is well worth it.)

The blue-marked trail loses 1100 ft of elevation in the next 0.9 mi. Sections are extremely steep, and in winter full crampons are essential. Views are frequent through the trees; the route levels briefly near the 3500 ft elevation DEC sign.

Yellow Jacket Lookout at 3.3 mi offers splendid views N. The trail descends through pretty birch woods and levels in hemlock woods before reaching the Batavia Kill Trail jct. (trail 6) at 3.7 mi. (The yellow-marked Batavia Kill Trail descends 0.25 mi to Batavia Kill Lean-to, where water is found, and continues to Big Hollow Rd., 1.5 mi from this jct.)

At 4.2 mi, an open ledge provides good views E to Cairo Roundtop Mt. The trail climbs gradual grades to another view E at 4.4 mi. At 5.6 mi, the trail reaches Acra Point, an open ledge at 3100 ft with views E and N.

A side trail L at 6 mi presents excellent views of the Blackhead Range and Burnt Knob from several rock ledges. Loss of elevation continues to the Acra Point/Burnt Knob Access Trail (trail 5) at 6.3 mi. (The red-marked Acra Point/Burnt Knob Access Trail runs 1 mi down to Big Hollow Rd. A stream is 0.7 mi from the jct.)

The trail climbs Burnt Knob steadily to 3100 ft and a spur path L at 6.6 mi leads to an open rock cliff top with excellent views to the Blackhead Range and the northern escarpment.

The trail continues W on level trail to a downgrade at 7.2 mi; sloped rock here is very slippery! After the trail levels, a path R leads to a cliff top with expansive viewing N, E, and W to Windham High Peak. Side trails L at 7.6 mi offer excellent views S and W. An interesting variety of forest and trail continue to a low point at 8.2 mi. Varying grades ascend to the 3500 ft sign at 8.9 mi.

In 100 ft a spectacular open rock ledge has views to Albany on a clear day and E to the Hudson River Valley. The trail ascends to a geodetic survey marker 90 yd higher at the true summit of Windham High Peak, elevation 3524 ft. Spur trails along the summit offer views, especially good to the Blackhead Range, L.

The trail then begins a gradual descent and reaches a brief section of steeper terrain where views are available through openings in the woods. Grades become more moderate as the trail swings R and slabs the hillside on rocky terrain. Crossing a stream, the trail swings L and nearly levels near a dark conifer forest; the footing improves. In winter, the Blackhead Range is in full view.

Then the trail enters the first of several scenic spruce and red pine forests, over planks, at 10.4 mi. A side trail L at 11.2 mi leads to the Elm Ridge Lean-to, and beyond, the jct. of the Elm Ridge Trail (trail 4). This connector trail leads 0.9 mi to the end of Peck Rd., which is 0.8 mi to Big Hollow Rd. A spring is 0.25 mi from the jct.

The blue trail switchbacks down through attractive forest with a few older growth hemlock, and then passes possibly wet areas on nearly level trail. It passes through stone walls, reaches a DEC trail register at 12.5 mi, and crosses a bridge to NY 23 at 12.6 mi. A parking area is on the opposite side of the highway.

🐾 Distances: To summit of Blackhead Mt., 2.8 mi; to Batavia Kill Trail, 3.7 mi; to Acra Point, 5.6 mi; to Acra Pt./Burnt Knob Access Trail, 6.3 mi; to view S from Burnt Knob, 6.6 mi; to view N, 7.2 mi; to Windham High Peak lookout, 8.9 mi; to Elm Ridge Lean-to and trail jct., 11.2 mi; to NY 23, 12.6 mi (20.2 km). From beginning of Escarpment Trail, 24.2 mi (38.7 km).

Kaaterskill Creek from top of Kaaterskill Falls. ADK Archives

Palenville, North-South Lake Section

Millions of years ago, it is believed, the outlet of North-South Lake drained SW to Lake Rip Van Winkle in Tannersville and the Schoharie Creek basin. A classic case of stream piracy occurred when Kaaterskill Falls eroded back into Lake Creek, stealing the Schoharie-bound waters that now flow to the Hudson.

In 1741, John Bartram, the famous Philadelphia botanist, sought out the Balm of Gilead, today's balsam fir that was in great demand for the gardens of Europe. He found an abundance of them around North and South lakes. Captivated by the region, he returned in 1753 with his son to study the area.

In 1823, the view from the escarpment was immortalized by James Fenimore Cooper's Natty Bumpo in *The Pioneers*. When asked what he could see when he got there, he replied, "Creation, all creation, lad."

Perhaps no other place in America had such significant impact in changing the prevailing view of nature held by eighteenth-century minds than did this region around Kaaterskill Clove. Before then, wilderness was evil—something to avoid or conquer. By the end of the nineteenth century, romanticists saw nature as a place of overpowering beauty, drawing one toward spiritual uplift. The magic of the Land of Falling Waters, where Rip Van Winkle tramped the hills with his dog Wolf, changed the image of these forests from dangerous to places of peaceful retreat.

Thomas Cole's Hudson River School of landscape painting centered on this region. Steamboats brought the elite and powerful of the world here. Carriages and later railroads carried them up the Great Wall of Manitou to the mountaintop with its Catskill Mountain House, Hotel Kaaterskill, Laurel House, and other hotels. Here, one became renewed and enjoyed nature.

It is the same today. The glades are as enchanting and the vistas as awe-inspiring as ever they were in the past. But let the hiker be cautioned. The cliffs and crags are rugged and can be extremely dangerous.

General access from the E is from Exit 21 (Catskill) off I-87, the New York State Thruway. One can get to NY 23A and Palenville via NY 23 and NY 32. One can also leave I-87 at Exit 20, but it is advisable to take NY 32 to Palenville rather than to go to West Saugerties and up Platte Clove Mountain Rd., which is officially closed from November to April each year and is hazardous to drive the rest of the time. From the W, this region can be reached via NY 23 and NY 23A.

❋ Trails in winter: North-South Lake State Campground is excellent for cross-country skiing and snowshoeing, except on trails near the escarpment. Crampons are necessary for a climb to North Point via Mary's Glen Trail, which is icy. When the campground is closed, the Rock Shelter Trail is a direct route to North

Point and the Escarpment Trail. A winter parking area is at the W end of South Lake, beyond the campground tollgate and R. Across the lawn past an information board, a broad trail is excellent for skiing or snowshoeing to North Lake. Beyond a road barrier, a marked path follows the S side of South Lake through the woods to South Lake beach. Continuing across the beach, pick up the trail again to North Lake. Nearby is the site of the Catskill Mountain House, with sweeping views of the Hudson Valley. Circle through North Lake beach and campground to return to the parking area on the broad ski trail (or retrace by South Beach road). These yellow-marked paths provide nice treks around both lakes in any season.

A winter walk to the base of Kaaterskill Falls is interesting, and may require crampons.

Below is a list of suggested hikes in this region.

SHORT HIKES

Kaaterskill Falls: 1.4 mi (2.2 km) round-trip (includes 0.5 mi from Molly Stark parking area to trailhead and back). A 350 ft climb to one of the most impressive waterfalls in New York State.

Boulder Rock: 1.4 mi (2.2 km) round-trip. Visit the site of the former Catskill Mountain House, 0.5 mi round-trip, and then climb the steep shoulder of South Mt. and enjoy excellent viewing. Continue just beyond to Split Rock.

Artists Rock: 0.6 mi (1 km) round-trip. A delightful walk on flat rock through pitch pine forest to the escarpment edge. Involves one steep ascent and sharp drops next to the trail. This vista inspired artists of the Hudson River School.

Ashley Falls: 0.3 mi round-trip to base; 0.4 mi to top (0.6 km). Visit the bottom and top of Ashley Falls, via a spur path to the boulder-filled bottom, or cross the creek on top for a good view. The trail is rocky and can be wet, and at times the falls are dry.

North-South Lake: 2.5 mi (4 km) loop. A pretty loop through woods and along the lakeshores on level terrain, featuring Dinosaur Rock and Alligator Rock. This can be started at any point, except in winter when you must start from the South Lake outlet parking area.

MODERATE HIKES

Inspiration Point Circuit: 4.7 mi (7.5 km) loop. Follow the Escarpment Trail from Schutt Rd. to Inspiration Point, a favorite spot of President Grant; continue along the Escarpment Trail with good views to the Hudson Valley, and return via the Schutt Rd. Trail.

Palenville Overlook loop from South Lake: 5 mi (8 km). Visit Catskill Mountain

House site and Boulder Rock, hike the scenic Escarpment Trail and Sleepy Hollow Horse Trail to spectacular Palenville Overlook, and return via Sleepy Hollow Horse Trail and the old carriage road to North Lake picnic area and nearby Catskill Mountain House.

HARDER HIKES

Escarpment Trail with Sleepy Hollow Trail: 8.2 mi (13.1 km) point-to-point trip; requires spotting second vehicle. Walk the Escarpment Trail from Schutt Rd., then the Sleepy Hollow Horse Trail to Palenville Overlook (0.6 mi round-trip spur path off the Horse Trail), ending at Mountain Turnpike Rd. in Palenville.

North Point Circuit: 9.7 mi (15.5 km) loop. Follow the Escarpment Trail from Schutt Rd. to North Point, returning via the Mary's Glen and Rock Shelter trails.

Buttermilk Falls: 7.7 mi (12.3 km) round-trip; take the side trail to beautiful Poet's Ledge, adding an extra 0.95 mi (round-trip). A full day trip, with a great deal of climbing, to two waterfalls. Both falls are mostly invisible (you are at the top), but the view from the top of Wildcat Falls is great.

	Trail Described (one way)	Total Miles		Page
10	Escarpment Trail (Schutt Rd. to Dutcher Notch)	11.6	(18.6 km)	49
11	Catskill Mountain House Site	0.2	(0.3 km)	55
12	North-South Lake Loop	2.5	(4.0 km)	56
13	Mary's Glen Trail	1.3	(2.1 km)	57
14	Rock Shelter Trail	1.8	(2.9 km)	58
15	Schutt Rd. Trail	1.0	(1.6 km)	58
16	Kaaterskill Falls Trail	0.45	(0.7 km)	59
17	Sleepy Hollow Horse Trail	4.9	(7.8 km)	60
18	Harding Rd. Trail	2.7	(4.3 km)	63
18Y	Harding Rd. Spur Trail	0.2	(0.3 km)	63
19	Long Path to Kaaterskill High Peak from Palenville	5.4	(8.6 KM)	64
20	Poet's Ledge Trail	0.5	(0.8 km)	65

Route Guide for Palenville and North-South Lake (see map p. 48)

Mileage E to W	Description	Mileage W to E
0.0	Intersection of NY 23A and NY 32A in Palenville	8.9
0.15	Bogart Rd. jct. (Sleepy Hollow Horse Trail)	8.75
0.2	Whites Rd. jct. (Harding Rd. Trail)	8.7
0.6	100 ft E of Catskill Park sign, three horse-trail markers on	

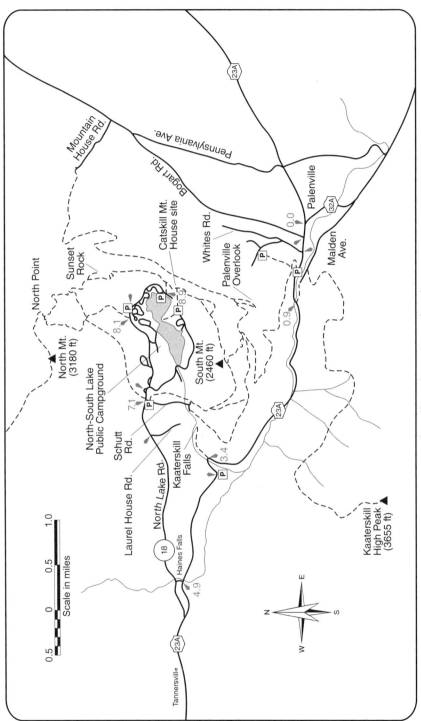

Palenville and North-South Lake

	telephone pole	
0.9	Malden Ave.	8.0
3.4	Bastion Falls, start of Kaaterskill Falls Trail at horseshoe turn	5.5
3.6	Molly Smith parking area	5.3
4.9	North Lake Rd. (CR 18)–NY 23A jct. Turn E onto CR18 toward North-South Lake Public Campground.	4.0
7.1	Schutt Rd., S side (200 ft to parking area; Rock Shelter trailhead, N side of road at same jct.)	1.8
7.2	Toll gate, North-South Lakes Public Campground (bear L at fork immediately past gate).	1.7
8.1	Trailhead, Mary's Glen Trail on L	0.8
8.2	Day-use parking on L for Mary's Glen Trail	0.7
8.9	Beach, bathhouses, picnic area	0.0

10 Escarpment Trail, Schutt Rd. to Dutcher Notch

Trails Illustrated Map 755: K18 / Map 141, North Lake Area: P4, trail ES

This section of the Escarpment Trail has some of the most beautiful and sustained vistas in the Catskills. Background information for the Escarpment Trail can be found in the chapter "Extended and Challenging Opportunities." Refer to the Black Dome Valley–Northern Escarpment Section for the description of the northern 12.6 mi of the trail from Dutcher Notch to NY 23 E of Windham village. North-South Lake Public Campground is a splendid place for recreation. Not only is the hiking very special, but one can also round out the trip with a swim and picnic. Boats can be rented at the South Lake beach (first R past the entrance gate). A small day-use charge per vehicle is levied for those entering through the campground gate; there is no charge for hikers parking outside the gate at the Schutt Rd. DEC parking area.

▶Trailhead: The trail originates on Schutt Rd. near the entrance gate to North-South Lake Public Campground. (See Route Guide, p. 47.) Trailhead parking is at the DEC parking area on the R, 200 ft down Schutt Rd. The trailhead is directly across the road from the parking area.◀

Carry plenty of water and allow yourself longer time for hiking than the distance suggests you need. You'll stop often to observe the views, and the cliff edges are no place to hurry. The trail in this section circles South Mt. to North Lake and then ascends North Point, turns W to Stoppel Point and NW to the approximate halfway point at Dutcher Notch.

Blue DEC trail markers lead through tall hemlocks and small spruces on a gradual descent, parallel to Schutt Rd. The trail crosses a narrow old railroad bed and then a wider railroad bed at 0.4 mi. Dropping down a small slope, the route passes over a bridge at Lake Creek. (If weather has been wet, the trail [also a

horse trail] is very muddy; if so, you can walk down Schutt Rd., turn L on a path paralleling the creek, cross bridge, and follow blue markers.)

A jct. past a second bridge on the trail is reached at 0.5 mi. (At the jct., a short L then R is the red-marked Schutt Rd. Trail [trail 15] to the old Hotel Kaaterskill site; an unmarked ski trail, L, goes to South Lake Rd.) The trail turns R down a rocky old road for 0.2 mi.

A trail register is located along the old road, where the road crosses a small stream on a narrow footbridge. (The faint trail R is the original, abandoned part of the Escarpment Trail; a Lake Creek dam is here.) The route reaches a height of land through maple/birch/oak forest. The trail swings R and begins to descend. (An obscure path L at a large rock is an overgrown crossover route, staying on contour, which rejoins the trail above Layman Monument.)

The blue trail descends quite steeply on a very rocky trail to Layman Monument at 1.2 mi. (Frank Layman lost his life here, fighting a forest fire on August 10, 1900.) A limited view down to Kaaterskill Clove and Rip Van Winkle Trail (NY 23A) opens up here. The trail makes a sharp turn L at the monument, now at the escarpment edge.

A short, steep ascent regains lost elevation to an open cliff ledge at 1.3 mi that provides excellent viewing S across Kaaterskill Clove and W to Haines Falls. We think this impressive place is really Sunset Rock with its western views (see below). Soon another view is reached.

At 1.5 mi, the trail ascends steeply, passing through interesting high ledges, and reaching a jct. at 1.6 mi. (The unnamed yellow trail L joins the Sleepy Hollow Horse Trail [trail 17] in 0.15 mi and the Schutt Rd. Trail [trail 15] in 0.5 mi.) The trail reaches Sunset Rock, a small ledge, at 1.8 mi and then descends down conglomerate rock to Inspiration Point, two extensive flat rock shelves with lots of space to enjoy the views, at 1.9 mi. Across the clove, Wildcat Ravine, Hillyer Ravine, and the cataract created by Buttermilk Falls are etched into the shoulder of Kaaterskill High Peak.

At 2 mi, beautiful viewing opens up to the E across the Hudson Valley. The walking is nearly level, but be watchful of your step, especially if you have children with you. The trail narrows in places and at 2.1 mi runs next to a sharp drop. This is a fascinating section.

The trail descends gradually, followed by a slight upgrade, before it joins the Sleepy Hollow Horse Trail (trail 17) at 2.7 mi. The trail turns R, coming to a second jct. 65 yd farther, where it turns L. (The horse trail continues straight ahead on the Harding Rd. Trail [trail 18], and the Long Path now joins the Escarpment Trail.)

The trail ascends about 200 vertical ft up South Mt. to another jct. at 3.2 mi. This area can be confusing with all the trails: the Escarpment Trail turns R at the DEC sign. (The red-marked Schutt Rd. Trail straight ahead [trail 15], turning L in 60 ft, runs 1 mi back to its first jct. with the Escarpment Trail. At this L turn, an unmarked wide trail R and a path straight ahead circle the old Hotel Kaaterskill site.)

The level roadbed trail now heading E is beautiful, adorned with mountain laurel, in spite of being away from the escarpment edge for a while. The trail passes a large rock outcrop L at 3.7 mi, just before a jct. at 3.8 mi. The blue-marked trail turns R. (The red cutoff trail straight ahead bypasses the Boulder Rock vista.) The blue trail passes Split Rock at 3.9 mi; huge blocks of a rock massif have split off. At 4 mi, Boulder Rock sits on a large open ledge. Beyond, the Hudson River Valley spreads out to the E and fine views of Kaaterskill High Peak and Roundtop Mt. are near to the S.

From here, level trail pitches upward and passes the other end of the red cutoff trail coming in from the L at 4.1 mi. Moderate pitches downward soon level off and the landscape is beautiful, filled with mountain laurel and pitch pine. There is another lookout near an enormous tilted boulder, which sports graffiti from the 1850s. The trail descends South Mt. on a switchback to the site of the former Catskill Mountain House in Pine Orchard at 4.5 mi.

Both hotel and pines are gone, but the view remains incomparable. Large exhibit boards provide maps and historical information about this famous spot. In its day, four U.S. presidents came here to rest. Night boats on the Hudson beamed spotlights on the hotel for their passengers. A railroad climbed the escarpment to deliver the cream of society to its doors. Now there is no trace of this illustrious past, save two stone posts at the entrance of the carriage road.

The trail leaves the open meadow opposite the view, following the old roadway. Partway along note the sign, "Historic Site: Catskill Mountain House," and turn R, following a scenic old carriage road marked with blue trail markers down to a yellow metal barrier gate just before reaching a DEC sign at 4.7 mi.

The route crosses an open area, another confusing place. Continue straight ahead under telephone wires to an unmarked dirt path that goes down a small gully and enters woods, where again you can see blue markers. (Do not turn R to the old railroad grade, or L to the parking area.)

The trail arrives at a picnic area; the beach is on the other side of this area. There is a universal access viewing platform here. A jct. near the beginning of a high wire mesh fence appears at 4.8 mi, the red-marked snowmobile trail (old Mountain House Rd.), which goes to the Sleepy Hollow Horse Trail (trail 17). The Escarpment Trail follows the L side of the fence: a yellow connecter trail leads to the parking area.

This is a fascinating trek on flat rock next to a dramatic drop. Take care if the rock is wet! Mountain laurel blooms in late June. Beyond a trail register, the trail steeply ascends large boulders. Then the route traverses lovely flat rock terrain, covered with pitch pine; the area is reminiscent of an oriental garden.

The trail then runs along the escarpment edge next to a drop of hundreds of feet to Artists Rock at 5.3 mi. The views of the Hudson Valley from here are breathtaking. Thomas Cole brought fellow artists here to point out his home, miles away on the Hudson in the village of Catskill.

A moderately steep climb up red shale soon levels through park-like woods to another large ledge, R, without views when leaves are on. The trail soon reaches the base of interesting conglomerate cap rock, atop which is Sunset Rock. The path ascends along the base of the cliff, passing under a large ledge, before reaching a jct. at 5.8 mi. (A yellow-marked scenic spur trail R leads less than 0.2 mi [sign, "0.3 mi," is incorrect] to Sunset Rock, a beautiful open rock zone cleaved with deep crevices requiring care, a place of magnificent views of North-South Lake and Kaaterskill High Peak, Roundtop, Plateau, and Hunter mts.)

The trail continues from the jct., climbing a steep pitch. It swings R on nearly level trail along the cliff top to spectacular Newman's Ledge at 6 mi. One can see N beyond Albany and enjoy the broad Hudson River Valley from precipitous cliffs. The route proceeds on varying grades, at times leveling and then resuming a steady ascent.

At 6.6 mi, just below Badman Cave, where it is thought eighteenth-century outlaws lived, there is a jct. with the yellow-marked Rock Shelter Trail (trail 14), which runs SW 1.8 mi to the Schutt Rd. parking area, near the campground gate. The trail steeply ascends R of the cave. Beyond the overhang, the slope becomes level in a beautiful spruce, hemlock, and pine forest. At 6.7 mi, ascending again, the trail enters a large open area with views of Kaaterskill High Peak and Roundtop, and in winter of the Hudson Valley. There is a level campsite beyond a large boulder.

The trail passes through a variety of landscapes on gradual grades: through lovely hemlock forest, over rock ledges, past wetlands, and through deciduous woods on a wide, level route, reaching a jct. at 7.3 mi. (The red-marked trail at L is the Mary's Glen Trail [trail 13], which leads 1.3 mi to the North-South Lake Campground.)

Above the jct. the trail climbs on new trailwork to a small cliff, turning R and very steeply ascending to the top. A short distance leads to an open ledge at 7.4 mi, with a view down to North-South Lake and mountains beyond. The trail ascends moderately to a vertical rock abutment, which it ascends 50 ft to the spacious rock shelf called North Point, at 7.55 mi.

From this spectacular spot, there are sweeping views of the Hudson River Valley and S over North-South Lake as far as the eye can see. Along the E edge, paths lead to another open area with views N to Albany and W to the Blackhead Range.

At the DEC sign, the trail continues gradually up to Moon Rock Shelter, a rock overhang, and then to Moon Rock, a large erratic on a second open rock shelf at

Milt's Lookout along trail to Stoppel Point. Mark Schaefer

7.7 mi. The route follows rock cairns and paint blazes. There is excellent viewing down to North Point at 7.8 mi, and again to the Blackhead Range.

A gradual SW ascent takes you into a hemlock forest and over the tree-covered, 3180 ft summit of North Mt. at 8.1 mi. A minor descent at 8.3 mi reaches a small saddle, where Winter Clove can be seen below to the N. In winter, there is a good view of the Blackhead Range. The trail passes through a beautiful hemlock forest on level trail, and then begins the ascent toward Stoppel Point at 8.9 mi. Ascending through ledges at 9.1 mi, it swings L and then climbs steeply to Stoppel Point at 9.3 mi. (A DEC sign says 8.9 mi, which is incorrect.) Elevation is 3420 ft.

From this section of Stoppel Point, views from a rock ledge are N and E to the Hudson Valley and to Albany on a clear day. The trail curves around the flat summit to an excellent view of the entire Blackhead Range at 9.5 mi. In 100 yd is a plane wreck, just before the trail begins its moderate to gradual descent to Milt's Lookout at 10.4 mi. (An informal trail R below the wreck descends to the Winter Clove House; only the lower reaches are easy to follow.)

Milt's Lookout presents excellent viewing N and E directly over Cairo Roundtop Mt. to the Hudson River Valley. The trail descends steeply from here, and then ascends gradually before finally dropping steadily to 2550 ft in a grassy wooded col at Dutcher Notch, where the Dutcher Notch and Colgate Lake trails meet at a four-way jct. at the 11.6 mi point of the trail. (A spring is located 0.3 mi down a gradual grade, E, on the Dutcher Notch Trail [trail 7]; the trailhead is N in Round Top village at 1.9 mi. The Colgate Lake Trail [trail 8] descends gradually S and then W on level terrain to a DEC parking area near Colgate Lake.)

The trail continues N another 12.6 mi to NY 23 E of Windham village. Refer

Cascades below Winter Clove Resort. Mark Schaefer

to the Escarpment Trail (Northern Section, trail 9) in the Black Dome Valley–Northern Escarpment Section of this book for the trail description.

🚶 Distances: To Schutt Rd. Trail jct., 0.5 mi; to Layman Monument, 1.2 mi; to Inspiration Point, 1.9 mi; to second Schutt Rd. Trail jct., 3.2 mi; to Boulder Rock, 4 mi; to Catskill Mountain House site, 4.5 mi; to picnic area, 4.8 mi; to Artists Rock, 5.3 mi; to jct. with yellow spur to Sunset Rock, 5.8 mi; to Newman's Ledge, 6 mi; to Rock Shelter Trail jct., 6.6 mi; to Mary's Glen Trail jct., 7.3 mi; to North Point, 7.55 mi; to Stoppel Point, 9.3 mi; to Milt's Lookout, 10.4 mi; to Dutcher Notch, 11.6 mi (18.6 km).

11 Catskill Mountain House Site

Trails Illustrated Map 755: K18 / Map 141, North Lake Area: P4

This short trek from the end of South Lake Rd. to the edge of the escarpment is one of the most visited areas in the Catskills to this day. The old carriage road brought the rich and famous to Pine Orchard, where the Catskill Mountain House flourished for over one hundred years.

▶Trailhead: Access to the trailhead is via South Lake Rd. (See Route Guide, p. 47.) Past the campground gatehouse, travel 0.8 mi to the end of South Lake Rd., taking the R fork to a parking area with a pavilion. The trail begins at the NE corner of the parking area past a barrier.◀

The broad path, an old carriage road to the Catskill Mountain House, gently ascends E, often on flat rock. Remnants of old foundations are off the path. Two stone posts and a sign, "Historic Site: Catskill Mountain House," are passed halfway along the route. At 0.2 mi, the open expanse of a meadow appears ahead. Originally this was a grove of pine, called Pine Orchard, and the hotel stood on the site. The foundation blocks are still evident; the exhibit board reveals the splendid hotel that stood here from 1824 to the 1960s, as well as information about competing Hotel Kaaterskill and Laurel House.

The front of the hotel was not far from the 1600 ft drop off the dramatic ledges found here, which afford views of the vast expanse of the Hudson River and valley. Names from the 1800s are carved in the rock. To the L, a path leads down through the woods to the top of the stationary engine Otis Railroad Line that brought passengers 1500 ft from the valley to the mountaintop. This technology and the fabulous hotel were a new experience even for the presidents and cream of society that came here. To the R near the exhibit board, the Escarpment Trail (trail 10) climbs 200 ft up South Mt. to Boulder Rock and Split Rock in 0.5 mi. (Returning toward the parking area, at the halfway point at the Historic Site sign, the Escarpment Trail turns R down a scenic old carriage road 0.2 mi to North Lake beach. A macadam lane, L of beachfront buildings, continues along North Lake and loops back to the parking area, passing a pretty lakeside area near islands.)

🚶 Distances: To Catskill Mountain House site, 0.2 mi (0.3 km).

12 North-South Lake Loop

Trails Illustrated Map 755: K18 / Map 141 NE Catskills: P4

The yellow-marked trail around North-South Lake can be hiked in either direction. It is described below, beginning at the parking area at the W end of South Lake, because there is a barrier beyond this parking area in seasons when the North-South Lake State Campground is closed. When the campground is open, the trail can be accessed from South Lake and North Lake beaches and from campsites and picnic areas near the lakefront.

▶Trailhead: From the campground toll gate, turn R on South Beach Rd. to the first parking area at the W end of South Lake. From the parking area, the route to the L of the lake is the easier route, running next to the lake on level terrain and reaching the far end of North Lake sooner than does the route on the R side of South Lake. This description starts on the R (S side), which begins through woods beyond the brown guardrail where there is a yellow marker and "Trail" sign (0.0 mi).◀

The trail ascends to level terrain and at 0.1 mi, the route goes R uphill. At 0.3 mi, the trail descends to the lake briefly. This area can be wet in seasonal runoff. At 0.5 mi, a bridge leads to South Lake beach. Cross the beach to where the trail again enters woods at 0.6 mi and crosses large flat rocks to a lovely stretch with many picnic tables; the footing in this section is excellent. At 0.7 mi, Dinosaur Rock appears R in the woods, worth a trip up for a close look.

At 0.8 mi the trail reaches a dirt road and turns L. (The route R passes Alligator Rock and reaches the final parking area on South Lake Rd., from where a 0.2-mi trail leads to the site of the famous Catskill Mountain House [trail 11].) Continuing L on the yellow trail, great flat rocks at lakeside soon appear, offering excellent lake views. The trail continues along a scenic stretch with shady pine and hemlock woods and next to the lake.

At North Beach at 1 mi, the route continues L, crossing the beach to the far end and resuming on a macadam path near the lake through camping areas, at times on roads or cross-trails. Throughout, be alert for yellow trail markers; avoid walking through campsites.

At 1.7 mi, the trail crosses a bridge over an inlet stream into a picnic area and reaches the first campsite loop, sites 4 and 5. At nearly 2 mi, a path goes out to the end of a peninsula. The yellow trail forks to the L, leaving the road, on a level trail mostly along the lakeside to the end of South Lake. Notable features are beaver activity and freshwater clamshells in the shallows of both lakes. At information boards, the trail comes to the end of South Lake and passes a yellow barrier gate at 2.5 mi.

🐾 Distances: To South Beach, 0.5 mi; to North Beach, 1 mi; to inlet stream, 1.7 mi; to information board, 2.5 mi (4 km).

13 Mary's Glen Trail

Trails Illustrated Map 755: K18 / Map 141, North Lake Area: P4, trail MG

Mary's Glen Trail is the shortest route to North Point from North Lake Rd. North Point offers dramatic 270-degree views from S to NW.

The Mary of Mary's Glen was Mary Scribner. Ira and Mary Scribner built the Glen Mary Cottage in 1844, near Lake Creek. Over the years, the little cottage was frequently used to care for the overflow of the large hotels, and Henry David Thoreau reportedly spent a night there.

▶Trailhead: Access to the trailhead is via North Lake Rd. (See Route Guide, p. 47.) A parking area is a short distance past the trailhead.◀

The trail runs N from the trailhead (0.0 mi), following the W side of Ashley Creek. The primary water source of North Lake, the creek once provided water for the Catskill Mountain House. The red-marked trail is crisscrossed by tree roots, but large stepping stones keep you dry in wet spots. An old-growth hemlock is L of the level trail as you near a trail register.

At a jct. at 0.15 mi, the whisper of a falls is heard. A short walk R on the spur trail brings you to the base of Ashley Falls. Many enormous boulders lean at sharp angles. Above, two upper pitches of the falls can be seen. In dry seasons there is often no water in the falls area.

The trail steeply ascends rocky ledges to the top of the falls, and then curves R through the hemlock woods to cross Ashley Creek at 0.2 mi. A short walk off-trail R reveals the top of Ashley Falls. The way is nearly level through the shady glen; the mossy stream edge, pleasant forest, and sounds of water create an enjoyable effect.

The way heads NW away from the stream, and then N before reaching a three-way jct. with the Rock Shelter Trail at 0.5 mi. New trailwork improves rocky, wet footing here. (The Rock Shelter Trail [trail 14] turns E for 0.5 mi to the Escarpment Trail [trail 10].) Passing a scenic high ledge on the R, the Mary's Glen Trail turns W briefly, sharing the route with the Rock Shelter Trail. (The Rock Shelter Trail departs L about 200 yd up from the first jct. and proceeds 1.3 mi to Schutt Rd.)

At 0.65 mi, the route ascends rock ledges moderately steeply on often-wet footing. In winter, this section above the Rock Shelter Trail jct. is extremely icy. The trail levels and meanders along the stream at 0.9 mi. Crossing runoff, it again steeply ascends rock ledges. It then levels and coal appears along the path. It passes below ledges where huge sedimentary rock slabs are tumbled together.

Another steep rock zone pitches up ledges where views of North Point become evident. The route passes next to a dark forest, and in the mossy understory you may spot pieces of an old iron stove. The rock type changes to red shale and the path steepens through deciduous woods; it can be muddy in wet weather.

At 1.3 mi, the trail joins the Escarpment Trail at a jct. (The Escarpment Trail [trail 10] heads steeply L 0.25 mi to North Point, and R 2.8 mi to the picnic and parking area at North Lake.)

🥾 Distances: To spur trail to Ashley Falls, 0.15 mi; to stream crossing at top of falls, 0.2 mi; to first Rock Shelter Trail jct., 0.5 mi; to Escarpment Trail jct., 1.3 mi (2.1 km).

14 Rock Shelter Trail

Trails Illustrated Map 755: K18 / Map 141, North Lake Area: P4, trail RS

The Rock Shelter Trail provides hikers on the Escarpment Trail or the Mary's Glen Trail with a means to reach the Schutt Rd. parking area without having to walk the paved roads of the North-South Lake Public Campground.

▶Trailhead: See Route Guide, p. 47, for access information. From the parking area on Schutt Rd., walk back up and cross CR 18 at its jct. with Schutt Rd.◀

The trail heads N from CR 18, crossing a wet area on large flat rocks, to a trail register at 0.05 mi. The route begins a broad swing E at 0.1 mi, gradually ascending as it winds through open deciduous forest. After losing ascent slightly, the trail becomes nearly level.

At 1.3 mi the trail joins the Mary's Glen Trail. (Mary's Glen Trail [trail 13] turns L to North Point in 0.9 mi.) The Rock Shelter Trail turns R and follows Mary's Glen Trail E down rocky terrain for 200 ft to another jct. (Mary's Glen Trail continues S, crossing Ashley Creek at the top of Ashley Falls in 0.3 mi, and reaching North Lake Rd. in 0.5 mi.) In this open area, a rock ledge with attractive mosses is found; in wet weather, they are a rich, lush green.

The last section of the trail has a much longer history than the relatively new part before this jct. Heading NE, it ascends 200 vertical feet before reaching its terminus at the Escarpment Trail. The trail climbs in steps of steep and level sections, where the forest is very attractive.

A campsite with a fire ring up against a boulder is at L at 1.6 mi. After topping the ridgeline, the path drops down slightly, passing rocky ledges L and reaching the Escarpment Trail (trail 10) at 1.8 mi. (From this jct., North Point is L, 0.9 mi; North Lake picnic area is R, 2.1 mi.)

🥾 Distances: To Mary's Glen Trail jct., 1.3 mi; to Escarpment Trail, 1.8 mi (2.9 km).

15 Schutt Rd. Trail

Trails Illustrated Map 755: K18 / Map 141, North Lake Area: P4, trail SC

The Schutt Rd. Trail is a short connector trail between two sections of the Escarpment Trail. It climbs gradually to the site of the old Hotel Kaaterskill, built on top of South Mt. after Catskill Mountain House owner Charles Beach refused to provide a chicken dinner for George Harding's daughter. Beach told Harding to build his own hotel if he didn't like it, so Harding built the Hotel Kaaterskill. The largest hotel of its time, it could handle 1200 guests. The hiking trail follows one of the routes to this old hotel, providing walking of little challenge but pleasant surroundings. The trail is named after Peter Schutt and his son, Jacob, who started the Laurel House Hotel in 1852 to provide rooms for vacationers who couldn't gain booking into the larger hotels.

▶Trailhead: Schutt Rd. Trail begins 0.5 mi S of the Schutt Rd. parking area at the first Escarpment Trail jct. over two bridges. From the jct., turn L and immediately R at the DEC sign onto the Schutt Rd. Trail. (The unmarked ski trail, L, heads to the South Lake perimeter road.)◀

From the jct. (0.0 mi), the red-marked DEC trail climbs the gradual grade of an old carriage road to the Hotel Kaaterskill site. It passes remnants of two stone gate posts in 200 ft, reaching a trail register on the R. Great hemlocks, attractive birches, and a rippling streamlet interest you until the trail reaches a second trail register at a jct. at 0.25 mi. (The unnamed yellow-marked trail R joins the Escarpment Trail 0.5 mi SE.)

The trail continues at comfortable grades, sometimes nearly level and sometimes slowly ascending the mountain. Large overhangs are seen L at 0.5 mi, where great rock outcrops stand out. The grassy road swings NE at 0.6 mi, and soon reaches an unmarked jct. Here a path L curves up to the area where the Hotel Kaaterskill once stood, while the unmarked trail straight ahead approaches the site from the opposite direction.

The trail turns R 20 yd to a DEC signpost at a jct. at 1 mi. Here, the blue-marked Escarpment Trail (trail 10) enters from the SE and turns ENE to Boulder Rock and the Catskill Mountain House site.

𝕄 Distances: To yellow crossover trail, 0.25 mi; to Escarpment Trail, 1 mi (1.6 km).

16 Kaaterskill Falls Trail

Trails Illustrated Map 755: K18 / Map 141, North Lake Area: O4, trail KF

Kaaterskill Falls is one of the most striking natural features in New York State. It has two great tiers: the upper falls drops 175 ft, the lower falls drops 85 ft. The overhang of the upper falls cap rock is so prominent that a great amphitheater exists behind the water flow. William Cullen Bryant immortalized the falls in his poem "Cauterskill Falls"; Currier and Ives prints were made of it; great painters made their reputations trying to duplicate its glory.

▶Trailhead: Access is from the Molly Smith parking area on NY 23A, 0.25 mi W of the trailhead. (See Route Guide, p. 47.) Down the hill from the parking area, at a sharp turn over the gorge bridge, a DEC signpost marks the trailhead (0.0 mi). Caution: Care should be taken while walking the section of NY 23A, which lacks shoulders by the cliff-side.◀

View from behind Katterskill Falls. Henning Vahlenkamp

Bastion Falls is the cataract at the trailhead. The trail proceeds steeply up new trailwork, which much improved the footing. The grade eases as it nears Lake Creek and a great boulder. Shale cliffs rise vertically across the stream and a great rock outcrop invites.

Moving away from the water, the trail climbs through picturesque territory, and then levels as it approaches the rocky talus at the base of the falls at 0.45 mi. The first full view of Kaaterskill Falls is breathtaking. It is a photographer's delight. Caution: Do not attempt to climb the falls from the base. Many deaths and injuries have occurred here.

🚶 Distances: To base of Kaaterskill Falls, 0.45 mi (0.7 km).

17 Sleepy Hollow Horse Trail

Trails Illustrated Map 755: K19 / Map 141, North Lake Area: P4

The Sleepy Hollow Horse Trail is a little-used but rewarding hiking route. The vale, where some have said Rip Van Winkle bowled ninepins with the ghosts of Henry Hudson's *Half Moon* crew, and vistas of the Hudson River are but two of the joys awaiting the walker.

Much of this historic path was part of the Little Delaware Turnpike. Passengers left ship at Catskill for stagecoaches that bounced and jostled their way up this road to North Lake. In time it became part of the second DEC horse trail developed in New York State. However, the upper reaches, beyond Palenville Overlook, are difficult for horses. Much of that section is seldom used by riders.

▶Trailhead: Access is off NY 23A at Bogart Rd. in Palenville. (See Route Guide, p. 47.) The Sleepy Hollow Horse Trail parking area is on the L side of Bogart Rd. at 2.1 mi, but this is not the hiker's trailhead. Continue past it, bearing L at the Pennsylvania Ave. jct. Note the old stone foundation on the L at 2.3 mi, the remains of a turnpike station, where horses were added to make six-horse teams before stagecoaches started up the mountain. Turn L onto Mountain House Rd. at 2.4 mi. The trailhead begins at the end of pavement, 0.8 mi up this road. Do not use the private home parking area at the road end. Use the wide shoulder of the road, 100 yd down the lane.◀

From the trailhead (0.0 mi) the old turnpike trail heads into Rip Van Winkle Hollow (Sleepy Hollow). It soon swings W, following the N bank of Rip Van Winkle Brook (Stony Brook). Sounds of falling water play in your mind as you watch the flow spill over the brinks of endless small cataracts amongst the deepening walls of the hollow.

Sometimes called the Mountain House Rd., this trail gradually ascends, being drawn into an ever-narrowing vale where hemlocks darken the way and eerie thoughts of times long past come to mind. At 0.5 mi the trail crosses tiny Black Snake Bridge. Moderate ascent leads to a trail register at a sharp horseshoe bend at 1 mi, where the roadway swings SE. This is Rip Van Winkle Hollow. Take time here to look at the stone foundation of the Rip Van Winkle House, once a small inn. Seek out Rip's Boulder, a large flat rock behind the inn site, where Rip allegedly slept away those twenty long years. If you have time, bushwhack up some 600 vertical feet to Rip's Rock, an extensive area of open ledges.

From here, the route ascends Dead Ox Hill. Initially, the way is gradual, and at 1.3 mi, a new wooden building is located just before the boundary between private and state land. Now the route becomes more rocky. Forbidding cliffs are on the R; a broadening valley floor is to the L. The grade becomes moderate; it is evident why two more horses were needed for a stage's climb and why passengers often had to get out to walk the steeper sections.

A spur road L at 1.6 mi leads to the Little Pine Orchard Picnic Area, with a fine view of the Hudson River Valley, and a fireplace and picnic table. Ascent to this area is 800 ft. A sharp switchback, called Cape Horn, heads N at 1.7 mi. It was possible to see the Catskill Mountain House on the escarpment from this point in the 1800s, but forests block the view of the site today.

The grade soon moderates as you travel through the Short Level. Another switchback S, at 2 mi, sends you up Featherbed Hill at moderate grades. At 2.4 mi, just before it levels off again, the trail becomes more rocky and curves L. The nature of the route greatly changes, as an almost flat grassy lane greets you. This is the Long Level. The roadway is nearly level or a gradual ascent to a jct. at 2.9 mi. (The old Mountain House Rd. continues another 0.6 mi to North Lake.)

The trail makes an abrupt turn L and descends at a moderate grade for 0.1 mi. A gradual downgrade finally levels as the trail passes under a high electric utility line at 3.3 mi, the site of the old stationary engine Otis Railroad Line that carried guests almost to the door of the Catskill Mountain House.

The trail is now level and straight, making a jog L at 3.4 mi. Areas are wet. At 3.75 mi, two marked trails lead to Palenville Overlook from the main trail. Separated by some 100 feet, the drier approach is the second yellow spur trail at an obvious jct., leading 0.3 mi on level terrain to the escarpment cliff with beautiful views and much to explore. There is a picnic table and fireplace, but the best lunch spot is 100 ft farther on several open ledges.

Continuing on the Sleepy Hollow Horse Trail, a series of switchbacks climbs steeply upward 0.1 mi to the next rock shelf level, some 150 vertical feet above. The route becomes an attractive level footpath surrounded by mountain laurel. The direction of travel is still S. Views of the Hudson eventually open up to the L rear.

At 4.5 mi, a swing NW offers views across Kaaterskill Clove. Gradual and moderate grades alternate as the wide path gains elevation. The trail crosses a creek, passes through a nice stand of hemlocks, and ends at a T-jct. at 4.8 mi. (The Harding Rd. Trail [trail 18] enters from the L, also with red trail markers; Palenville is 2.7 mi down this trail.) Bear R to a second T-jct. at 4.9 mi. The blue-marked trail running each direction from this jct. is the Escarpment Trail (trail 10).

🌠 Distances: To Rip Van Winkle Hollow, 1 mi; to Little Pine Orchard Picnic Area, 1.6 mi; to North Lake spur jct., 2.9 mi; to Palenville Overlook spur jct., 3.9 mi; to Harding Rd. Trail T-jct., 4.8 mi; to Escarpment Trail T-jct., 4.9 mi (7.8 km).

View of North-South Lakes from Sunset Rock. David White

18 Harding Rd. Trail
18Y Harding Rd. Spur Trail

Trails Illustrated Map 755: J18 / Map 141, North Lake Area: P5, trail HR

This trail has very nice walking over a little-used old carriage road. A group with two vehicles can have a through trip by starting at the Schutt Rd. parking area near North Lake and then walking the Schutt Rd. Trail and short sections of the Escarpment and Sleepy Hollow trails to connect with the Harding Rd. Trail. The group will travel on nearly level or downhill grades for the whole trip.

When George Harding built the Hotel Kaaterskill near the top of South Mt. in 1880–81, he also built Harding Rd. for access. Considered an engineering marvel in its time, this road snaked its way up South Mt. from Palenville to the hotel. In more recent years it became part of the Sleepy Hollow Horse Trail network and then part of the Long Path trail.

▶Trailhead: An older trailhead is 100 ft E of the large wooden "Entering Catskill Park" sign on NY 23A in Palenville, and just W of the Palenville village limit sign. (See Route Guide, p. 47.) The location is the unmarked old carriage road where state land signs are posted. A new trailhead is up Whites Rd., 0.2 mi W of the jct. of NY 23A and NY 32A in Palenville; take a L fork to the parking area. Walk S on the lane (trail 18Y) to a T intersection, descend briefly to meet the Harding Rd. Trail at 0.2 mi. Turn R.◀

The older trailhead begins on the unmarked gravel carriage road, the original Harding Rd. (Mileages are calculated from this trailhead.) The route climbs gradually, curving W at 0.2 mi and passes the new approach to this red-marked trail (trail 18Y) at 0.3 mi. The trail enters state land at 0.5 mi.

Interesting views open up to the L into Kaaterskill Clove, while the bank sweeps steeply upward on the R side of the road. The grade eases and the trail passes a trail register and horse tie rail just short of 1 mi. There is a splendid lookout into Kaaterskill Clove. The route curves R around the hillside and passes a large fireplace cleverly built into the cliff.

Now the trail heads N, ascending gradually near a major tributary of Kaaterskill Creek. The birches are lovely in this section. Tall hemlocks and stately pines give off entrancing scents as cool breezes waft up from the valley below.

At 1.2 mi the route crosses the boulder-filled tributary and gradually ascends to the escarpment edge with high rock cliffs on the R. At 2 mi, at a major switchback, the trail sharply turns ENE and climbs moderately another 350 vertical feet past interesting rock slabs. It must have been a fascinating trip by stagecoach. The trail nearly levels, and at 2.7 mi, the Harding Rd. Trail joins a section of the Sleepy Hollow Trail that was once part of the old Mountain Turnpike Rd. (The Sleepy Hollow Trail [trail 17] turns R here, descending to Rip Van Winkle Hollow, where Rip bowled ninepins with the ghosts of Henry Hudson's *Half Moon* crew, and then goes on to Mountain House Rd.)

Those walking the trail as part of the Long Path should continue L on the

Sleepy Hollow Trail to join the Escarpment Trail (trail 10) at a jct. 0.1 mi SW.

🏃 Distances: To first lookout, 1 mi; to tributary, 1.2 mi; to switchback, 2 mi; to Sleepy Hollow Trail, 2.7 mi (4.3 km).

19 Long Path to Kaaterskill High Peak snowmobile trail from Palenville

Trails Illustrated Map 755: J18 / Map 141, NE Catskills: P5, trail LP

This route is the access to Poet's Ledge and passes Wildcat Falls and Buttermilk Falls, which sit far up the shoulder of Kaaterskill High Peak. It is beautiful in June and early July, when the mountain laurel is in bloom.

▶Trailhead: The actual trailhead is 0.35 mi E on Malden Ave., off NY 23A in Palenville just W of the bridge on the W edge of town. The parking space at this trailhead is not open for public use. The closest area to park is described above for the Harding Rd. Trail, at the unmarked old carriage road (the original Harding Rd.), 100 ft E of the "Entering Catskill Park" sign on NY 23A and just W of the Palenville village limit sign. From this spot, walk 0.3 mi W on NY 23A over the bridge, turning E past a barrier onto Malden Ave. Note the occasional turquoise paint blazes indicating the Long Path. The trailhead is just past the Fernwood Restaurant, R for a few yards up a dirt road to another turn R (which passes above the restaurant).◀

Turquoise blazes on a large tree mark the trailhead (0.0 mi). The rocky old Red Gravel Hill Rd., now the Long Path, is turquoise-blazed to state land, where blue DEC markers then continue. The footing is initially rocky, but improves quickly above the switchback. State land is reached at 0.4 mi. Blue DEC trail markers now guide you.

The trail reaches impressive rock ledges and soon leaves the road, turning R at a sign, "Long Path," at 0.7 mi. Steady climbing continues to a turn N, where at 1 mi the route almost levels on a scenic mossy path. Mountain laurel abounds here in early summer.

At 1.2 mi, the trail begins another broad swing W, entering a hemlock grove and then climbing quite steeply to 1.5 mi. Soon, the route swings R past scenic ledges covered with moss and peeling paint fungus to a short spur path R at 1.75 mi. Here is a great view across Kaaterskill Clove to the ledges of Palenville Overlook. Mountain laurel blooms as late as July up here.

The trail now switchbacks L and ascends steadily to 1.9 mi, where it swings R and levels at the height of land. At 2.1 mi, the trail reaches the jct. with the Poet's Ledge Trail (trail 20). Continuing W on the Long Path, a very gradual downgrade on sometimes-wet trail reaches the Hillyer Ravine area at 2.9 mi, crossing a brook of two sections 100 ft apart. This is the main flow that enters Hillyer Ravine.

The trail is now level and swings closer to the edge of the escarpment. The path briefly turns L at 3.2 mi near a large boulder and overhang, then passes through narrow, multitiered rock outcrops and turns R.

The trail breaks out of the woods at 3.4 mi and crosses the stream atop Wildcat Falls. This is a spectacular place. The view looks across the distant Hudson River directly at artist Frederick Church's home, Olana. One feels a part of one of his Catskill paintings in this setting. The falls, however, drop invisibly from a great rock ledge. While there is no vantage point from which to see the falls, there is a large area to sit and enjoy the vista.

The trail continues westerly on level terrain to Buttermilk Falls at 3.9 mi. Here, very limited views of the top tier of the falls can be seen as the trail reaches the area. Extreme care is needed in this area with its sharp drops. Directly across Kaaterskill Clove is a view of the northern escarpment from North Mt. to Stoppel Point.

From Buttermilk Falls, the trail passes through attractive woods of older-growth hemlock and large oak, moving nearer the drop than previously. At 4.1 mi the route swings S. A trail from the Twilight Park area enters.

The Long Path ascends briefly and then becomes gradual or level to a jct. at 4.4 mi, marked by double turquoise blazes, indicating a sharp turn L. (At 4.5 mi, a trail goes R; if descending the Long Path, note this fork and go R.)

The trail climbs a series of rock ledges and passes a mossy rock wall at 4.6 mi. Good trailwork assists the ascent at 4.7 mi, passing rock overhangs. The route climbs very steeply through scenic rock ledges to a lovely clearing with great boulders.

The grade eases to a flat area at 4.8 mi; climbing becomes gradual or level through an attractive forest at 5.2 mi. The jct. with Kaaterskill High Peak snowmobile trail is reached at 5.4 mi. The Long Path continues straight 3.3 mi to Platte Clove (trail 22). The snowmobile trail turns R and climbs to another jct. in 0.1 mi, continuing in both directions around Kaaterskill High Peak and Roundtop Mt; see trail 21 for Twilight Park Trail to the summit.

❦ Distances: To state land, 0.4 mi; to view N, 1.75 mi; to Poet's Ledge Trail jct., 2.1 mi; to Hillyer Ravine double brook, 2.9 mi; to Wildcat Falls, 3.4 mi; to Buttermilk Falls 3.9 mi; to turn S, 4.1 mi; to second L turn, 4.4 mi; to snowmobile trail on Kaaterskill High Peak, 5.4 mi (8.6 km).

20 Poet's Ledge Trail

Trails Illustrated Map 755: J18 / Map 141, NE Catskills: P5, trail PL

The Poet's Ledge Trail starts at the 2.1 mi point of the Long Path from Palenville to the Kaaterskill High Peak snowmobile trail (trail 19). The yellow-marked trail is a R turn from the Long Path. It descends 300 ft in stages through older growth hemlock and giant mountain laurel, reaching an interesting open flat-rock area, a mossy path to a view N, and final descent through scenic narrow ledges to Poet's Ledge. This large rock shelf offers outstanding views of Kaaterskill Clove and Kaaterskill High Peak near to the S.

❦ Distances: To Poet's Ledge, 0.5 mi (0.8 km).

Stream along the Overlook Trail. Mark Schaefer

Platte Clove Section

This section offers the hiker some of the most fascinating outings in the Catskills, and its trailheads are among the easiest to reach.

The Mohawk Joseph Brant marched his Revolutionary War prisoners along Overlook Rd. in the 1700s, and Mink Hollow Rd. was used for hauling in the early 1800s. Summer visitors of the nineteenth century visited Plattekill Clove.

Several of the trails were created by the Twilight Park Association and Elka Park members. The Devil's Path begins in this section, running over Indian Head, Twin, Sugarloaf, and Plateau mts. before heading over a section of Hunter and West Kill mts. Platte Clove Preserve is a 208-acre nature preserve on Platte Clove Rd., owned by the Catskill Center for Conservation and Development. It is home to an artist-in-residence program, with a modest cabin, left of which is a steep path to the base of Plattekill Falls.

Plattekill Creek has headwaters on the shoulder of Kaaterskill High Peak, while Schoharie Creek begins on neighboring Indian Head Mt. Plattekill Creek water flows E to Esopus Creek and then to the Hudson. The Schoharie flows W and N, first entering the Mohawk on its way to the Hudson. Its water has to flow 175 mi to reach the same point in the Hudson where the Plattekill's water enters, though they start their journeys within 3 mi of each other.

❄ Trails in winter: Climbers have to be careful on the steep rock along the Devil's Path in winter, especially on the E side of Indian Head Mt. and the W sides of Twin and Sugarloaf mts. Cliffs and very steep grades make full crampons essential.

Kaaterskill High Peak (alternative trail to Hurricane Ledge) is not recommended in winter because of the steepness of the trail in the upper reaches. However, a 0.3-mi descent from the wooded summit to Hurricane Ledge for excellent viewing is rewarding. The N approach up the informal Twilight Park Trail to High Peak is icy into spring; a mild, sunny season might entirely melt the snow and ice from the steep but S-facing trail under Hurricane Ledge, so consider the conditions in making your choice of descent.

Cross-country skiing on Kaaterskill High Peak's snowmobile trail and Long Path at 3000 ft is excellent, as well as on the Old Overlook Rd. Trail.

Below is a list of suggested hikes in this region.

SHORT HIKES

Dibbles Quarry on Sugarloaf: 2 mi (3.2 km) round-trip. Visit a fascinating quarry with many rock chairs and other stonework, with beautiful views, not far up a mountain trail.

Devil's Kitchen Lean-to: 2.4 mi (3.8 km) round-trip; to quarry, 3.8 mi (6.1 km) round-trip. Walk the Platte Clove Preserve's Old Overlook Road Trail past an in-

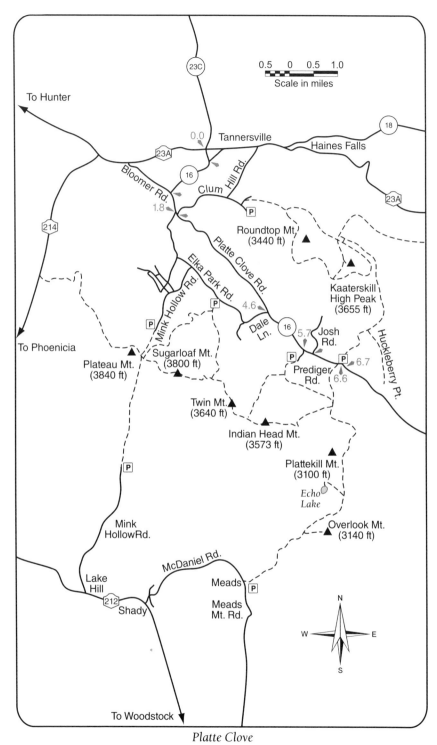

teresting old quarry to the Devil's Kitchen Lean-to by the scenic Cold Kill. Cross the bridge and hike another 0.7 mi to an interesting large quarry on a yellow-marked spur path, L, with excellent views of the Hudson Valley.

MODERATE HIKES

Huckleberry Point: 4.8 mi (7.7 km) round-trip. Plan on arriving at lunch time, so you can spend lots of time at this magnificent vista.

Twin Mt. E lookout via Jimmy Dolan Notch Trail: 4.6 mi (7.4 km). A good introduction to the Devil's Path, with sweeping views from several open ledges.

HARDER HIKES

Kaaterskill High Peak: 7.8 mi (12.5 km) loop trip. A long hike through attractive forest to an isolated mountaintop, descending the alternative trail from Hurricane Ledge to a plane wreck on a snowmobile trail. Involves a 0.25 mi bushwhack E from wreck back to Long Path.

Indian Head Mt.: 6.4 mi (10.2 km) loop trip. Several outstanding vistas and two very steep ascents up cliff-sides in a variety of terrain and forest.

Sugarloaf Mt.: 7.1 mi (11.4 km) loop trip. Visit an extensive quarry, enjoy a summit view, and hike one of the Devil's Path's most rugged and scenic sections on the W side of Sugarloaf.

	Trail Described	*Total Miles* (one way)		*Page*
21	Kaaterskill High Peak	0.7	(1.1 km)	70
	From Long Path via N			
	From Long Path via S	2.5	(3.5 km)	
22	Long Path to Kaaterskill High Peak from Platte Clove	3.3	(5.3 km)	71
23	Huckleberry Point Trail (Friends Nature Trail)	1.4	(2.2 km)	72
24	Overlook Trail	4.7	(7.5 km)	73
25	Echo Lake Trail	0.7	(1.1 km)	76
26	Jimmy Dolan Notch Trail	1.6	(2.6 km)	77
27	Pecoy Notch Trail	1.8	(2.9 km)	77
27Y	Roaring Kill Connector Trail	0.3	(0.5 km)	79
28	Mink Hollow Trail (Northern Section)	2.6	(4.2 km)	79
29	Mink Hollow from Elka Park—old trail	0.8	(1.3 km)	81
30	Devil's Path, Eastern Section (Indian Head to Plateau)	10.2	(16.3 km)	81

Route Guide for Platte Clove (see map p. 68)

Mileage W to E	Description	Mileage E to W
0.0	Traffic light, NY 23A in Tannersville Turn S; road becomes CR 16.	6.7
0.3	Going S, bear R at Spring St. jct.	6.4
1.3	Going S, bear L at Bloomer Rd.	5.4
1.8	Elka Park Rd. jct., S side; Bloomer Rd. becomes Platte Clove Rd.	4.9
1.9	Clum Rd. jct., N side.	4.8
4.6	Dale Lane jct., S side.	2.1
5.7	Prediger Rd., S side.	1.0
6.0	Josh Rd., N side.	0.7
6.6	Kaaterskill High Peak trailhead, N side; Platte Clove Preserve, N and S.	0.1
6.7	Parking turnabout, S side, on level at top of Platte Clove Mountain Rd. hill.	0.0

21 Kaaterskill High Peak from Long Path via N

Trails Illustrated Map 755: J18 / Map 141, NE Catskills: O5

The Kaaterskill High Peak snowmobile trail is reached by the Long Path from Platte Clove (trail 22) at its 3.3 mi point, turning L uphill for 0.1 mi; and from Palenville (trail 19) at its 5.4 mi point, turning R uphill for 0.1 mi. Here, a DEC sign marks the beginning of the 7.6 mi snowmobile loop around High Peak and Roundtop Mt.

At this snowmobile trail jct., the route turns R for 0.1 mi; the informally marked Twilight Park Trail leaves the loop trail L just before a dip that crosses a small brook. A small rock cairn may be seen here in summer, but look carefully because blue markings are now scant; the Twilight Park Trail's beginning here crosses a short rocky wet area and is nearly indiscernible.

The route soon steepens, climbing through a rock cut where views N begin to open up. The route passes between large boulders, jogging E and then back S before ascending steeply up another rock cut in a cliff wall. This N-facing trail

Long Path over Kaaterskill High Peak. Joan Dean

can be extremely icy in winter, making good crampons necessary. At the top of the rock cut, the path circles L where at 0.5 mi a boulder top provides a clear lookout N to Stoppel Point and the Blackhead Range.

The grade becomes more gradual. After minor pitches up, the trail reaches the wooded summit at 0.7 mi (1.1 km) in a small clearing, an ascent of 1705 ft from Platte Clove Rd. The careful searcher can find a USGS bench mark embedded in a rock some 10 ft SE. Remnants of a plane can be found on a path. From the summit, the trail descends to Hurricane Ledge at 1.1 mi, offering excellent views S from grassy open ledges. The hiker is encouraged to walk the extra distance.

A route marked by blue disks descends very steeply from Hurricane Ledge to the snowmobile trail at 1.5 mi; the Long Path is accessed by turning L to a downed airplane at 2.1 mi and reaching the DEC-marked jct. at 3.1 mi, turning R 0.1 mi. (The snowmobile trail is very wet in the last mile.) However, a map reveals that a 0.25 mi bushwhack E from the airplane brings the hiker directly over to the Long Path at about its 2.2 mi (3.5 km) point (see trail 22). This route eliminates 2 mi (continuing on the wet snowmobile trail to the jct., then looping back an equal distance, also very wet).

22 Long Path to Kaaterskill High Peak from Platte Clove

Trails Illustrated Map 755: J18 / Map 141, NE Catskills: O5, trail LP

Kaaterskill High Peak stands apart from other Catskill mountains, making it appear higher than it really is, and gives climbers superb views from Hurricane Ledge. Originally called Roundtop (Roundtop was called High Peak then), it was renamed Liberty Cap by the French Revolutionist Pierre DeLabigarre in 1793. By the 1820s, it was referred to by many as Mrs. Montgomery's Cap, after the widow's cap worn by Janet Montgomery, widow of General Richard Montgomery, who died leading the attack on the city of Quebec in 1775. Today, local people call it Cauterskill High Peak.

This trail to the base of the mountain and the snowmobile loop around Roundtop would be excellent for skiing. The first 3.3 mi of the route is part of the Long Path. (The Long Path continues to Buttermilk Falls, Wildcat Falls, Poet's Ledge and Palenville, described in trail 19.)

▶Trailhead: Access is via an old woods road/snowmobile trail off the N side of Platte Clove Rd. (See Route Guide, p. 70.) This is 0.9 mi E of Prediger Rd. (just W of a bridge near Platte Clove Rd.'s descent). A DEC sign (partially obscured by trees) marks the woods road where a large parking area is located a few yards in.◀

The trail follows blue DEC trail markers, snowmobile markers, and Long Path aqua blazes N from Platte Clove Rd. The woods road climbs steadily at first through hemlock forest. Nearly leveling at 0.5 mi, the rocky road then climbs more gradually, reaching a fork at 0.65 mi. Bear R.

At Steenburg Rd. jct. at 0.9 mi, the trail again bears R. At 1 mi, there is a third jct. where a yellow-marked trail leads 1.4 mi SE to spectacular Huckleberry Point (trail 23).

The High Peak Trail continues N, crossing a wet area and then two branches of Upper Plattekill Creek at 1.4 mi. The route climbs gradual and moderate grades. As elevation is gained, the slopes are drier. Trees change to maple and birch.

At 2.2 mi, the route levels out in Pine Plains at 3000 ft elevation. Spruce and balsam fir now dominate, with blueberries in season, in this beautiful section. Beginning where the Long Path levels out at 3000 ft where the terrain L levels at this point, a 0.25-mi bushwhack NW, L, brings the hiker directly over to the S section of the snowmobile trail (look for a downed airplane where the snowmobile trail swings W). This route eliminates 2 mi (continuing on the Long Path to a jct. at 3.3 mi, then looping back an equal distance from the 3.4 mi jct.; both the Long Path and the snowmobile trail are wet in these sections). Hurricane Ledge is 1.1 mi and the summit 1.4 mi from the plane wreck.

Continuing on the Long Path, the trail becomes very wet in places following a gentle downgrade. Brooks now flow N. At 3.3 mi, at a jct., the trail turns sharply L, leaving the Long Path. See trail 21 for the informal trail to Kaaterskill High Peak summit. (Straight ahead the Long Path merges with the old Twilight Park Trail in 0.2 mi, and then descends 700 ft, turning sharply R near the drop to Kaaterskill Clove and reaching Buttermilk Falls 1.5 mi from this jct. See trail 19 for continuation to Malden Ave. in Palenville.)

🐾 Distances: To fork, 0.65 mi; to Steenburg Rd. jct., 0.9 mi; to Huckleberry Point Trail jct., 1 mi; to Pine Plains, 2.2 mi; to divergence from Long Path, 3.3 mi (5.3 km).

23 Huckleberry Point Trail

Trails Illustrated Map 755: J18 / Map 141, NE Catskills: O5, trail HP

Huckleberry Point, formerly known as Friends Nature Trail, has one of the truly magnificent vistas in the Catskills. From its precipice one looks directly S to Overlook Mt.; to the SE and E are the Hudson River and New England; to the W is the awesome steepness of the Plattekill Clove walls abutting the shoulder of Indian Head Mt. Straight down, over 1000 ft, is the narrow ribbon of Plattekill Creek, cutting through its narrow canyon, spilling over waterfalls, shimmering in the sunlight.

▶Trailhead: Trail access is via the Kaaterskill High Peak Trail (trail 22) at its 1 mi point. Yellow DEC trail markers lead R to the SE.◀

The nearly level trail gradually loses elevation, passing several rock piles at 0.1 mi. Plattekill Creek must be rock-hopped at 0.35 mi; this can be difficult in high water. There is a moderate climb up ledges at 0.5 mi, and the trail approaches a high point at 0.6 mi. At 0.7 mi, mountain laurel adorns the mostly level path, which descends a steep slope at 0.8 mi, losing more than 200 vertical feet to Huckleberry Point. The trail becomes very scenic, winding through oak, pitch pine, and mountain laurel, which makes a trip in mid-June to July especially nice.

Several side trails go in different directions along the way; look for yellow markers before proceeding too far, especially when retracing. At a T-jct. at 1.2 mi, the trail turns R. A level section soon leads to Huckleberry Point, where the trail descends a short distance down ledges to the precipice edge, at 1.4 mi.

A sheer drop of over 1000 ft into Plattekill Clove immediately draws your attention; you are captivated by the view SE across the Hudson, and views across the clove to Overlook Mt. with its towers, and R to Plattekill Mt. and Indian Head Mt. Another ledge to the L permits a more directly E view. This is a wonderful place to have lunch while watching hawks, ravens, and vultures glide on air currents.

👣 Distances: To creek crossing, 0.35 mi; to height of land, 0.6 mi; to T-jct., 1.2 mi; to Huckleberry Point, 1.4 mi (2.2 km) (2.4 mi from Platte Clove Rd.).

24 Overlook Trail

Trails Illustrated Map 755: I18 / Map 141, NE Catskills: O6, trail OL

The Overlook Trail runs from Platte Clove Rd. to the jct. of the Overlook Mt. Trail (trail 55; see Woodstock-Shandaken Section). Until the mid-1980s, the trail began at the Indian Head Mt. jct. of the Devil's Path Trail. When the Catskill

Overlook Mt. fire tower. David White

Center for Conservation and Development created the Platte Clove Preserve, the trail system included a section of this old road, which is included here as part of the trail description. The trail makes a delightfully easy and attractive day hike to a large quarry on a spur path, or to Echo Lake or Overlook Mt. (If the skier starts on the Devil's Path at Prediger Rd. trailhead [trail 30] and picks up this trail at the 1.7 mi point, this is also a very nice intermediate cross-country trail all the way to the summit of Overlook Mt.)

Perhaps no other Catskill trail conjures up so much history in such a short distance. The route was used by Indians to force-march their Revolutionary War prisoners to their stronghold at Echo Lake.

▶Trailhead: Trail access is off the S side of Platte Clove Rd., 0.6 mi E of Prediger Rd. (See Route Guide, p. 70.) Continue E to the parking area 0.8 mi E of Prediger Rd., L, on an old woods road marked by a DEC sign that is obscured by shade trees. (L turn is before final bridge.) Limited parking is available on Platte Clove Rd. at the trailhead.◀

The trailhead location (0.0 mi) has Platte Clove Preserve signs posted on trees. Follow the green arrow trail markers. The trail drops down a bank 30 ft to Plattekill Creek. (Note beautiful waterfall, L on path.) An impressive King Post bridge crosses the creek.

Across the creek, the new trail diverges R briefly and enters an attractive hemlock forest. At 0.15 mi, the route approaches a creek on the R; the route crosses the creek at 0.25 mi. The trail swings L at 0.3 mi where there are double green square markers, crossing two other drainages; in winter or spring runoff, this area is wet.

At 0.6 mi, the trail passes the brushed-in old route and continues on gradual grades up the old Overlook Rd. trail, leaving the Platte Clove Preserve property at 0.75 mi. At 0.9 mi, look for a way into a stone quarry before a deep pit, L. The area has several chairs, built of the rock, on which to relax.

In 45 yd, the Devil's Path (trail 30) enters from the R. The route follows red DEC trail markers to a jct. in another 110 yd, where the Devil's Path turns R up Indian Head Mt. Continue straight ahead, following the blue trail markers of the Overlook Trail.

Another quarry, R, is just before the Devil's Kitchen Lean-to at 1.2 mi. The lean-to sits above Cold Kill in a picturesque location. This is a high-use lean-to. Hikers are strongly urged to carry out anything they carried in, plus a bit more. If the lean-to is occupied, overflow campsites are located across the bridge. Do not use the sites that are marked "No Camping."

The trail crosses Cold Kill on a bridge 50 yd farther along the way. Gradual upgrades on sometimes wet and rocky trail continue to a jct. at 1.9 mi, where a yellow-marked spur path L leads shortly to the remains of the very large Codfish Point quarry, well worth a trip to explore and relax on stone chairs with an excellent view of the Hudson Valley. Snakes might enjoy the rock, so approach watchfully.

Platte Clove near Artists Residence. David White

At 2 mi, the route begins to swing from SE to SW around the shoulder of Plattekill Mt. The trail contours the slope for the next 1.2 mi.. The main trail passes next to the quarry for a considerable distance.

At 2.5 mi, the trail comes to Skunk Spring, now an unreliable pipe spring, R. As the terrain drops off on the L, views of the Hudson Valley are seen through trees when leaves are off. The trail continues S on very gentle undulating grades on good footing, surrounded by mountain laurel. A path to a clearing for camping is reached at 3.15 mi and at 3.3 mi, a large boulder marks the jct. of the Echo Lake Trail (trail 25). (The Echo Lake Trail descends R on mostly gradual, rocky grades 0.7 mi to Echo Lake Lean-to. Total descent is 450 ft.)

The trail continues straight ahead over gradually rising terrain. At 3.7 mi, the trail swings R under Overlook Mt. on gradual or level grades. Views to Indian Head Mt. are excellent over the drop to the R when leaves are off. A large, balanced rock adorns the trail at 4.1 mi. At the base of a small cliff is a spring at 4.4 mi.

The trail reaches the jct. with the Overlook Mt. Trail (trail 55) at 4.7 mi. (To the R the Overlook Mt. Trail descends 2 mi to Meads Mountain Rd.; the Overlook Mountain House ruins are 0.1 mi.) To the L the Overlook Mt. Trail leads to the summit; the old road ascends 0.4 mi on moderate grades to the fire tower. A path near the jct. diverges R from the road and ascends 0.5 mi over open rock ledges with splendid views, and then to the fire tower. Rattlesnakes have been observed in this region.

🐾 Distances: To Devil's Kitchen Lean-to, 1.2 mi; to quarry spur path, 1.9 mi; to Skunk Spring, 2.5 mi; to Echo Lake Trail jct., 3.3 mi; to Overlook Mt. Trail jct., 4.7 mi (7.5 km).

25 Echo Lake Trail

Trails Illustrated Map 755: I18 / Map 141, NE Catskills: O6, trail EL

The Echo Lake Trail is a short spur trail to Echo Lake off the Overlook Trail (trail 24). It is also accessed from the Overlook Mt. Trail (trail 55). Echo Lake is the headwaters of the Saw Kill. Formerly Shue's Pond, it is the only natural lake in a designated Wilderness Area in the Catskills. It was here that the last Indian encampment in the Catskills was located. Many legends were generated about the lake in the heyday of the Overlook Mountain House.

▶Trailhead: From the 3.3 mi point on the Overlook Trail (trail 24) from Platte Clove, or the 1.4 mi point on trail 24 from the Overlook Mt. Trail jct., the Echo Lake Trail (0.0 mi) descends NW to Echo Lake following yellow DEC trail markers.◀

The route has a constant gradual-to-moderate grade on a rocky old road through open deciduous woods. At the bottom of the slope, the trail curves SE. It reaches the rear of Echo Lake Lean-to at 0.7 mi, having descended 450 ft. The lean-to sits 50 ft back from the shoreline. Tall trees around the lean-to are widely spaced, allowing excellent views across the lake. Informal paths wind around the lake.

👣 Distances: To lean-to, 0.7 mi (1.1 km).

26 Jimmy Dolan Notch Trail

Trails Illustrated Map 755: I17 / Map 141, NE Catskills: O5, trail JD

▶Trailhead: The Jimmy Dolan Notch Trail branches R from the Devil's Path (trail 30) at its 0.3 mi point. It climbs 1.6 mi SW to rejoin the Devil's Path at that trail's 4.6 mi point. The trail provides the hiker with several options for varying trip distances.◀

From the 0.3 mi point of the Devil's Path (0.0 mi), the trail crosses a stream and proceeds along a grassy woods road, following blue DEC trail markers. The trail crosses several intermittent brooks. In 0.5 mi, the trail heads L up a gradual grade into hemlocks on a softer footpath. The slope increasingly steepens and the trail becomes rocky into the notch. It finally becomes nearly level approaching the jct. at 1.6 mi. Elevation here is 3098 ft.

The Devil's Path, L, leads 0.6 mi to the summit of Indian Head Mt., with limited first view; 1 mi to sweeping views from Pulpit Rock; and R, 0.45 mi to the E summit of Twin Mt. (with beautiful vista), and 1.15 mi to the true summit of Twin Mt. (also excellent views).

👣 Distances: To jct. with Devil's Path, 1.6 mi (2.6 km).

27 Pecoy Notch Trail *(via Roaring Kill Connector Trail)*

Trails Illustrated Map 755: J17 / Map 141, NE Catskills: N5, trail PN

▶Trailhead: Trail starts at a jct. at the end of the Roaring Kill Connector Trail (trail 27Y). Bear L (0.0 mi). The trail leads 1.8 mi to the Devil's Path and 2.5 mi to Twin Mt. (The blue trail R leads 2.6 mi to the Devil's Path in Mink Hollow [see trails 28 and 30], forming part of a loop over Sugarloaf Mt.) ◀

The trail continues S from the jct., soon beginning a short, moderate climb along a former quarry road through a steep area. At 0.15 mi, the grade eases, and the trail passes a large mossy ledge and an intermittent spring about 70 yd beyond.

The trail traverses Mudd Quarry at 0.35 mi, after a short, steep pitch up through the talus slope below the quarry. The next 0.3 mi is mostly level through a mature hardwood forest with cliffs to the R. The trail enters a hemlock grove and turns L (this turn is not obvious) to descend to the quarry.

At 0.75 mi, the trail emerges into the open expanse of Dibbles Quarry, an excellent destination for families with children. The quarry has been transformed with large and amazingly comfortable thrones made of rock, and has much else to explore. In addition, there are excellent views of the upper Schoharie Valley

Beaver meadow on the Pecoy Notch Trail. Henning Vahlenkamp

in the foreground, to Round Top and High Peak in the NE and to the Hudson Valley in the E. A cave can be found below to the R of the talus slope.

The trail reenters the woods through additional sections of the quarry and crosses a large stream at 1 mi. (A bridge here was destroyed, but the crossing is not difficult; a short side trip L on the other side takes you to the top of a waterfall.) The trail climbs steadily E of the stream through a lovely hemlock woods. Look for bear claw marks on large beech trees farther up.

The trail reaches a small wet-weather pond at 1.2 mi. Turning easterly, the trail passes just below the extensive dam of a large beaver pond at 1.3 mi, with good views of Twin and Sugarloaf mts. This is an interesting place, with much beaver activity. Beyond, crossing a rocky drainage, the trail reenters the woods and reaches the old Pecoy Notch Trail at 1.4 mi; turn R. The route climbs toward the notch on rocky ground, passing a drainage at 1.6 mi and reaching the Devil's Path in Pecoy Notch at 1.8 mi. (The red-marked Devil's Path leads L to Twin Mt. in 0.75 mi and R to Sugarloaf Mt. spur path to views in 1.3 mi.)

❀❀ Distances: To Mudd Quarry, 0.35 mi; to Dibbles Quarry, 0.73 mi; to beaver meadow, 1.3 mi; to Devil's Path, 1.8 mi (2.9 km).

78 *Catskill Trails*

27Y Roaring Kill Connector Trail

Trails Illustrated Map 755: J17 / Map 141, NE Catskills: N5, trail RK

▶Trailhead: Access to the trailhead is off Platte Clove Rd. Turn S onto Dale Lane at a trailhead sign 3.7 mi from Tannersville. At a jct. at 0.5 mi, bear R, crossing a small stream onto Roaring Kill Rd. Follow this road NW 0.7 mi to a parking area on the L. Roaring Kill (worth a look) is about 200 ft beyond. The road continues into Elka Park becoming Elka Park Rd., but this section of road is closed in winter.◀

A trail register is 50 ft up the trail. From the rear of the parking lot, the yellow-marked trail heads SW through a small grassy area before crossing a small drainage and entering the woods. It crosses a second small drainage at 0.2 mi before reaching the trail jct. at 0.3 mi (0.5 km). Trail L goes to Dibbles Quarry and Pecoy Notch (trail 27) and trail R goes to Mink Hollow (trail 28).

28 Mink Hollow Trail (Northern Section)

Trails Illustrated Map 755: J17 / Map 141, NE Catskills: N5, trail MK

▶Trailhead: Same as trail 27, p. 77. This section of the trail makes a wonderful loop trek over Sugarloaf Mt., combined with the Devil's Path (trail 30) and the Pecoy Notch Trail (trail 27).◀

From the parking lot on Roaring Kill Rd., follow yellow markers 0.3 mi to a jct. To the L, the Pecoy Notch Trail (trail 27) leads 1.8 mi to the Devil's Path in Pecoy Notch. The Mink Hollow Trail leads R from this jct. 2.6 mi to the Devil's Path in Mink Hollow. These two new blue-marked trails create an opportunity for a loop hike totaling 7.1 mi over Sugarloaf Mt. from the trailhead.

From the jct. (0.0 mi), bear R on level ground through open hardwoods on a gentle grade to the first of two quarries. The trail crosses two small streams (not reliable) and reaches the first quarry in dense woods at 0.3 mi. The trail swings around the E side of the quarry on level terrain before beginning a gradual ascent to a scenic second quarry at 0.6 mi.

This second quarry is interesting, with old walls built from the tailings, set in a dense hemlock woods with 20 ft mossy cliffs. It is quite extensive, spreading to the W several hundred feet into private property. The trail turns nearly 180 degrees at this spot, and climbs moderately to steeply through hemlock woods, reaching a good woods road at 0.7 mi. Limited seasonal views can be had to the N and the Blackhead Range.

The trail turns L and ascends moderately, then bears R on level terrain below rocky outcrops. It climbs a short rise to yet another woods road at 1 mi. The trail follows this road L to the high point of the trail at 1.2 mi. (Approximate elevation 2750 ft.)

Mink Hollow. Bill Chriswell

The route turns S and heads toward Mink Hollow. It continues mostly level through mixed woods. The hemlocks thin out by 1.3 mi, offering limited seasonal views across the Roaring Kill valley to Spruce Top and Plateau Mt.

At 1.6 mi, there is an open view W to Spruce Top, then from the top of a ledge an open view toward Plateau and Mink Hollow. Here the trail makes a sharp switchback R and descends steeply to a cut-over area. At 1.8 mi, the trail enters an overgrown area, joining a skidder road to the L. This route descends for a short distance before reentering the woods and crossing a stream on a bridge in a hemlock-lined ravine at 2 mi.

At 2.2 mi, the trail bears L and passes through young hardwoods before climbing steeply to a level stretch. Heading S with the notch sometimes in sight, the trail passes through a hemlock grove before emerging onto an old road at 2.3 mi, continuing with slight ups and downs to the jct. with the Devil's Path at 2.6 mi. (The red-marked Devil's Path [trail 30] leads L to Sugarloaf Mt. in 0.95 mi, and R to Plateau Mt. in 1.1 mi [ledge view, 1 mi].)

To continue S on the trail, descend R for 175 yd to a second jct.; turn L 2.5 mi on the Mink Hollow Trail to Lake Hill parking area (trail 54). (Mink Hollow Lean-to is 0.05 mi L from the second jct.; straight ahead 1 mi for Plateau Mt.; the woods road R at the second jct. is the old N portion of the trail, [trail 29].)

❈ Distances: To second quarry, 0.6 mi; to height of land, 1.2 mi; to bridge, 2 mi; to Devil's Path, 2.6 mi (4.2 km). Total distance from trail register, 2.9 mi (4.6 km).

29 Mink Hollow Trail from Elka Park—former trail

Trails Illustrated Map 755: J16 / Map 141, NE Catskills: N5

Mink Hollow Rd. was a route used by the tanning industry to transport hides from Saugerties to Tannersville and Prattsville, and today this is the former trail to the Devil's Path. The best access is from Tannersville.

▶Trailhead: (See Route Guide p. 70.) Turn S off Platte Clove Rd. onto Elka Park Rd., pass Green Hill Rd. at 0.5 mi, and bear L at 1 mi at the DEC signpost at Park Rd. Turn R on Mink Hollow Rd. at 1.4 mi. The trailhead is at a large parking area another 1.4 mi along Mink Hollow Rd.◀

The trail proceeds on the level and crosses possibly wet areas before ascending 0.8 mi to the jct. with the Devil's Path (trail 30). (Trail R leads to Plateau Mt, 0.9 mi; trail L ascends to the more recent Mink Hollow Trail jct. [trail 28] in 0.1 mi, and to Sugarloaf Mt. in 1.1 mi).

30 Devil's Path, Eastern Section *(Indian Head to Plateau)*

Trails Illustrated Map 755: J16 / Map 141, NE Catskills: O5, trail DP

The Devil's Path is presented in four parts in this book. Trails 30 and 31 describe the eastern section; trails 33 and 39 describe the western section.

This 10.2 mi section of the Devil's Path climbs Indian Head, Twin, Sugarloaf, and Plateau to the Daley Ridge Trail (trail 32), in a total of 4275 ft elevation gain. This trail offers exceptional viewing and exciting hiking, featuring precipitous slopes and extremely rugged terrain. One must be well-conditioned, cautious, and well-prepared. It is particularly precarious when ice may be present. Backpackers should carry plenty of water as the only spring is W of Mink Hollow. Sections can be hiked using access trails 26 through 29.

▶Trailhead: Access to the E end of the Devil's Path is at the end of Prediger Rd., 0.6 mi off Platte Clove Rd. at a large DEC parking area 0.2 mi beyond the last house. (See Route Guide, p. 70.) The best approach to Prediger Rd. is from Tannersville, rather than from West Saugerties, because Platte Clove Rd. from West Saugerties climbs a treacherously steep, narrow route and is not open November to April.◀

A DEC information board and trail register are on the L side of the parking area. Small intermittent streams cross the trail in several places in wet weather and it approaches a stream at 0.2 mi.

At 0.3 mi at a trail jct. the Devil's Path goes L, following red trail markers. (The Jimmy Dolan Notch Trail [trail 26] goes R with blue trail markers.)

Gradual inclines continue and the woods road narrows to a footpath at 0.5 mi. The trail crosses a brook on an intriguing rock bridge at 0.9 mi. A general downgrade begins at 1.4 mi and the trail merges with the Overlook Trail (trail 24) at 1.7 mi. (The Overlook Trail, L, runs 1 mi to Platte Clove Rd., passing through the Catskill Center's Platte Clove Preserve. Note an interesting old quarry, R, 150 ft down this old road.)

The Devil's Path turns R, merged with the Overlook Trail, and at 1.8 mi turns R again at the Indian Head Mt. jct., with a sign obscured under trees. (Devil's Kitchen Lean-to is 0.1 mi on the blue-marked Overlook Trail, which goes to the Overlook Mt. Trail [trail 55], 0.5 mi from that summit.)

The Devil's Path, R, heads W and soon ascends scenic mossy ledges amidst old-growth hemlock. The grade steepens and is interspersed with level sections. The trail crosses a wet section and swings S beyond rock ledges, beginning a steady ascent. At 2.5 mi, the trail becomes steep, passing fine examples of multilayered sedimentary rock, to Sherman's Lookout (the chin of the Indian) at 3 mi. Here is an expansive 180-degree view of the Hudson River Valley and Kaaterskill High Peak to the N.

The route continues to a sharp drop-off, with limited views through the trees of nearby Plattekill and Overlook mts. Ascending large rock ledges, the trail continues its circuit around the area next to the drop, and levels before reaching another excellent view S at 3.3 mi to Ashokan Reservoir, the Burroughs Range, and Peekamoose and Table mts.

From here, the scenic trail passes over flat bedrock on high ledges, then begins a gentle downgrade to a short, extremely steep climb to the top of a cliff at 3.5 mi. Known as Pulpit Rock, this large ledge juts out over the area, affording spectacular views from N to S. A section of Indian Head Mt. is near to the E.

Minor climbing and level sections lead at 3.7 mi to the bottom of a 60 ft cliff, which the trail scales up tree roots with precarious hand- and foot-holds. In winter, the narrow trail along the cliff top requires great care, with crampons or snowshoes with crampons.

Catskill fiddleheads. Alan Via

The grade is easy along the long, wooded summit ridge, reaching the 3500 ft sign at 3.8 mi. Ups and downs over ledges on the summit ridge lead to an imperceptible high point at about 4 mi, with a nice view S. Ascent from the parking area is 1573 ft; summit elevation is 3573 ft.

The trail begins its 475 ft descent into Jimmy Dolan Notch at 4.2 mi on varied grades, but there are no cliffs. Twin Mt. and the Blackhead Range can be seen from a ledge. The Jimmy Dolan Notch Trail (trail 26) enters from the R at 4.6 mi. (It descends 1.6 mi to rejoin the Devil's Path, 0.3

View to Hudson Valley from the Devil's Path on Twin Mountain. David White

mi from the Prediger Rd. parking area.) Col elevation is 3100 ft.

The trail heads W through the small notch. At a large overhanging ledge L, note that the trail turns R up a pitch, and soon red markers are evident. After traversing rugged rocky terrain, the trail passes under a large rock overhang at 4.7 mi, and then ascends tree roots up 10 ft of nearly vertical rock.

Climbing continues to the 3500 ft elevation sign at 4.8 mi. An open ledge offers excellent views of Indian Head Mt., Kaaterskill High Peak (NE), and Overlook Mt. (SE). The trail levels and heads SW between windswept spruces and blueberry bushes as it skirts the edge of the mountaintop. Suddenly, it reaches extensive open-rock ledges with sweeping 180-degree views far S, E, and W to Twin's summit and Sugarloaf Mt. This is the lower of the two summits of Twin Mt. at 5 mi.

The trail descends gradually and ascends several pitches up rock ledges to the true summit of Twin Mt. at 5.7 mi. Summit elevation is 3640 ft. A flat rock ledge provides excellent views S and W.

The trail descends the bluff to the L, turning R below it, and begins an initially gradual descent to a viewpoint at 5.8 mi. Here, the trail reaches dramatic terrain, dropping steeply between narrowly spaced boulders, known as a "lemon-squeezer," to an enormous overhanging ledge. Past the 3500 ft sign, an open rock offers views N and W, with Sugarloaf Mt. near to the W.

A short, gradual grade then passes through another lemon-squeezer, and at 6.1 mi becomes one of the steepest sections of the whole Devil's Path, down boulders to the top of a 50 ft cliff. Extreme caution must be exercised in the descent from the cliff. Below, the trail passes a tank-like rock ledge and then maneuvers down a jumble of massive boulders that offer a view to Sugarloaf Mt.

The steep descent continues to Pecoy Notch at 6.4 mi. Col elevation is 2810 ft. The Pecoy Notch Trail (trail 27) enters from the R. (It descends 2.1 mi to Elka Park Rd. parking area, including the 0.3 mi Roaring Kill Connector Trail.)

The red-marked trail continues straight ahead toward Sugarloaf Mt. Initially level, it soon turns L and ascends the mountain, becoming steep and rocky in places. Good views to Twin Mt. and the Ashokan Reservoir occur at 6.7 mi and 6.9 mi. The grade becomes gradual again as the trail passes the 3500 ft elevation marker at 7.1 mi.

Near the summit the trail almost levels; low evergreens and ferns are abundant. At 7.6 mi, the trail reaches the true summit of Sugarloaf (wooded) at 3800 ft, an ascent from Pecoy Notch of 822 ft. At 7.7 mi, a spur trail L leads to excellent views E and S from a large rock ledge.

The trail remains nearly level before descending over large boulders, from which there are good views NW toward Plateau Mt. at 7.8 mi. It passes a 3500 ft elevation mark at 7.9 mi, just before reaching a spring (which fails in dry weather).

The trail drops with varying grades between boulders that close in on it in places. Several caves are found here. At 8.1 mi, the trail passes through a lemon-squeezer; at 8.4 mi, it runs across the top of a 50 ft cliff, descending on intermediate sections. (It is easy to miss this route, from the bottom if ascending, because the trail appears to continue straight instead of climbing the cliff soon after passing under a massive overhang. Look for red markers and take care in this terrain.)

This is spectacular territory, the trail turning L under the towering overhang and next to a high natural wall, always interestingly wet. Swinging R, the route soon crosses a crevice atop narrow rock ledges and passes under a natural rock arch, turning L amidst tank-sized sedimentary boulders at all angles along the slope.

The grade then moderates to a three-way jct. with the new Mink Hollow leg of the Sugarloaf Mt. loop trail, at 8.65 mi. To the R, the Mink Hollow Trail (trail 28) follows blue markers 2.6 mi to the jct. with the Roaring Kill Connector Trail, which leads 0.3 mi N to the Roaring Kill Rd. parking area.

The Devil's Path gradually descends to a trail jct. in the Mink Hollow col at 8.75 mi. Elevation is 2600 ft. Descent from Sugarloaf Mt. is 1200 ft. A trail register is located here. (To the L, the Mink Hollow Trail [trail 54] follows blue markers less than 0.1 mi to the Mink Hollow Lean-to and another 2.4 mi S to a parking area at the end of Mink Hollow Rd., N of Lake Hill. To the R, the old Mink Hollow Trail [trail 29] leads 0.8 mi N to the end of Mink Hollow Rd., S of Elka Park.)

The trail heads W from Mink Hollow Notch toward Plateau Mt., swings R and soon passes a spring and crosses a stream at 8.9 mi. New trailwork creates steps up the steep slope. The route slabs a shoulder that drops off to the R. At 9.1 mi, the route begins the ascent up a steep rock bluff, followed by switchbacks and a climb up through a rock cut. Moderate and steep grades continue to a rock overhang at 9.4 mi, followed by a partial view E. This is a scenic section of the Devil's Path.

A grassy section gives the hiker a breather at 9.5 mi, and the trail passes a 3500

Blackheads, Roundtop, Kaaterskill High Peak, and Plattekill views from Overlook Mountain tower. Mark Schaefer

ft sign. Stone steps lead up through one last rock cut to a large flat boulder at 9.6 mi with good views NE to Kaaterskill High Peak and Roundtop Mt. Gentle grades lead through attractive spruce forest to the high point of the Plateau ridge (rather than a discernible summit) at 9.7 mi. Summit elevation is 3840 ft. Ascent from Mink Hollow Notch is 1240 ft.

The reason for its name is obvious—the top of Plateau Mt. is nearly flat, with only mildly undulating grades. The Daley Ridge Trail (trail 32) enters at 10.2 mi from the S. (A private trail from Spruce Top Mt. enters here from the N.)

The next 3 mi are described in trail 31 from W to E, but here is an E to W summary from the Daley Ridge Trail jct. to NY 214: The trail across Plateau Mt reaches a lookout N to Kaaterskill High Peak at 11.4 mi, and at 11.7 mi, Danny's Lookout with its large erratic offers excellent views N to the Blackhead Range. Orchard Point at 11.9 mi offers panoramic views, with Hunter Mt directly across. The trail drops down the large ledge, crosses a wetland on rocks, and passes a spring L at 12.1 mi. Moderate and steep grades switchback down to a second spring R at 12.7 mi. Passing above a brook, the trail descends to a register and reaches NY 214 at Notch Lake in Stony Clove at 13.2 mi.

🍁 Distances: To Jimmy Dolan Notch Trail jct., 0.3 mi; to Overlook Trail jct., 1.7 mi; to Indian Head Mt. jct., 1.8 mi; to Sherman's Lookout, 3 mi; to Indian Head Mt. summit, 4 mi; to second Jimmy Dolan Notch Trail jct., 4.6 mi; to Twin Mt. E summit, 5 mi; to Twin true summit, 5.7 mi; to Pecoy Notch, 6.4 mi; to Sugarloaf Mt. summit spur trail, 7.7 mi; to Mink Hollow Trail N, 8.65 mi; to Mink Hollow Trail S, 8.75; to Plateau Mt. high point, 9.7 mi; to Daley Ridge Trail, 10.2 mi (16.3 km); to Orchard Point, 11.9 mi; to NY 214 trail register, 13.2 mi (21.1 km). 🍁

Stony Clove ADK Archives

Stony Clove Section

Hunter Mt., the principal feature in this section, was named after a landlord, John Hunter—a rascal who endlessly sought back-rent from his tenants in the mid-1800s. There was a movement to change its name to Mount Guyot, in honor of Arnold Guyot, the great mapmaker of the Catskills. His August 1871 ascent proved Kaaterskill High Peak was not the highest in the Catskills, though he was yet to find that Slide Mt. was even higher than Hunter.

Raging forest fires swept the mountain in 1893, eight years after the Forest Preserve was created. The first fire tower was built in 1909 at the 4010 ft level, where the Becker Hollow Trail joins the Hunter Mt. Trail. The foundation bolts are still visible. The current tower is at the 4040 ft summit and is open to the public.

Of the four major trails on Hunter Mt., the Becker Hollow Trail and Devil's Path (and Hunter Mt. Trail) are described in this section. The Spruceton Trail (trail 40) and the Colonel's Chair Trail (trail 41) are described in the Lexington to Shandaken Section.

Stony Clove more clearly demonstrates the concept of a notch than any other rock cut in the Catskills. It was so narrow before the building of a railroad and road, that in the 1840s the painter Charles Lanman said, "It is the loneliest and most awful corner of the world that I have ever seen—none other, I fancy, could make a man feel more utterly desolate...in single file did we pass through it and in single file must we pass to the grave." Now, of course, we delight in its scenic and challenging trails.

Take your time and explore it, for you will see, from NY 214, high on a cliff of Hunter (best viewed from the S), the stone face of the Devil himself. The Devil's Tombstone is at Devil's Tombstone Campground. Notch Lake was formerly called Stygian Lake (mythical source of the River Styx, across which the souls of the dead are ferried into Hades).

✣ Trails in winter: Very steep initial pitches up the Devil's Path from Notch Lake require full crampons. The Hunter Mt. Trail, between the summit and Devil's Path, is beautiful in winter, curving around the slope on gradual grades through snow-blanketed evergreen, permitting skiing to the flat summit of Hunter Mt. Plateau Mt. from Stony Clove is steep for the first 0.7 mi and becomes icy above 1 mi, requiring crampons, especially on the descent.

Below is a list of suggested hikes in this region.

SHORT HIKES

Becker Hollow to concrete dam: 1 mi (1.6 km) round-trip. A pleasant walk on mostly level terrain by a brook to a 50 ft concrete dam.

Hollow Tree Brook into Diamond Notch Hollow: 1.4 mi (2.2 km) round-trip. Route to trailhead requires high-clearance vehicle. Hike next to a beautiful brook. The route steepens at 0.7 mi; turn around here.

MODERATE HIKES

Orchard Point and Danny's Lookout on Plateau Mt.: 2.8 mi (4.5 km) round-trip. A short very steep climb to Orchard Point for spectacular 180-degree views; then visit a large erratic and take in another fine view to the Blackhead Range at Danny's Lookout. Ascent 1600 ft.

Diamond Notch: 3 mi (4.8 km) round-trip, with total ascent 1000 ft. Route to trailhead requires high-clearance vehicle. Walk next to Hollow Tree Brook and hike up the notch past Elephant Rock to a lookout spot at a large flat rock at 1.3 mi; proceed to the top of the notch, 1.4 mi, and beyond to a lean-to in a scenic setting, 1.5 mi.

HARDER HIKES

Hunter Mt. Loop from Stony Clove: 6.1 mi (9.8 km). 2200 ft ascent to the summit of Hunter Mt. from Becker Hollow, descent via Devil's Path to NY 214 (if done in reverse direction, a day-use parking permit from Devil's Tombstone Public Campground office, 0.2 mi S, is required to park at Notch Lake when the campground is open). Spot second vehicle or road-walk past Notch Lake 1.6 mi back to Becker Hollow trailhead.

Plateau Mt. Loop via Daley Ridge Trail: 8.3 mi (13.3 km) loop trip. Hike a beautiful new section of the Long Path with many views and a nice traverse across the summit to two more excellent views.

	Trail Described	*Total Miles* (*one way*)		*Page*
31	Devil's Path, Eastern Section (Plateau Mt. from NY 214)	3.0	(4.8 km)	89
32	Daley Ridge Trail to Plateau Mt.	3.0	(4.8 km)	93
32Y	Notch Inn Rd. Connector Trail	0.9	(1.4 km)	94
33	Devil's Path, Western Section (Diamond Notch Falls from NY 214)	4.3	(6.9 km)	94
34	Hunter Mt. Trail	1.35	(2.2 km)	96
35	Becker Hollow Trail	2.2	(3.5 km)	97
36	Becker Hollow Connector Trail	0.35	(0.6 km)	98
37	Diamond Notch Trail	2.0	(3.2 km)	98

Route Guide for Stony Clove (see map p. 90)

Mileage E to W	Description	Mileage W to E
0.0	Jct. of NY 23A and NY 214, E of village of Hunter	13.5
0.7	Ski Bowl Rd. to Hunter Mt. (to Colonel's Chair trailhead [trail 41])	12.8
1.3	Parking, Becker Hollow Trail	12.2
2.6	Devil's profile on Hunter Mt. cliff	10.9
2.8	Notch Lake	10.7
2.9	Parking, Devil's Path to Hunter and Plateau mts.	10.6
3.1	Office of Devil's Tombstone Campground, W side of road	10.4
3.3	Devil's Tombstone with DEC Forest Preserve Centennial Plaque, E side of road	10.2
4.2	Notch Inn Rd.; Daley Ridge Trail	9.3
7.5	Diamond Notch Rd., Lanesville; Diamond Notch Trail	6.0
10.5	Ox Clove (West Kill Mt. Wilderness Area)	3.0
11.5	Chichester	2.0
13.5	Phoenicia, NY 214–NY 28 jct.	0.0

31 Devil's Path, Eastern Section *(Plateau Mt. from NY 214)*

Trails Illustrated Map 755: J16 / Map 141, NE Catskills: N5, trail DP

The Devil's Path is presented in four parts in this book. Trails 30 and 31 describe the E section; trails 33 and 39 describe the W section.

This 3 mi section of the Devil's Path is described to the jct. of the Long Path near the summit of Plateau (Daley Ridge Trail, trail 32), passing outstanding views at Orchard Point and Danny's Overlook. The rest of the Devil's Path E section is described in trail 30 from Prediger Rd. to Plateau Mt., in some of the most rugged and challenging territory in the Catskill Forest Preserve.

▶Trailhead: The trailhead is on the E side of NY 214 at the Notch Lake parking area of Devil's Tombstone State Campground. (See Route Guide, above.) A day-use parking permit must be obtained from the campground office, 0.2 mi S of the parking area, when the campground is open.◀

The trail ascends log steps (0.0 mi) to a trail register in 65 yd. Red DEC trail markers guide you toward a rushing brook. The trail turns L and then R, beginning a series of steep switchbacks from 0.25 to 0.7 mi. A spring is to the L at 0.25 mi.

Moderate to steep grades slab the mountainside through a talus slope, with good views down through open woods at 0.8 mi. Passing large, flat boulders, the trail executes a sharp turn L at 0.9 mi, where it climbs rocky terrain, now well-maintained by trailwork.

Swinging L again, the trail becomes wet (icy in winter) from a spring and passes the 3500 ft sign at 1 mi. It reaches a wet meadow-like area, crossed on

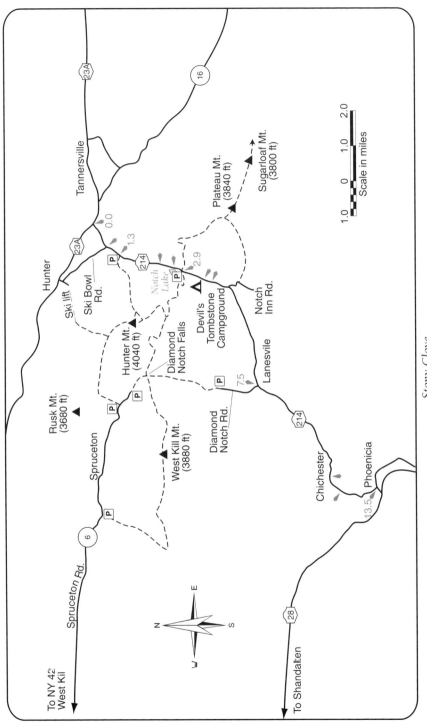

large, flat rocks.

The trail swings L below interesting ledges at 1.1 mi. The rocky route ascends to 1.3 mi, where it reaches the base of Orchard Point. It is a large stretch to scramble up; bushwhacking R offers an alternative. From this broad ledge are magnificent views from S to N. Directly across Stony Clove Notch is Hunter Mt. with its fire tower. West Kill Mt. can barely be seen over Hunter's L shoulder. The elevation is near 3600 ft.

The trail continues on level terrain to Danny's Lookout at 1.4 mi, offering excellent views N to the Blackhead Range, E to the northern escarpment region, and to the broad valley below. An enormous erratic boulder adorns the lookout. The trail swings R and continues on a nearly level route, reaching a second lookout to the NE at 1.6 mi, with good views of Kaaterskill High Peak and Roundtop Mt. From this point to the Plateau Mt. summit, the spruce woods close in. The undulating trail on often-level terrain in the evergreen forest doesn't suggest the top of a mountain, but it is a very pleasant walk. At 3 mi, the new Daley Ridge Trail (trail 32) and Long Path enter from the S.

The Devil's Path E to W (trail 30) is described in detail in the Platte Clove Section. Here is a summary W to E to Prediger Rd.: The viewless Plateau Mt. true summit is at 3.4 mi; a gradual downgrade leads to an overlook at 3.5 mi. A spring is at 4 mi; a stream is crossed at 4.2 mi; Mink Hollow is reached at 4.35 mi. (Mink Hollow Lean-to is near to the R and blue-marked Mink Hollow Trail [trail 54] ends 2.5 mi S in Lake Hill. To the L, the old Mink Hollow Trail leads 0.8 mi N to the end of Mink Hollow Rd. S of Elka Park.)

At 4.5 mi is a three-way jct. with the new Mink Hollow leg of the Sugarloaf Mt. loop. (Mink Hollow Trail [trail 28] follows blue markers 2.6 mi to the Roaring Kill Connector Trail jct.) The route reaches a cliff and towering overhang. Look carefully for a red marker on a tree after the overhang and another marker on top of the cliff for the safe ascent; proceed with caution.

At 5.3 mi, boulders offer good views; at 5.4 mi, a yellow-marked spur path, R, soon reaches Sugarloaf's excellent summit views.

The trail ascends to the true summit at 3800 ft, an ascent from Mink Hollow of 1200 ft. The trail remains nearly level across the summit through fragrant hemlock and balsam woods and gradually descends, passing the 3500 ft sign at 6 mi. At 6.2 and 6.4 mi, excellent views toward Twin Mt. and the Ashokan Reservoir open up.

Descent steepens through picturesque ledges and rocky footing, leveling as the trail approaches Pecoy Notch at 6.7 mi. Col elevation is 2810 ft, a descent of 1000 ft from the summit. (The Pecoy Notch Trail [trail 27] enters from the L; it descends 2.1 mi to the Roaring Kill parking area, including the 0.3 mi Roaring Kill Connector Trail.)

The Devil's Path traverses perhaps its most rugged section, climbing over massive boulders that offer a first view back to Sugarloaf. The trail reaches a 50 ft cliff that requires extreme caution to ascend. Footholds and handholds are evident, but the vertical pitch means some exposure.

Above, the climb continues unabated through boulders, reaching a lemon-squeezer, and briefly offers a more gradual section. Passing the 3500 ft sign and an enormous overhanging ledge, the route squeezes through another lemon-squeezer and pitches up to a viewpoint at 7.3 mi.

At the base of a large rock bluff, the trail climbs to its top, the Twin Mt. summit at 7.4 mi, an ascent of 830 ft from Pecoy Notch. A large rock ledge provides excellent viewing from 3640 ft. The route descends rock ledges and then climbs gradually to beautiful open ledges of the lower summit of Twin Mt. at 8.1 mi. Sweeping 180-degree views are seen far S, E, and W to Twin's summit and to Sugarloaf Mt.

The trail now heads through windswept spruces and blueberry bushes, skirting the edge of the mountaintop. At 8.3 mi, an open ledge offers excellent views E to Indian Head Mt., Kaaterskill High Peak, and Overlook Mt. The trail passes the 3500 ft sign and continues a steep descent, reaching a 10 ft pitch down nearly vertical rock covered with tree roots and passes under a rock overhang at 8.4 mi.

The route passes over boulders tilted at every angle, requiring nimble footwork and care, and swings R reaching a small pitch down. Turn L here; the large cave-like area straight ahead might look like trail but is just fun to explore. Jimmy Dolan Notch is at 8.55 mi. The Jimmy Dolan Notch Trail (trail 26) is L; it descends 1.6 mi to rejoin the Devil's Path 0.3 mi from the Prediger Rd. parking area. Col elevation is 3100 ft.

The Devil's Path ascent to Indian Head Mt. is more moderate, only 475 vertical feet from Jimmy Dolan Notch. A final steep ascent leads to the imperceptible summit of Indian Head at 9.1 mi with a good view S. Elevation is 3573 ft.

Minor ups and downs continue across the long summit, with a 3500 ft sign at 9.3 mi. The trail swings L across the top of a cliff (in winter full crampons and nerve are required to traverse this side of Indian Head Mt.) Precarious hand- and foot-holds and tree roots assist descent before trail levels near the dramatic 60 ft cliff base at 9.4 mi. (Go off-trail to see it best.)

The trail continues E on level terrain or minor descents to the next fascinating geological feature—a large, flat rock ledge that juts out over the area far below, at 9.6 mi, known as Pulpit Rock. This spot offers spectacular views; near to the E is a lower section of Indian Head Mt. To the R, the trail descends precipitously some 30 ft to the base.

The trail ascends very gradually through scenic territory, passing over flat rock on high ledges and reaching an excellent view S at 9.8 mi to the Ashokan Reservoir, the Burroughs Range, and Peekamoose and Table mts. The route passes next to a sharp drop-off, descending rock ledges and continuing past the drop to Sherman's Lookout (the Indian's chin) at 10.1 mi, with expansive 180-degree views.

A steep descent begins to 10.6 mi, passing fine examples of multilayered sedimentary rock. Descent continues to a wet section and then level sections are interspersed with downgrades; old-growth hemlock and mossy ledges provide scenic territory.

The trail merges briefly with the Overlook Trail (trail 24) at 11.4 mi. (The

Last light on Blackhead Range. Henning Vahlenkamp

Devil's Kitchen Lean-to is 0.1 mi to the R from this jct.) The Devil's Path turns L for 100 yd and then forks L (the Overlook Trail and Platte Clove Preserve Trail go straight ahead 1 mi to Platte Clove Rd. A quarry is past the jct., R, off the Overlook Trail.)

From the fork, L, the Devil's Path ascends gradually to 11.8 mi. The route is eroded and can be wet. The trail crosses a brook on an interesting rock bridge at 12.3 mi, and very gradually descends to a jct. at 12.9 mi. (The blue-marked Jimmy Dolan Notch Trail [trail 26] goes L 1.6 mi to rejoin the Devil's Path in Jimmy Dolan Notch.)

The trail turns R, passes near a stream, and terminates at the new parking area 0.2 mi from Prediger Rd. at 13.2 mi.

🥾 Distances: To first spring, 0.25 mi; to Orchard Point, 1.3 mi; to Danny's Lookout, 1.4 mi; to Daley Ridge jct., 3 mi (4.8 km); to Plateau Mt. summit, 3.4 mi; to Mink Hollow, 4.3 mi; to Sugarloaf spur path, 5.4 mi; to Pecoy Notch, 6.7 mi; to Twin Mt. summit, 7.4 mi; to lower Twin summit, 8.1 mi; to Jimmy Dolan Notch, 8.5 mi; to Indian Head Mt. summit, 9.1 mi; to Pulpit Rock, 9.6 mi; to Sherman's Lookout, 10.1 mi; to Overlook Trail jct., 11.4 mi; to second Jimmy Dolan Trail jct., 12.9 mi; to Prediger Rd. trailhead, 13.2 mi (21.1 km).

32 Daley Ridge Trail to Plateau Mt.

Trails Illustrated Map 755: I16 / Map 141, NE Catskills: M5, trail WC

▶Trailhead: The blue-marked new section of the Long Path from Silver Hollow Notch to Plateau Mt. begins at the height of land of an old road, just a few yards W of the jct. of the Warner Creek Trail (trail 53) section of the Long Path coming from the S. To access the Long Path from Notch Inn Rd., see the description for trail 32Y below.◄

Double markers mean a turn in the trail. The first switchback reaches scenic ledges and climbs gradual grades to a yellow-marked side path with a good lookout to Edgewood Mt. The trail now moves away from the viewpoint on the level, then climbs more steeply to an imposing 25 ft cliff. Climbs on varying grades reach a second lookout; the soft path enters a lovely ferny area on mostly level trail, passes a ledge with peeling paint fungus, and on very gentle grades reaches and traverses an extensive section with shady, often older-growth hemlock.

When the trail swings L, a gradual downgrade continues and swings R to Daley Ridge toward the mountain, regaining ascent to an imposing view in winter. Soon a magnificent vista opens up atop the enormous cliff. The trail swings L and reaches a large rock ledge with a side trail, R, to a spring—at present lacking a pipe or accessible flow. A very steep climb veers R on top to another sweeping vista to the S. Climbing moderates through evergreen forest to the jct. with the Devil's Path, 0.4 mi W of the true summit of Plateau Mt. at its E end.

🕷 Distances: To jct. with the Devil's Path, 3 mi (4.8 km).

32Y Notch Inn Rd. Connector Trail

Trails Illustrated Map 755: I16 / Map 141, NE Catskills: M5

This old road to Silver Hollow Notch gives access to the Warner Creek Trail (trail 53) and Daley Ridge Trail (trail 32). This allows for a nice loop hike over Plateau Mt.

▶Trailhead: Notch Inn Rd. is on the E side of NY 214, 1.3 mi S of the Notch Lake parking area. (See Route Guide, p. 89.) There is parking on the N side of Notch Inn Rd. before a bridge.◄

The trail follows the road for 0.4 mi from NY 214 to a private drive R to a house; cross a dirt pile straight ahead. Yellow DEC markers now mark the trail to the jct. with the Long Path in 0.9 mi from NY 214. (Much of the trail is in a rocky streambed; there are occasional softer side paths.) The Daley Ridge Trail turns N (L), and yards farther, the Warner Creek Trail turns S (R).

33 Devil's Path, Western Section
(Diamond Notch Falls from NY 214)

Trails Illustrated Map 755: J16 / Map 141, NE Catskills: M5, Trail DP

The Devil's Path is presented in four parts in this book. Trails 30 and 31 describe the eastern portion; trails 33 and 39 describe the western portion. (For trail 33 from W to E, see Diamond Notch Falls Trail [trail 38].)

▶Trailhead: The trailhead is at a parking area on NY 214, 2.9 mi S of NY 23A

Diamond Notch Falls. Henning Vahlenkamp

(see Route Guide, p. 89), where the Devil's Path crosses the road. A day-use parking permit must be obtained from the Devil's Tombstone campground office, 0.2 mi S of the parking area, when the campground is open. ◀

Leaving the L rear of the parking area (0.0 mi), the trail follows red DEC trail markers as it enters the Hunter–West Kill Mountain Wilderness. The trail drops down a bank and crosses the outlet of Notch Lake on a bridge below a small cement dam, reaching a trail register in 100 yd. The trail approaches a cliff at 0.1 mi, surrounded by immense boulders. Continue straight ahead on the sloping rock.

The grade steepens, with some excellent stone trailwork, to a second rock bluff at 0.35 mi. After following the base of the cliff, the trail climbs very steeply up a 50 ft vertical zone known as the Devil's Portal, passing a small stone overhang before reaching the top of this wall.

At 0.5 mi, the trail passes through a shady hemlock woods and continues to climb at varying grades to 1.4 mi, where it turns L around a rock ledge and suddenly levels, having ascended 1500 ft from Stony Clove. The route contours the slope of Hunter Mt. through scenic birch woods and reaches the Hunter Mt. Trail jct. at 2.1 mi at about 3550 ft elevation. (Hunter Mt. summit is R 1.65 mi, including 1.35 mi from this jct. via the yellow Hunter Mt. Trail [trail 34], and 0.3 mi on the blue Spruceton Trail [trail 40; see Lexington to Shandaken Section]. From the jct. to the summit is a 500 ft ascent.)

The red-marked Devil's Path continues L; the Devil's Acre Lean-to is 100 yd farther at 2.2 mi. There is a good spring here. Informal camping spots can be found past the wet area.

The trail then ascends to a height of land at 2.4 mi, where the herd path to Southwest Hunter Mt. heads L along an old railroad bed. There are remnants of logging railroad equipment used by Fenwick Lumber Co. in the early 1900s to transport logs to its Diamond Notch sawmill.

The route continues on level terrain and then descends moderately to 2.55 mi, where it swings R and contours the slope between 3400 and 3500 ft N to Geiger Point at 2.8 mi. A spur trail L leads to a fine lookout to Southwest Hunter Mt. from a sizeable overhang split off from the edge.

At 3.2 mi, the trail passes two large boulder ledges and rushing water in the ravine at L can be heard at 3.3 mi. The trail climbs briefly, passing a large rock overhang. A spur trail leads L at 3.4 mi, through an informal campsite to a large flat boulder overlooking the West Kill valley. Excellent views invite a rest.

At a stream crossing at 3.7 mi, the grade becomes more gradual. Several more drainages and a large brook at 4.1 mi make this a wet section during wet seasons. The trail crosses a substantial tributary on rocks. In winter, this crossing can be difficult; bushwhack upstream for best crossings. At 4.3 mi, a large clearing is reached next to the West Kill, atop Diamond Notch Falls. (The bridge destroyed in Tropical Storm Irene will be rebuilt.)

(The Devil's Path [trail 39] continues across the brook to its western terminus, initially running next to the West Kill. Also across the brook, the S leg of the Diamond Notch Trail [trail 37] continues uphill to the Diamond Notch Lean-to at 0.45 mi, and 2 mi S to the trailhead at the end of Diamond Notch Rd., 1.5 mi from NY 214 in Lanesville. The N leg of the Diamond Notch Trail [trail 38] continues straight ahead [not crossing the brook] 0.7 mi to the end of Spruceton Rd. A parking area is 0.1 mi W on Spruceton Rd. In 0.4 mi a parking area is located at the Spruceton Trail [trail 40]. See end of trail 38 for a Devil's Path summary in reverse.)

🥾 Distances: To trail register, 100 yd; to Devil's Portal, 0.35 mi; to level section, 1.4 mi; to Hunter Mt. Trail jct., 2.1 mi; to Devil's Acre Lean-to, 2.2 mi; to Geiger Point, 2.8 mi; to Diamond Notch Falls, 4.3 mi. (6.9 km). The Devil's Path continues for 7.1 more mi to the western terminus at Spruceton Rd. (See West Kill Traverse [trail 39].)

34 Hunter Mt. Trail

Trails Illustrated Map 755: J15 / Map 141, NE Catskills: M5, trail HU

The original fire tower on Hunter Mt. was where the Becker Hollow Trail (trail 35) now ends, 0.3 mi from the summit of Hunter Mt. Both the Hunter Mt. Trail (formerly Hunter Mt. Spur Trail) and the Spruceton Trail (trail 40; Lexington to Shandaken Section) ended at this tower. When today's tower was constructed at the actual summit, the trails were never adjusted to end at the new tower. Consequently, the trail markers are the same as originally set out, and the Hunter Mt. and Spruceton trails still both end at the original tower site. This is why hikers sometimes become confused when the trail markers they have been following suddenly change color on Hunter Mt.

▶Trailhead: The Hunter Mt. Trail connects the Devil's Path (trail 33) to the Becker Hollow Trail (trail 35) and the Spruceton Trail (trail 40).◀

Original Becker Hollow trailhead
David White

The Hunter Mt. Trail leaves its jct. with the Devil's Path (0.0 mi) and gradually ascends Hunter Mt., swinging to the NW at 0.3 mi, following an old woods road through increasingly dense balsam and spruce. This high trail is especially beautiful in winter.

At 1 mi, the trail steepens briefly as it climbs two switchbacks. It then resumes its nearly flat grade to the jct. with the Becker Hollow Trail (trail 35) at 1.35 mi. At the jct., a short level walk 75 yd L (W) brings you to one of two large open ledges with extensive views from SE to W.

🐾 Distances: To beginning of swing to NW, 0.3 mi; to switchbacks, 1 mi; to Becker Hollow Trail jct., 1.35 mi (2.2 km).

35 Becker Hollow Trail

Trails Illustrated Map 755: J15 / Map 141, NE Catskills: M5, trail BH

This is the shortest trail to the summit of Hunter Mt., at 4040 ft the second-highest peak in the Catskills, and therefore is a tough climb. It ascends 2200 ft in 2.2 mi and the first 0.5 mi is on nearly level trail to an old concrete dam.

▶Trailhead: Trail access is off NY 214 (see Route Guide, p. 89) at the DEC trail sign and parking area 1.3 mi S of NY 23A. A trail register is at the trailhead (0.0 mi).◀

The trail heads W on a wide lane past an interesting stone arch (the top now removed), following blue DEC trail markers. The route passes through open areas and woods, and then parallels a brook well below the trail. A footbridge crosses the brook at 0.3 mi. (Avoid an unmarked path R to camping areas, as the trail swings L.)

At 0.4 mi, the trail passes a three-tiered cascade of the brook and then a 50 ft

Stony Clove Section **97**

concrete dam. Across a small creek at 0.5 mi, a pitch up leads to a pretty hemlock glade above the brook. The route then moves away from the water through beautiful hemlock and ascends steadily.

The grade eases briefly at 0.9 mi before resuming the steady ascent, which becomes steep up rocky terrain at 1.8 mi, where a 3500 ft sign is located. The trail comes to a jct. with the Becker Hollow Connector Trail (trail 36) at 2 mi. (The yellow-marked Becker Hollow Connector Trail leads 0.35 mi to the fire tower on the Hunter Mt. summit. A spring is 100 yd R along the trail.)

The blue Becker Hollow Trail continues straight ahead up several steep pitches to the jct. with the Hunter Mt. Trail (trail 34) at 2.2 mi. Steel rods of the former fire tower protrude from the bedrock here. (The true summit is 0.3 mi R, or NW, along the blue-marked Spruceton Trail. The Hunter Mt. Trail heads L 1.35 mi to its jct. with the Devil's Path and nearby Devil's Acre Lean-to. An unmarked path straight ahead at 75 yd ends at a magnificent view S and W.)

🥾 Distances: To concrete dam, 0.4 mi; to 3500 ft sign, 1.8 mi; to Becker Hollow Connector Trail, 2 mi; to Hunter Mt./Spruceton Trail jct., 2.2 mi (3.5 km).

36 Becker Hollow Connector Trail

Trails Illustrated Map 755: J15 / Map 141, NE Catskills: M5

This short trail provides a source of water for hikers who need to refill their water bottles. The condition of the trail is less stable than that of other trails on the mountain, but it is pleasant to walk.

▶Trailhead: The trail begins at the 2 mi point of the Becker Hollow Trail (trail 35) and climbs to the summit of Hunter Mt. (the 3.4 mi point of the Spruceton Trail [trail 40]; Lexington to Shandaken Section).◀

From the jct. (0.0 mi), the yellow-marked trail very gradually descends NW 100 yd through a wet area to good spring water delivered from a metal pipe. The trail then travels on contour, passing an interesting large ledge at 0.2 mi. The trail swings L and pitches upward through conifers. One has to be careful to follow trail markers here. It enters the clearing at the summit of Hunter Mt. at 0.35 mi.

🥾 Distances: To spring, 100 yd; to Hunter Mt. summit clearing, 0.35 mi (0.6 km).

37 Diamond Notch Trail

Trails Illustrated Map 755: J15 / Map 141, NE Catskills: L5, trail DN

The Diamond Notch Trail, sometimes called the Hollow Tree Brook Trail, follows the route of an old wagon trail connecting Lanesville to Spruceton.

▶Trailhead: Access to the Lanesville trailhead is at the end of Diamond Notch Rd., 1.5 mi N of NY 214. (See Route Guide map, p. 90.) Drive 1.5 mi on Diamond Notch Rd. to a parking area. (The last 0.4 mi of this road is unpaved and in places very rough, requiring a high-clearance vehicle.) ◄

The blue-marked DEC trail leaves the parking area (0.0 mi) and heads N. It crosses a footbridge at 0.1 mi, 50 yd before reaching a trail register. The woods road follows the course of Hollow Tree Brook into Diamond Notch. At 0.4 mi, the route passes a deep pool; the brook cascades over mossy flat red rock.

The trail ascends gradually to a bridge at 0.45 mi, and climbs stone steps steeply. Then the trail becomes level to 0.7 mi, where the ascent steepens, leaving the brook far below in the ravine. It crosses a flow from a good spring at 1 mi, and passes Elephant Rock at 1.15 mi.

Hemlock grove in the Catskills. Tony Versandi

At 1.2 mi, the route becomes fully open and offers good views back down the valley. The talus slope at the base of Southwest Hunter Mt. spills onto the trail; a large, flat rock offers a good view S.

The top of Diamond Notch is at 1.4 mi, elevation 2650 ft. The view S is now obscured by trees, but the terrain is interesting between the talus slope of Southwest Hunter Mt. and the rising ledges of West Kill Mt. across the narrow ravine. (If ascending from Diamond Notch Falls, continue past the top of the notch to the flat rock for a view S.)

The trail passes through a beautiful hemlock grove and a second spring at 1.5 mi, reaching Diamond Notch Lean-to shortly. (A spur trail R leads to the lean-to, set in attractive terrain above a brook.)

Long, winding stretches gradually sweep downward from here, passing an old-growth hemlock at 1.8 mi. The trail swings W and footing becomes rockier under nettles. Descent continues to the West Kill Mt. jct. of the Devil's Path at 2 mi (see trail 39, Lexington to Shandaken Section). From this jct., the Diamond Notch Trail crosses the West Kill brook (bridge to be rebuilt) and turns L as trail 38, following the West Kill for 0.7 mi to Spruceton Rd. (Trail L, immediately before the brook crossing, is the Devil's Path to West Kill Mt. [trail 39]. Trail R, after the bridge, is the Devil's Path to NY 214 [trail 33].)

🍁 Distances: To bridge, 0.45 mi; to spring, 1 mi; to Elephant Rock, 1.15 mi; to top of Diamond Notch, 1.4 mi; to Diamond Notch Lean-to, 1.5 mi; Devil's Path jct., 2 mi (3.2 km). 🍃

Hunter Mountain view. Hardie Truesdale

Lexington to Shandaken Section

The northwest Catskills, described in this section, include Spruceton Valley with its approaches to Hunter and West Kill mts., western sections of the Devil's Path, and Diamond Notch. The NY 42 corridor farther S is referred to as Deep Notch, and its name is well deserved near the height of land. There is a pull-off, W, to the start of the Halcott Mt. bushwhack at 5 mi from Shandaken, and a parking area also referred to as Shaft 7 on the E side at 3.7 mi from Shandaken to bushwhack to Mt. Sherrill.

Spruceton Rd. is a long walk, so be sure you go in with a full gas tank; the last part of Spruceton Rd. is dirt. In winter, a second DEC parking area 0.2 mi past the Spruceton trailhead is to be used (not the area at road's end, often used in summer; it is the plow turnaround).

❋ Trails in winter: All trails in this section are frequently climbed in winter. The loop to Hunter Mt. is an excellent winter hike, with no cliffs or high ledges to negotiate; the high summit with conifer forest is especially beautiful when blanketed with snow. The approach to West Kill Mt., via the Devil's Path from Diamond Notch Falls, is up the N face; a steep, wet section partway toward the ridge becomes very icy and crampons are essential.

Trailless North Dome and Sherrill mts., often done together, are a long trip in winter. Sherrill is very steep from the col between the two mountains—avoid conditions where snow is hard-glazed, for descents can be hazardous and ascents require packable snow to make "steps."

Parking on Spruceton Rd. can be uncertain; the unmarked North Dome parking area at 2.9 mi and the Mink Hollow parking area for West Kill Mt. at 3.8 mi may not be plowed. The parking area for Halcott Mt. on the W side of NY 42 is generally plowed. The next parking area is 1.3 mi S on NY 42, at Shaft 7; crossing NY 42 from here, a good approach to Halcott is following the gradual ridge up.

Below is a list of suggested hikes in this region.

SHORT HIKE
Diamond Notch Falls: 1.4 mi (2.2 km) round-trip. A gradual ascent up an attractive woods road along the West Kill to a 12 ft waterfall. The flat rock above the falls is interestingly etched, but very slippery. Take care.

MODERATE HIKES
Diamond Notch: 3 mi (4.8 km). Continue past Diamond Notch Falls (above), cross West Kill brook (bridge to be rebuilt), proceed straight ahead (not R) up to the notch high point and beyond to a great flat rock with a nice view S. Enjoy a scenic lean-to and the Southwest Hunter Mt. talus slope.

Colonel's Chair Trail: Take a ski chairlift to a ski lodge, then go on a 4.2 mi (6.7

km) round-trip to the summit of Hunter Mt. Return by chairlift.

HARDER HIKES
Hunter Mt. Loop: 8.4 mi (13.4 km) (includes a 0.4 mi road walk). A steady moderate grade to the fire tower; scenic conifer forest, views, lean-tos, and Diamond Notch Falls back to parking area. This is a recommended winter trip.

West Kill Mt.: 7.8 mi (12.5 km) through trip; requires two vehicles. Steep climbing up the Devil's Path, beautiful lookout ledges in two directions, and a variety of terrain.

	Trail Described	Total Miles (one way)	Page
38	Diamond Notch Falls from Spruceton Rd.	0.7 (1.1 km)	103
39 E-W	Devil's Path (West Kill Mt. Traverse)	7.1 (11.4 km)	105
39 W-E	Devil's Path (West Kill Mt. Traverse)	7.1 (11.4 km)	106
40	Spruceton Trail	3.4 (5.4 km)	108
41	Colonel's Chair Trail	1.1 (1.8 km)	109
42	Rusk Mt.	trailless	110
43	Southwest Hunter Mt.	trailless	110
44	North Dome Mt.	trailless	111
45	Mt. Sherrill	trailless	112
46	Halcott Mt.	trailless	113

Route Guide for Lexington to Shandaken (see map p. 104)

Mileage N to S	Description	Mileage S to N
0.0	Jct. NY 42 and NY 23A W of Hunter	10.5
0.2	Cross Schoharie Creek bridge at NY 42 jct.	10.3
3.1	West Kill hamlet and Spruceton Rd. (see separate route guide for Spruceton Rd.)	7.4
4.5	Height of land in Deep Notch	6.0
5.5	Unmarked parking area, W side of road; starting point for Halcott Mt.	5.0
6.8	Forest Preserve access parking; alternate starting point for Mt. Sherrill	3.7
10.5	Jct. NY 42 and NY 28 at Shandaken	0.0

Route Guide for Spruceton Rd. (see map p. 104)

Mileage N to S	Description	Mileage S to N
0.0	Spruceton Rd. (CR 6) and NY 42 jct. at hamlet of West Kill (look for flag pole)	7.0

0.05	Post Office	6.95
1.8	Bridge over West Kill	5.2
1.9	Shoemaker Rd. (good starting point for Mt. Sherrill)	5.1
2.8	Bridge over West Kill	4.2
2.9	Unmarked DEC parking area, S side (good starting point for North Dome Mt.)	4.1
3.8	Mink Hollow trailhead for West Kill Mt.	3.2
6	Paved road narrows and becomes dirt.	1.0
6.7	Large DEC parking area, N side, for Spruceton Trail	0.3
6.9	DEC parking area, S side; use for West Kill Mt., Diamond Notch, Devil's Path, Hunter Mt.	0.1
7	Snowplow turnaround; no parking in winter.	0.0

38 Diamond Notch Falls from Spruceton Rd.

Trails Illustrated Map 755: J15 / Map 141, NE Catskills: L5, trail DN

▶Trailhead: There is space for several vehicles at the end of Spruceton Rd. at 7 mi, but in winter this is a snowplow turnaround. The Spruceton Trail (trail 40) parking area is 6.7 mi from NY 42; additional parking is at 6.9 mi on the R. (See Route Guide to Spruceton Rd., above.)◀

The blue-marked Diamond Notch Falls Trail (0.0 mi) begins past a barrier cable at the snowplow turnaround at the end of Spruceton Rd. A trail register is reached where there are views down to the nearby West Kill; evidence of an old mill can be seen. The brook meanders away briefly, but soon reappears with many delightful cascades and pools. The old woods road ascends gradually and reaches a large clearing at 0.7 mi. A steep path down to the base of Diamond Notch Falls is just before the clearing. From the clearing, the Devil's Path (trail 33, described below from W to E), continues straight ahead with red markers.

Across the West Kill, the Diamond Notch Trail (trail 37) continues 2 mi to Lanesville. The red-marked Devil's Path (trail 39) turns R and ascends 2.5 mi to West Kill Mt. Above the falls is a scenic section of flat rock (very slippery) and water-carved channels where the stream plunges over a 12 ft waterfall into a shallow pool.

🥾 Distances: To Diamond Notch Falls, 0.7 mi (1.1 km).

Because the Devil's Path (trail 33) is often used to climb Hunter and Southwest Hunter mts. from the end of trail 38, the W to E summary is included here:

The Devil's Path (0.0 mi) continues E up a rise to the L of the information board, following red trail markers. It reaches a rushing tributary that is easily rock-hopped but can be challenging in high water. Crossing spots can be found upstream.

An unmarked path at 0.9 mi leads R to an informal campsite. A spur trail R at 1.5 mi leads to Geiger Point, a ledge with good views to Southwest Hunter Mt. A gradual downgrade to 1.8 mi is followed by a pitch up to a height of land,

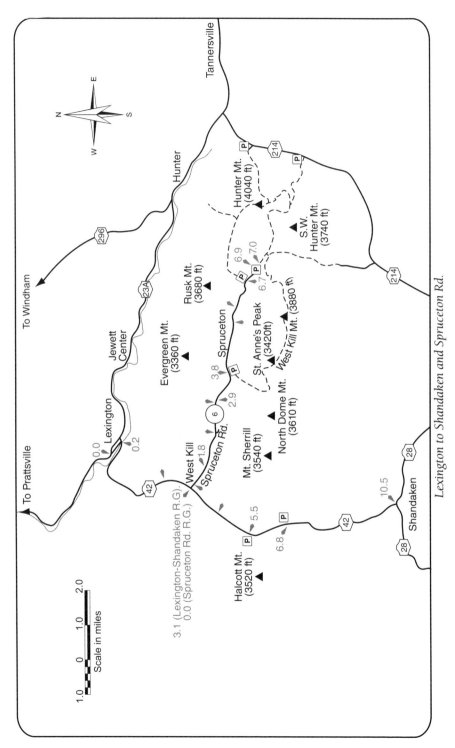

Lexington to Shandaken and Spruceton Rd.

where at 2 mi an old railroad path to Southwest Hunter begins.
    The trail descends, passes outflow from a spring, and reaches the Devil's Acre Lean-to at 2.2 mi. The Devil's Path ascends 100 yd to the jct. of the Hunter Mt. Trail (trail 34), which leads L in 1.4 mi to the Spruceton Trail (trail 40) and the Becker Hollow Trail (trail 35), and 1.7 mi to the Hunter Mt. summit.
    The Devil's Path turns R at the jct. and contours Hunter's S slope to 3 mi, then descends steadily. At 4 mi, the trail drops precipitously down a cliff known as the Devil's Portal. Passing a trail register and crossing a bridge over the Notch Lake outflow, the trail reaches the parking area on NY 214 at 4.3 mi. (The Devil's Path [trail 31 and 30] continues up wood steps across NY 214 to its eastern terminus at Prediger Rd.)
    🚶 Distances: To Geiger Point, 1.5 mi; to path to Southwest Hunter, 2 mi; to Devil's Acre Lean-to, 2.2 mi; to Notch Lake parking area, 4.3 mi (6.9 km).

39 E-W Devil's Path
(West Kill Mt. Traverse)

Trails Illustrated Map 755: J14 / Map 141, NE Catskills: L5, trail DP

The Devil's Path is presented in four parts in this book. Trails 30 and 31 describe the eastern section; trails 33 and 39 describe the western section. Here the trail is described E to W; see trail 39 W-E for reverse.

▶Trailhead: Access this section of the Devil's Path from the Diamond Notch Falls Trail (trail 38) unless backpacking the Devil's Path.◀

Starting at Diamond Notch Falls (0.0 mi), the Devil's Path crosses the West Kill and immediately turns R and follows the S bank of the brook downstream. The red-marked DEC route veers away from the water at 0.1 mi and begins moderate upgrades to the SW. Lush ferns and other ground cover make this an attractive walk through open deciduous forest. A section with large hemlock follows.
    A small outcrop on the L at 0.7 mi has a wet-weather spring. At 0.9 mi, the trail pitches steeply up (can be very icy) and then passes through a scenic area of mossy ledges. It climbs varying grades and occasionally levels for a breather. The grade becomes gradual approaching a large rock overhang called the "Cave" at 1.4 mi with a wind-protected rock wall and fire ring.
    Above the Cave is a 3500 ft sign. Gradual ascents and nearly level rolling terrain lead to another short downgrade. There are two more knolls to cross before the last climb to the summit.
    At the Buck Ridge Lookout at 2.4 mi, a large, flat rock ledge provides magnificent views to the E and SE over Diamond Notch Hollow toward Hunter, Indian Head, and Overlook mts. The Blackhead Range is NE. To the R, a path leads 100 ft across the area to a boulder that offers good views to Hunter, Rusk, and Evergreen mts. and down to Spruceton Valley. At 2.5 mi, the wooded West Kill Mt. summit is identified by a large cairn; the summit sign—long the only sign on

the summits—is now gone.

A spring R in a wet spot at 2.8 mi marks the start of a gradual downgrade. The 3500 ft elevation sign is at 3.3 mi. From 3.4 mi, the route is again nearly level; a short, moderate rocky downgrade at 4 mi is followed by a steady gradual descent. At 4.5 mi, St. Anne's Peak (no views) is topped after a steep rocky upgrade. Beyond, varying grades become a steady descent to a trail sign at 5.5 mi in Mink Hollow.

Bearing R, the trail reaches the E bank of Mink Hollow Brook at 5.9 mi. A long and very gradual upgrade through a significant hemlock grove gives evidence of what the early Catskills were like before the tanning industry left the forest denuded of this magnificent tree in the early 1800s.

Avoid a side trail on the E. A final downgrade leads to a DEC trail register 100 yd before the Spruceton Rd. trailhead at 7.1 mi. (This trailhead is 3.8 mi from NY 42, West Kill hamlet, and has parking for several vehicles.)

🐾 Distances: To spring, 0.7 mi; to Cave, 1.4 mi; to Buck Ridge Lookout, 2.4 mi; to West Kill Mt. summit, 2.5 mi; to St. Anne's Peak, 4.5 mi; to Mink Hollow, 5.5 mi; to western terminus on Spruceton Rd., 7.1 mi (11.4 km).

39 W-E Devil's Path
(West Kill Mt. Traverse)

Trails Illustrated Map 755: J14 / Map 141, NE Catskills: K4, trail DP

Here the trail is described W to E; see trail 39 E-W for reverse.

▶Trailhead: The trailhead is 3.8 mi E of West Kill hamlet on Spruceton Rd. (see Route Guides p. 102). A parking area is on the S side of Spruceton Rd. across from a large DEC sign. (Note: Mileages on the double-sided sign to Hunter Mt. and Prediger Rd. are reversed on opposite sides.)◀

The DEC trail register is 100 yd up the red-marked Devil's Path. Avoid unmarked side trails. Heading S through Mink Hollow, the trail very gradually descends through stately older-growth hemlock groves, reminiscent of the landscape prior to logging for the tannery industry in the early nineteenth century.

North Dome Mt. is often accessed from this general section of the Devil's Path. The trail approaches the bank of Mink Hollow Brook at 1.2 mi. Runoff and wetland areas can make the trail wet. A trail sign is at 1.6 mi, where the trail turns L and steadily ascends to 3000 ft.

Turning S again, the trail climbs a ridge spur more moderately to St. Anne's Peak at 3420 ft and 2.5 mi. As it swings E toward West Kill, the trail loses 200 ft, passing interesting rock ledges and, in wet seasons, falling water. A brief level section, sometimes wet, follows.

After gradually ascending again to 3400 ft, the trail pitches up a rock ledge at 3.1 mi and again levels out. It passes the 3500 ft sign at 3.8 mi as it continues to climb. A spring is L in a wet spot at 4.3 mi. Climbing to 3800 ft through berry bushes, the trail swings NE, leveling before reaching the wooded summit of West

Kill Mt. at 4.55 mi.

Pitching down rock ledges, the trail comes to the Buck Ridge lookouts at 4.7 mi. A large, flat rock shelf affords splendid views SE to Indian Head and Overlook mts. over Diamond Notch, E to Hunter Mt., and NE to the rolling Blackhead Range. A path leads L 30 yd to a boulder with views to Hunter, Rusk, and Evergreen mts. over the Spruceton Valley.

The Devil's Path pitches down mossy ledges and then continues E, ascending briefly before the very gradual descent to the 3500 ft sign above the "Cave," a large overhang, at 5.7 mi; the trail pitches down a narrow opening in the rock ledge.

Swinging N at 3400 ft, the trail begins its 1100 ft descent to Diamond Notch Falls. Sections

Diamond Notch Falls. David White

of this N-facing trail, especially a very steep short descent, become icy in transitional seasons. A small outcrop in 6.4 mi has a wet-weather spring. After more descent, this becomes an attractive hike by occasional large hemlock and then fern-filled open deciduous woods.

As the trail nears the cascading West Kill, the grade nearly levels, following the S bank of the stream to 7.05 mi, where a bridge needs replacement. The etched flat rock above Diamond Notch Falls is irresistible, but extremely slippery if wet. Cross the West Kill to a large clearing.

(Before the stream crossing, the southern Diamond Notch Trail [trail 37] turns R for 0.45 mi to the Diamond Notch Lean-to, 0.7 mi to a view S beyond the notch, and 2 mi to the trailhead near Lanesville. After the crossing, the northern Diamond Notch Falls Trail [trail 38] turns L and follows the West Kill 0.7 mi to the end of Spruceton Rd. Across the West Kill, heading E up a rise from the clearing, the Devil's Path continues for 4.3 mi to NY 214 [see end of trail 38 for a summary description]; across NY 214, it continues for 13.2 more mi to its eastern terminus off Prediger Rd.)

❧ Distances: To trail sign in Mink Hollow, 1.6 mi; to St Anne's Peak, 2.5 mi; to summit of West Kill Mt., 4.55 mi; to Buck Ridge lookouts, 4.7 mi; to the Cave, 5.7 mi; to Diamond Notch Falls, 7.1 mi (11.4 km).

40 Spruceton Trail

Trails Illustrated Map 755: K15 / Map 141, NE Catskills: L5, trail SP

The Spruceton Trail follows the Hunter Mt. fire tower jeep road to the summit and beyond to the former tower site where the Becker Hollow Trail (trail 35) terminates. Relatively easy to climb, this route is an attractive and enjoyable hike.

▶Trailhead: The DEC parking area trailhead is at the 6.7 mi point on Spruceton Rd. (See Route Guide for Spruceton Rd., p. 102.) The level trail leaves the NE end of the parking area with DEC blue trail markers. A yellow barrier gate blocks vehicles; the route soon parallels the E side of rushing Hunter Brook, reaching a trail register at 0.2 mi.◀

At 0.5 mi, the trail turns L and crosses Hunter Brook on a wide bridge. A steady moderate upgrade reaches a sharp switchback at 0.6 mi. (This is where the bushwhack to Rusk Mt. begins; see below.) Occasional switchbacks and a gradual, steady grade end at a col between Rusk and Hunter at 1.7 mi, where the trail turns R. (Avoid continuing straight ahead on the old Hunter Rd. [now a path] down Taylor Hollow.)

The trail begins a moderate grade curving up the mountainside. At 2.2 mi, a pipe spring is on the trail followed by a spur trail R leading 100 yd to a good spring. This trail continues some way to the John Robb Lean-to, but the main access trail to the John Robb Lean-to is at 2.3 mi up the Spruceton Trail on a yellow-marked spur path, R. This spur path is challenging for those with a full pack, who must squeeze down through rocks. Just beyond the lean-to is an excellent lookout. The Catskill 3500 Club partially funded this project and helped build it in 2009.

A short distance up the Spruceton Trail, there are good views W atop a great boulder. Just above here is the 3500 ft sign, marking the highest point where camping is permitted on the mountain in non-winter conditions.

At a jct. at 2.4 mi, the yellow-marked Colonel's Chair Trail (trail 41) heads N 1.1 mi to the Hunter Mt. Ski Lodge and ski chairlift, at the Colonel's Chair. (This is a good emergency escape route.)

The trail levels at 2.5 mi, with occasional short upgrades. A brook runoff at 2.9 mi leads 40 ft to the top of an old glacial melt-off waterfall. Almost dry now, it shows evidence of once having had more water.

The Spruceton Trail now climbs a moderate grade at 3.3 mi, reaching the Hunter Mt. fire tower and fire observer's cabin at 3.4 mi in a large summit clearing surrounded by conifers. From the renovated fire tower, a 360-degree panorama awaits. The Blackhead Range is to the NE; Kaaterskill High Peak is E; the Devil's Path mountains are S; West Kill Mt. is W. The Becker Hollow Connector Trail (trail 36) leaves the clearing near the fire tower.

The Spruceton Trail was built to end at a fire tower 0.3 mi SE of the current tower, so the trail continues along the flat summit ridge amid dark conifers and ends at the Becker Hollow Trail (trail 35) and Hunter Mt. Trail (trail 34) jct. at

3.7 mi, where the original fire tower stood. A spur path R leads to two excellent ledge overlooks.

✻ Trail in winter: This trail is an excellent winter snowshoe loop combined with the Hunter Mt. Trail, Devil's Path, and Diamond Notch Trail back out to Spruceton Rd. The moderate grade of the trail above the Rusk-Hunter col is suitable for expert skiers only.

🥾 Distances: To Hunter Brook bridge, 0.5 mi; to Hunter/Rusk col, 1.7 mi; to spring, 2.2 mi; to John Robb Lean-to spur trail, 2.3 mi; to Colonel's Chair Trail jct., 2.4 mi; to summit fire tower and Becker Hollow Connector Trail, 3.4 mi (5.4 km); to jct. of Becker Hollow Trail and Hunter Mt. Trail, 3.7 mi (5.9 km). Summit elevation, 4040 ft (1231 m); ascent, 1950 ft.

41 Colonel's Chair Trail

Trails Illustrated Map 755: K15 / Map 141, NE Catskills: M4, trail CC

This spot on the shoulder of Hunter Mt. was named for Col. William Edwards, a major leather tanner in this region in the early 1800s. From the valley floor, this bump on Hunter's shoulder resembles a chair.

On Saturdays and Sundays from early July to Columbus Day and in winter, the Sky Ride ski lift from Hunter Mt. Main Lodge to Summit Lodge will take you to the Colonel's Chair trailhead area. The hiker should verify chairlift operating hours (usually 10 AM to 5 PM), especially in inclement weather. Snowshoes are available for rent at the main lodge. The trail ends at the Spruceton Trail (trail 40), 1 mi from the Hunter Mt. fire tower.

▶Trailhead: After the Sky Ride, follow signs for the Z lift, passing it and following Hunter Mt. yellow markers to a sign that guides you to the Colonel's Chair Trail. The route passes picnic tables and starting points of ski runs. At 0.1 mi, a monument commemorates John Clair for his contributions to skiing, and Jean Wald, who lost his life serving with the ski patrol.◀

The route follows a grassy path L of the service road a short distance before rejoining it. Look for a new and wonderfully detailed sculpture of Rip Van Winkle to the L. Continue along the flat trail to a jct. at 0.5 mi.

At a trail register, the yellow-marked DEC trail bears L and ascends varying grades to the 3500 ft elevation at 1 mi. The moderate grade levels before the trail reaches the Spruceton Trail (trail 40) jct. at 1.1 mi, for an ascent of 530 ft.

(The blue-marked Spruceton Trail leads L 1 mi to the fire tower summit of 4040 ft Hunter Mt.; to the R, it leads in 0.1 mi to John Robb Lean-to spur trail, L, and ends at Spruceton Rd. 2.4 mi from the jct. Total distance to Hunter Mt. summit is 2.1 mi, with an ascent of 940 ft. On the return from the summit, remain alert for the jct. of the Colonel's Chair Trail in 1 mi, to the R. Many Colonel's Chair hikers reportedly end up in Spruceton, 18 mi from Hunter village.)

👣 Distances: To monument, 0.1 mi; to jct., 0.5 mi; to Spruceton Trail jct., 1.1 mi (1.8 km). Ascent to Spruceton Trail jct., 530 ft (162 m).

42 Rusk Mt. *(bushwhack)*

Trails Illustrated Map 755: K14 / Map 141, NE Catskills: L4

Rusk Mt. is the fourth of five peaks that make up the Lexington Chain. It is named for Samuel E. Rusk, an assistant of the early mapmaker Arnold Guyot. Rusk wrote one of the first guidebooks for this section of the Catskills.

The Rusk Mt. that appears on today's USGS maps is not the mountain Guyot actually named Rusk. Guyot's Rusk was one peak to the E. Guyot's names for the peaks, W to E, were Lexington (3100 ft), Pine Island (3140 ft), Bee Line (3360 ft), Evergreen (3680 ft), and Rusk (3640 ft). Today's USGS maps list them, W to E, as nameless, though climbers use Packsaddle Mt. (3100 ft), nameless (3140 ft), Evergreen (3360 ft), Rusk (3680 ft), and nameless (3640 ft). The latter is considered the E summit of Rusk. The whole chain makes an interesting day's outing.

▶ Trailhead: The easiest approach to Rusk Mt. is via the Spruceton Trail (trail 40) up Hunter Mt. (see above). The most direct route leaves the Spruceton Trail at 0.6 mi, at a notable switchback. Leave the trail here and head up Ox Hollow; partway up bear L toward the summit. Near the top, one needs to negotiate a way around ledges. Occasional views look out to the Spruceton Trail area and Southwest Hunter Mt.

Another approach to Rusk Mt. is from the col between Rusk and Hunter at 1.7 mi, where the Spruceton Trail levels and turns E (see trail 40). For Rusk Mt., head NW up the ridge from this spot. From a high point which is the E summit, it is necessary to continue W, losing ascent slightly to a col between Rusk's two summits, before climbing to the true summit. A herd path between the summits may be found. ◀

👣 Ascent from Spruceton Rd., 1577 ft. Summit elevation, 3680 ft (1122 m).

43 Southwest Hunter Mt. *(bushwhack)*

Trails Illustrated Map 755: J15 / Map 141, NE Catskills: M5

Clearly higher than 3500 ft in elevation, the peak SW of Hunter Mt. was not placed on the Catskill 3500 Club's original list of 3500 ft peaks. It seems to meet at least one of the other criteria: being at least one-half mile from any other 3500 ft summit or having a drop between it and neighboring peaks of at least 250 ft. Why was it left off the list?

Current maps are more accurate than the maps originally used. The peak had no official name on USGS maps. It has been surmised by at least one of the original compilers that some Catskill 3500 Club founders didn't agree that the peak

Rusk Mountain bushwhack. Moonray Schepart

was separate, but felt that it was a spur ridge of Hunter Mt. In 1987, the Catskill 3500 Club voted to include the mountain in its climbing list for membership; it has been officially required by all climbers accepted after April 1, 1990.

▶Trailhead: The easiest approach to the mountain is from Spruceton Rd. via the Diamond Notch Falls Trail (trail 38) and the Devil's Path (trail 33, summarized from W to E in trail 38). Beyond Geiger Point, after a 0.3 mi gradual downgrade, the Devil's Path climbs to a height of land and significant flat area; before the trail descends look for a prominent old railroad path to Southwest Hunter Mt. that might be marked by a cairn. Follow the nearly level grade of the old railroad for nearly 20 minutes, passing a couple of paths upward, to a good path up a drainage for about 0.2 mi to the summit.

Southwest Hunter can also be approached from Stony Clove via the Devil's Path (trail 33). At the jct. with the Hunter Mt. Trail (trail 34) at 2.1 mi, turn L for 0.25 mi past the Devil's Acre Lean-to up a rise; when the Devil's Path levels out, look for the SW Hunter railroad path, L (see above).◀

🚶 Summit elevation, 3740 ft (1140 m).

44 North Dome Mt. *(bushwhack)*

Trails Illustrated Map 755: J13 / Map 142, Central Catskills: K5

North Dome Mt. is part of the Hunter–West Kill Mountain Wilderness area. The mountain was formerly called Blue Bell Mt.

▶Trailhead: Access is from the 2.9 mi point of Spruceton Rd., where a small DEC parking area (unplowed in winter) is located. Forest Preserve Wilderness signs are on the trees and the area is marked for anglers. (See Route Guide for Spruceton Rd., p. 102.)◀

The legal route from this parking area travels S up the ravine, staying E of a private property line, then ascends to the ridge. Another approach is from the Mink Hollow end of the Devil's Path (trail 39). From the Devil's Path, determine the best ascent route to bushwhack the steep E face of North Dome. The summit area is fairly open but nearly flat. The summit "bump" and canister can be hard to spot.

👥 Summit elevation, 3610 ft (1100 m).

45 Mt. Sherrill *(bushwhack)*

Trails Illustrated Map 755: K13 / Map 142, Central Catskills: K5

Mt. Sherrill is part of the Hunter–West Kill Mountain Wilderness. The mountain is named after Col. Sherrill, a Shandaken tannery owner who lost his life at Gettysburg during the Civil War.

▶Trailhead: A good access point is on the E side of NY 42 at the DEC Forest Preserve Access parking area, 3.7 mi S of the hamlet of West Kill and 3.7 mi N of the jct. of NY 42 and NY 28 at Shandaken. (See Route Guide, p. 102.)◀

Old woods road. Mark Schaefer

Typically, parties climb an old woods road until it runs out and then continue along the crest of the spur ridge to the summit. The mountain can also be climbed from North Dome for a long day trip, but climbers in winter may find it impossible to complete both peaks in a day. If heading for Sherrill from North Dome, travel W into the col between the two mountains; a compass bearing must be followed with care in order to hit the narrow col. The climb out of the col up the E side of Sherrill is very steep.

A descent off Sherrill back to Spruceton Rd. can be made if the hiker drops down the spur ridge crest from the summit, W of Bennett Brook. Stay W of any yellow paint blazes on trees or stone fences to avoid a very narrow

Meadow near Halcott and Sleeping Lion mountains. Alan Via

band of private property near Spruceton Rd. It may be difficult to cross the West Kill at roadside in times of high water.

❧ Summit elevation, 3540 ft (1079 m).

46 Halcott Mt. *(bushwhack)*

Trails Illustrated Map 755: J12 / Map 142, Central Catskills: J5

The village of Halcott Center was named after George W. Halcott, an early settler. So, it seems, was Halcott Mt. This peak is part of the Forest Preserve's 4900-acre Halcott Mt. Wild Forest.

▶Trailhead: The usual starting point on state land is an unmarked parking area off the W side of NY 42, 2.4 mi S of the hamlet of West Kill. This point is also 5 mi N of the NY 42–NY 28 jct. in Shandaken and 1 mi S of the height of land in Deep Notch. The parking area is usually plowed in winter.◀

From the parking area, a path leads SW up a small grade and after 100 ft turns abruptly R to continue up a steep bank to the top of a nice waterfall. Cross the stream, then traverse S and cross a second stream. Ascend to the ridge and climb to the summit ridge; head N for about 5 minutes to attain the summit.

Other approaches are from Upper Birch Creek Rd. out of Pine Hill, the shortest and easiest non-private route to the summit; from Beech Ridge Rd. going over Northeast Halcott; and from Brush Ridge Rd. (Townsend Hollow Rd.) out of Fleischmanns, requiring permission to cross short stretches of private land.

❧ Summit elevation, 3520 ft (1073 m).

Looking East from Wittenberg Mt. Henning Vahlenkamp

Woodstock-Shandaken Section

The trails of the Woodstock-Shandaken area date back to 1783, when the Schoharie Rd. was built up through Mink Hollow on its way to Prattsville. At that time, it was believed the region's hollows were filled with witches and wizards. People sought out the "witch doctor," Jacob Brinks, to deal with them. It was a region where, much later, a favorite pastime for Overlook Mountain House guests was to push huge boulders off the escarpment's cliffs, just so they could watch the boulders as they crashed through the forest below. One would ride the Ulster and Delaware Railroad in pampered luxury almost to the doorstep of the Tremper House in Phoenicia, and then climb Tremper Mt. for exercise. In a time when Woodland Valley was still called Snyder's Hollow, today's Phoenicia–East Branch Trail was being used by pioneers.

❋ Trails in winter: The following sections of the Burroughs Range are a challenge in winter, requiring full crampons and winter experience: the 1.3 mi above the Wittenberg–Terrace Mt. jct. to Wittenberg Mt.; from the Wittenberg-Cornell col to Cornell Mt.; from the Cornell-Slide col to Slide Mt. Each of these sections has cliffs. Panther Mt. from Fox Hollow is a great winter trip with better viewing compared to seasons when leaves are on; the undulating trail takes longer than it would seem from the maps. Get an early start. Sections of both trails to Tremper Mt. are icy in low snow conditions and require crampons; otherwise the ascents are moderate.

Overlook Mt. is not only an excellent snowshoe climb, but the trail ascends a dirt roadway that is suitable for intermediate skiing. Mink Hollow is also excellent for skiing.

Below is a list of suggested hikes in this region.

SHORT HIKES
Mink Hollow from Lake Hill: 2 mi (3.2 km) round-trip. Walk up a beautiful wooded hollow by a river to its crossing at 1 mi.

Onteora Lake Loop: 2.6 mi (4.2 km). A pleasant hike through a variety of forest. A second and third loop can be added to extend the hike.

MODERATE HIKES
Overlook Mt.: 5 mi (8 km) round-trip. Great views from a fire tower, passing Overlook Mountain House ruins up the old carriage road trail. After jct. at 2 mi, path R off road leads to excellent views short of the summit. Total ascent, 1400 ft.

Phoenicia Trail to Tremper Mt.: 6.2 mi (9.9 km) round-trip. A steady 2000 ft ascent to a newly renovated fire tower. If second vehicle is available, a great traverse over the summit to the village of Willow.

HARDER HIKES

Wittenberg, Cornell, and Slide mts: approx. 15 mi (24 km) loop trip from Woodland Valley State Campground. One of the toughest day trips on a trail in the Catskills. Great views and variety of trail. Can be shortened to a through trip to Slide Mt. trailhead on CR 47 with two vehicles. Wittenberg Mt. itself, a 7.8 mi round-trip, is a challenging 2430 ft ascent to a summit that offers magnificent 180-degree views of Ashokan Reservoir and Devil's Path peaks.

Panther Mt. from Fox Hollow: 9.8 mi (15.7 km) round-trip. A tough trip with ups and downs, but a chance to get away from the crowd. Long but nice winter trip on snowshoes, with vistas not seen when leaves are on the trees.

	Trail Described	*Total Miles* (*one way*)		*Page*
47	Panther Mt. Trail (Fox Hollow)	4.9	(7.8 km)	117
48	Woodland Valley Trail to Giant Ledge–Panther Mt. Trail	2.8	(4.5 km)	119
49	Wittenberg-Cornell-Slide Trail (to Cornell) (9.8 mi to Slide Mt. parking area)	4.7	(7.5 km)	120
50	Terrace Mt. Trail	0.9	(1.4 km)	122
51	Phoenicia Trail to Tremper Mt.	3.1	(5.0 km)	123
52	Willow Trail	1.6	(2.6 km)	124
53	Warner Creek Trail–Long Path	7.5	(12.0 km)	125
54	Mink Hollow (S of Devil's Path)	2.6	(4.2 km)	126
55	Overlook Mt. Trail	2.4	(3.8 km)	127
56	Onteora Lake	varies		128
57	Jockey Hill (4.8 mi round-trip)	3.5	(5.6 km)	129

Route Guide for Woodstock-Shandaken (see map p. 118)

Mileage E to W	*Description*	*Mileage* W to E
0.0	Jct. NY 212 and CR 33; village of Woodstock	20.5
1.9	Bearsville; road turns N-S	18.6
3.2	Jct. Glasco Turnpike, E side	17.3
3.7	Jct. Hutch Hill Rd.; leads to Meads Mountain Rd. and Keefe Hollow Rd.	16.8
5.0	Jct. Mink Hollow Rd., N side; village of Lake Hill	15.5
7.4	Jct. Van Wagner Rd., W side; hamlet of Willow	13.1
11.4	Jct. CR 40 (old NY 28), W side; hamlet of Mount Tremper	9.1
11.6	Jct. NY 28 and NY 212; turn NW if driving W; turn E if driving E.	8.9
15.5	Jct. NY 28 and NY 214; Phoenicia 0.1 mi N on NY 214	5.0
16.0	Jct. Woodland Valley Rd., S side	4.5

19.5	Hamlet of Allaben	1.0
19.9	Jct. Fox Hollow Rd., S side	0.6
20.5	Jct. NY 28 and NY 42, village of Shandaken	0.0

47 Panther Mt. Trail *(Fox Hollow–Panther Trail)*

Trails Illustrated Map 755: I12 / Map 142, Central Catskills: J6, trail GP

The climb up Panther Mt. from Fox Hollow may take longer than the distance suggests. False peaks may discourage the novice; the poorly defined summit is not an obvious goal. In winter, however, the views are excellent. The shorter trip to the summit, from the S over Giant Ledge (trail 71), provides much open viewing for less effort. The Fox Hollow route gives the climber a longer day of hiking, with less contact with other hikers.

▶Trailhead: Access to the trailhead is via Fox Hollow Rd. off the S side of NY 28 in Allaben. (See Route Guide, p. 116.) A trailhead parking area is on the R, 1.6 mi along Fox Hollow Rd. A path to the rear of the parking area leads to a privy.◀

From the trailhead (0.0 mi), the trail leaves a barrier boulder at Fox Hollow Rd. and follows blue DEC trail markers NW up a woods road. Moderate to steep climbing begins immediately. The trail passes a trail register at 0.1 mi, crosses a stream over a bridge and reaches the jct. of a spur trail to the Fox Hollow Lean-to at 0.3 mi. The 150 ft spur trail R leads to a spring just beyond the lean-to.

The woods road winds back and forth, continuously ascending. Grades ease at 1.1 mi as the route gradually turns S. At 1.25 mi, the route loses elevation slightly, but stays generally on contour between 2600 and 2700 ft for a nice breather. The route becomes a footpath at 1.4 mi and the footing is rocky.

Having reached a high point on a ridge, the trail descends slightly at 1.75 mi. Steep climbing begins at 1.9 mi and moderates at 2 mi. The moderate slope climbs over boulders at 2.6 mi. A view E opens up at 2.8 mi. The route passes over a ledge and reaches a high point of 3300 ft on the ridge at 2.95 mi. There is no open view here.

The trail loses 100 ft of elevation and then traverses a flat "tableland" before regaining elevation to a second false peak at 3.6 mi. At 3400 ft, especially in winter here, views toward Panther and the surrounding area are outstanding. Flat rock ledges invite a rest stop.

The trail loses elevation again to 4.1 mi, then ascends and passes the 3500 ft elevation sign at 4.4 mi. Conifers close in on the trail; care must be taken to watch trail markers in winter. An open ledge at 4.7 mi offers nice views E, and at 4.9 mi the trail reaches the summit rock outcrop, with outstanding views E. Looking across to the Burroughs Range, a giant glacial cirque stands out before you; Wittenberg, Cornell, and Slide mts. are impressive. The Giant Ledge–Panther Mt. Trail (trail 71) continues another 2.6 mi to the jct. with the Phoenicia–East Branch Trail. (See Giant Ledge–Panther Mt. Trail [trail 71] in the

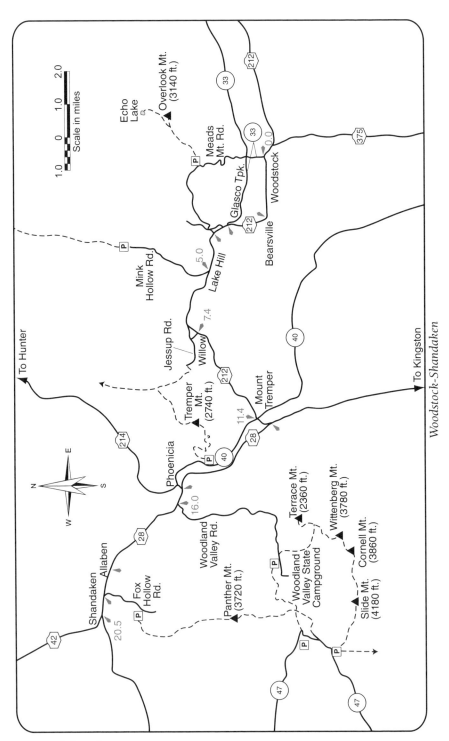

Big Indian–Pine Hill to Denning Section.)

🥾 Distances: To lean-to spur trail, 0.3 mi; to level section, 1.1 mi; to view E, 2.8 mi; to first false peak, 2.95 mi; to second false peak, 3.6 mi; to summit, 4.9 mi (7.8 km). Summit elevation, 3720 ft (1134 m). Ascent, 2420 ft.

48 Woodland Valley Trail to Giant Ledge–Panther Mt. Trail

Trails Illustrated Map 755: G13 / Map 143, Southern Catskills: K7, trail PE

This trail connects to the Giant Ledge–Panther Mt. Trail (trail 71), offering access to Panther Mt. from Woodland Valley. (It is the N end of the Phoenicia–East Branch Trail [trail 68]; see Big Indian–Pine Hill to Denning Section.) It is a challenging but rewarding trail.

▶Trailhead: Trail access is from Woodland Valley State Campground near Phoenicia. (See Route Guide, p. 116.) Turn S off NY 28, 0.5 mi W of Phoenicia, on Woodland Valley Rd. Travel 0.3 to a bridge crossing Esopus Creek and a road jct. Turn R and follow Woodland Valley Rd. 4.7 mi to a large parking area on the R at Woodland Valley State Campground. (Parking permits must be obtained at an office 500 ft farther along the road during the camping season.)◀

The trail (0.0 mi) leaves the rear of the parking area, climbing wooden steps up a short pitch. Yellow DEC trail markers lead 50 yd to a trail register. From there a pleasant footpath climbs W through deciduous forest. Occasionally moderate in grade, the incline is generally gradual.

Leveling at 0.7 mi, the footpath joins the beginning of a flat rock shelf. The shelf widens greatly as the trail progresses. Several yards to the R a cliff juts up, while only a few yards to the L the shelf ends and your gaze plummets into the valley below.

At 0.9 mi, the trail turns sharply L and descends very steeply. First, it clambers over large rocks and boulders; then some 100 stone steps lead to the valley floor. The path winds a bit before crossing Woodland Creek at 1 mi, and then steeply ascends some switchbacks. The trail soon levels, but the hiker needs to keep trail markers in sight in this section.

Breaking out of the woods at 1.2 mi, the trail reaches a jct. with an old woods road. (The original trail was on this road from Woodland Valley, but the current first 1.2 mi of this trail was added so that the route could be entirely on state land.)

Turning R, the trail follows the old woods road W, climbing at moderate grade, with occasional easier stretches. It climbs a ridge with a large talus slope at R and the valley wall dropping off sharply to the L. At 1.8 mi, the trail turns S at a rocky section where a spring and waterfall are R, and the route crosses another branch of Woodland Creek.

The ascent becomes more gradual. Birch and beech abound here. Beyond an undependable water flow at 2.4 mi, the trail curves W again, reaching height of land at 2.6 mi. (Avoid a side road L.) The now-level route joins the Giant Ledge–

Panther Mt. Trail (trail 71) at 2.8 mi, after an ascent of 1350 ft. Elevation at this jct. is 2750 ft.

(The trail to Giant Ledge, 0.75 mi, and Panther Mt., 2.6 mi, follows blue DEC trail markers N. The Phoenicia–East Branch Trail [trail 68] continues straight and descends 500 ft to CR 47; see Big Indian–Pine Hill to Denning Section. The unmaintained former Denning–Woodland Valley Trail [trail 68Y] heads L before the Phoenicia–East Branch Trail begins to descend. The Winnisook Club granted an easement to follow this former trail to Winnisook Lake, thus avoiding the 500 ft descent and re-ascent up CR 47. The old route enters private property near Winnisook Lake; the club asks hikers to stay on the trail.)

🥾 Distances: To Woodland Creek bridge, 1 mi; to woods road jct., 1.2 mi; to spring, 1.8 mi; to height of land, 2.6 mi; to jct. of Giant Ledge–Panther Mt. Trail, 2.8 mi (4.5 km).

49 Wittenberg-Cornell-Slide Trail (to Cornell)

Trails Illustrated Map 755: G13 / Map 143, Southern Catskills: K7, trail WS

The Wittenberg-Cornell-Slide Trail is one of the hardest, but most rewarding, Catskill trails. The hiker needs good boots and plenty of water. Springs along the trail are not dependable. The Wittenberg-Cornell-Slide Trail continues on as trail 70 to Slide Mt. and the Phoenicia–East Branch Trail (trail 68); trail 70 is summarized below from E to W for those wishing to continue on.

▶Trailhead: Trail access is from Woodland Valley. (See Route Guide, p. 116.) From NY 28 just W of Phoenicia, turn L to Woodland Valley State Campground, crossing the Esopus Creek bridge and reaching a T-jct. Turn R and follow Woodland Valley Rd. 4.7 mi to the Woodland Valley State Campground. A large parking area is on the R, a short distance beyond the trailhead. Parking permits must be purchased during the camping season at an office 500 ft farther along the road. Camp restrooms are across from the parking area. The trailhead is L just before the parking area, where a barrier prevents vehicle entry to a service road.◀

The trail leaves the trailhead (0.0 mi) on a macadam service road before the parking area. It turns L and follows red DEC trail markers between campsites 45 and 46, crossing the Woodland Creek bridge. Turning L, it climbs quite steeply to a trail register at 0.2 mi. The trail passes interesting rock ledges and at 0.5 mi the route levels in a very attractive hemlock grove. Across from scenic ledges there is a view over the great Wittenberg bowl to Terrace Mt. Continuing S, the trail climbs gradually to a sharp L uphill at 1 mi. (Avoid continuing on the level route straight ahead here.)

The trail ascends the rocky area quite steeply and follows the edge of the cliff in a hemlock grove, then climbs a bluff at 1.15 mi, where the grade eases. There is a spring 100 yd R of the trail at 1.45 mi. The route crosses several drainages and climbs mostly gradually, swinging E at a high point at 2.1 mi. The route loses

Samuels Point with Ashokan Reservoir in the distance. Henning Vahlenkamp

100 ft before resuming its course E to the T-jct. with the Terrace Mt. Trail (trail 50) at 2.6 mi. (The Terrace Mt. Trail leads 0.9 mi L on a gradual downgrade to a lean-to.)

Turn R at the jct. The gradual upgrade swings back W and here a new Long Path section will continue over Cross Mt., Mt. Pleasant, and Romer Mt. to Phoenicia. At 3 mi, the trail begins a relentless but fascinating and scenic climb to the summit of Wittenberg. After a second pitch up at 3.1 mi, a side path L leads to a view N. The trail climbs up through a sharp rock cut at 3.2 mi, with a view N at the top. Shortly it ascends a very steep rock bluff.

This N-facing trail is lined with beautiful mossy ledges. Steep pitches of varying size lead past the 3500 ft sign at 3.4 mi. A spring is 250 ft R of the trail at 3.6 mi. As the trail nears the summit, the terrain levels out on wet (or icy) sections. Ahead, an opening in the conifers reveals broad rock shelves. The spectacular summit of Wittenberg is at 3.9 mi. Summit elevation is 3780 ft. Ascent from Woodland Valley is 2430 ft.

The sweeping view is nearly 180 degrees, from the Blackhead Range and Devil's Path peaks in the N to Peekamoose and Table mts. in the S. Ashokan Reservoir stands out in full glory from the large open rock bluff. The isolated peak between Wittenberg and Ashokan Reservoir is Samuels Point. Nearby Cornell and Slide mts. cannot be seen.

The trail heads W from the lookout, descending gradually to a col. The trail crosses some log walkways before reaching a large rock bluff at 4.6 mi. A short vertical climb is followed soon by a sizeable ascent through a deep V-cut in the cliff top, a challenge without handholds or footholds, except wedging boots into the cut. (Winter climbers should use a rope to descend here for a safeguard. An easier way up this cliff may be found if conditions are not icy, by following L around the base to possible ascents.)

Gradual grades lead this "Bruin's Causeway" to a blue-marked spur trail L at 4.7 mi. This leads in 90 yd to the technical "Crown of Cornell" summit, elevation 3860 ft. The view is to the N and E here, with a good view of Wittenberg.

From the jct., the red trail shortly descends easily to a spectacular 180-degree lookout toward Slide Mt. at 4.8 mi. Views are to Table and Peekamoose mts. in the SW, Slide Mt. (impressive) and the great valley, Panther Mt., and N to Sherrill, North Dome, West Kill, and Hunter. This is followed by a second good lookout in the same direction.

Refer to the Slide-Cornell-Wittenberg Trail (trail 70) in the Big Indian–Pine Hill to Denning Section for the description of this trail W to E from the Phoenicia–East Branch Trail (trail 68) to Cornell. Here, from Cornell over Slide, is E to W summary of trail 70: The trail passes through a "lemon-squeezer." A spring is R of the trail at 5 mi, and water across the trail at 5.3 mi shows that a spring is 130 yd L. A spur trail leads to a designated campsite, N, and two more spur trails lead to designated campsites S. The col between Cornell and Slide mts. is at 6.2 mi, followed by three more designated campsites in attractive flat rock and grassy areas. A 35 ft vertical rock outcrop at 6.5 mi is followed by a 15 ft vertical bluff; both require care. A blue-marked spur trail R at 6.8 mi leads in 25 ft to an excellent spring. Four ladders ascend vertical rock. The summit rock is at 7 mi, with a commemorative plaque to John Burroughs. At 7.1 mi. a ledge offers magnificent viewing to Panther, Wittenberg, and Cornell. The trail reaches the Curtis-Ormsbee Trail jct. (trail 69) at 7.8 mi and terminates at 9.1 mi (14.6 km) at the Phoenicia–East Branch Trail (trail 68). The Phoenicia–East Branch Trail continues another 0.7 mi to the Slide Mt. parking area.

🐾 Distances: To L turn, 1 mi; to spring, 1.45 mi; to Terrace Mt. Trail jct., 2.6 mi; to summit of Wittenberg Mt., 3.9 mi (6.2 km); summit elevation, 3780 ft (1152 m); to spur to summit of Cornell Mt., 4.7 mi (7.5 km); to lookout toward Slide Mt., 4.8 mi. Cornell Mt. summit elevation, 3860 ft (1176 m).

50 Terrace Mt. Trail

Trails Illustrated Map 755: G13 / Map 143, Southern Catskills: K7, trail TM

A trail up Wittenberg Mt. formerly started from Woodland Valley Rd., 1.4 mi closer to Phoenicia than today's trail. (The suspension bridge across Woodland Creek can still be seen.) It ascended the NE slope of Terrace Mt. to the flat tree-covered Terrace summit at the 1.45 mi point. Here, a nice lean-to made a good overnight spot for backpackers. Today, this trail is no longer used. However, the portion from the lean-to, which leads 0.9 mi to a jct. at the 2.6 mi point of the Wittenberg-Cornell-Slide Trail (trail 49), is still maintained so Wittenberg Mt. hikers have access to the lean-to.

View from Tremper Mt. Joan Dean

▶Trailhead: From the jct. at the 2.6 mi point of the Wittenberg-Cornell-Slide Trail (trail 49), a very gradual grade leads downward to the lean-to.◀

There is a large bare rock clearing at 0.3 mi. A bench mark (2556 ft) is in a rock 100 yd R of the trail. There are good views N to Tremper Mt. Blueberries abound. The trail continues to descend, swinging R at a small clearing at 0.5 mi. It levels just before reaching a large clearing at 0.9 mi, where a sign points R to the lean-to 40 yd away.

The lean-to (1987) is old but in fair condition, considering its age. Water is not available. The large clearing is attractive and the hike in is very pleasant.

𝄞 Distances: To clearing, 0.3 mi; to second clearing, 0.5 mi; to lean-to, 0.9 mi (1.4 km) (3.5 mi from Woodland Valley State Campground). Descent to lean-to, 310 ft (94 m).

51 Phoenicia Trail to Tremper Mt.

Trails Illustrated Map 755: H14 / Map 141, NE Catskills: L6, trail PA

The Phoenicia Trail is the shorter of the two trails to the Tremper Mt. summit. The mountain is named after Major Jacob H. Tremper of Kingston, who, with Captain William C. Romer, owned the Tremper House. This large hotel was one of the first to offer visitors to the Catskills an opportunity to arrive at its door by railroad, with no bumpy stagecoaches needed for transport.

▶Trailhead: The trailhead is on the N side of CR 40 (old NY 28), 2.2 mi E of Phoenicia.◀

From the trailhead (0.0 mi), the red-marked trail slabs upward NE, crosses a short footbridge, then turns R up rock steps and over a knoll. It then loses some altitude to a jct. with the old jeep road route at 0.5 mi, where there is a trail register. Turn R and follow the old road uphill at moderate grades. The road grade becomes gradual at 0.8 mi, swinging SE and then S.

The trail passes a spring L and reaches an old quarry at 1.2 mi, then levels and begins a slight downgrade. An old woods road heads downhill at 1.4 mi. Continue on the red-marked trail as it begins a series of switchbacks and passes another old road with a "posted" sign at 1.9 mi. Just after a sharp switchback, a spur trail R at 2.2 mi leads 75 ft to the Baldwin Memorial Lean-to.

The trail heads uphill to 2.3 mi, where a side trail L runs 10 yd to a large boulder where water from a spring rushes out from a long metal pipe (except in drought periods). At 2.7 mi, the route levels, swinging NE on a grassy lane.

The Tremper Mt. Lean-to is on the L side of the trail at 3 mi and the summit is 50 yd beyond. Views from the renovated fire tower are magnificent (also see trail 53).

Rattlesnakes are occasionally seen on this mountain.

🐾 Distances: To trail register, 0.5 mi; to first spring, 1.2 mi; to Baldwin Memorial Lean-to, 2.2 mi; to second spring, 2.3 mi; to Tremper Mt. Lean-to, 3 mi; to summit, 3.1 mi. (5 km). Summit elevation, 2740 ft (835 m). Ascent, 2030 ft.

52 Willow Trail

Trails Illustrated Map 755: H15 / Map 141, NE Catskills: L6, trail WI

The Willow Trail, combined with the Warner Creek Trail (trail 53), is a longer but more interesting approach to the Tremper Mt. summit. The Phoenicia Trail (trail 51) is a somewhat monotonous steady ascent of 2000 ft, while the Willow Trail offers an interesting variety of terrain and forest as it ascends Hoyt Hollow and contours a slope toward Tremper Mt. If two vehicles are available, a through trip ascending the Phoenicia Trail and descending the Willow Trail is a nice 7 mi outing.

▶Trailhead: Access is off NY 212 in the hamlet of Willow. (See Route Guide, p. 116.) Turn W onto Van Wagner Rd. and drive 0.4 mi to Jessup Rd., where the turn is L. A post office is possibly the last parking area. Permission may be given to park along Jessup Rd., or space to pull off may be found along the road where land is not posted. There is no official parking area. It is about 1 mi to the end of Jessup Rd., beyond "no parking" signs and a second pond. From there a woods road gradually ascends 0.2 mi to a DEC sign.◀

The trail turns L (0.0 mi), crossing a grassy area to a barrier and woods road. Yellow DEC trail markers now guide you. Avoid all side roads on the climb to state land. The steady ascent abates as the road swings R. From 0.2 mi to 0.5 mi, mountain laurel abounds along the trail in early summer.

Yellow paint blazes mark the beginning of state land at 0.6 mi. At 0.9 mi, the trail becomes a moderate grade. The wall of the hollow drops sharply off on the R. Great ledges to the L meet the ascending trail. The route gradually loses altitude to a low point at 1.15 mi, then climbs at first gradually and then moderately to a jct. with the blue-marked Warner Creek Trail (trail 53, the Long Path route) at 1.6 mi. (The Warner Creek Trail leads S 2.2 mi to Tremper Mt. fire tower and N 5.3 mi to Silver Hollow Notch. The Daley Ridge Trail [trail 32] continues from Silver Hollow Notch to Plateau Mt. Trail 32Y describes 0.9 mi via Notch Inn Rd. to NY 214 in Edgewood, from which the Long Path can be accessed.)

🥾 Distances: To state land, 0.6 mi; to low point, 1.15 mi; to Warner Creek Trail jct., 1.6 mi (2.6 km).

53 Warner Creek Trail–Long Path

Trails Illustrated Map 755: I15 / Map 141, NE Catskills: L6, trail WC

The Warner Creek Trail, a section of the Long Path, runs from the summit of Tremper Mt., elevation, 2740 ft., to Silver Hollow Notch. Views from the top of the fire tower are magnificent to the Devil's Path peaks, the Burroughs Range, and the Ashokan Reservoir. (The red-marked Phoenicia Trail [trail 51], continues S for 3.1 mi to CR 40 near Phoenicia. The Tremper Mt. Lean-to is 50 yd from the tower.)

▶Trailhead: From the jct. with trail 51 at the Tremper Mt. fire tower (0.0 mi), the trail crosses Tremper Mt.'s mostly level summit, swings R at scenic ledges and descends nearly 400 ft to a low point at 1 mi. Ascending gently, it slabs the W side of an unnamed high point on slightly rolling territory to 2550 ft; when leaves are off, occasional views E can be seen. The trail then descends steeply to the jct. of the Willow Trail (trail 52) at 2.2 mi.◀

The trail continues N on contour at about 2450 ft. At 2.6 mi, the trail begins a descent of nearly 500 vertical ft; at 3 mi, it heads W on contour around Carl Mt. and begins another steady descent at 3.5 mi. The route turns W at a cairn at 3.65 mi, crosses a waterfall, passes a quarry, and descends to an old foundation. At 3.9 mi, it crosses a stream, ascends then descends to run beside and above Warner Creek to the crossing at 4.3 mi, which may be challenging in high water.

Now following an old road, possibly a wet section, the route begins a long 1400 ft ascent to 3000 ft. At 5.3 mi, the trail passes a large hemlock and an interesting 4-ft burl (knot) on a tree. At 6.3 mi, a pleasant ridge walk reaches the small high point, Edgewood Mt., and the trail skirts private property with a view toward Stony Clove at 6.8 mi.

At 7.1 mi, an attractive area is reached, where the route follows alongside a headwall and then ascends and traverses on top of the smooth rock wall. A view of Silver Hollow is R. In 120 yd, another ledge has a fire ring and offers a second viewing spot. Views continue, especially if leaves are off. The trail descends to

2300 ft and reaches Silver Hollow Notch at 7.5 mi. (The Long Path continues N to Plateau Mt. on the Daley Ridge Trail [trail 32], a few yards W; see "Extended and Challenging Opportunities." Yellow-marked trail 32Y leads to Notch Inn Rd. in 0.5 mi and to NY 214 in 0.9 mi.)

    🕊 Distances: To Willow Trail jct., 2.2 mi; to Warner Creek, 4.3 mi; to private property and view, 6.8 mi; to Silver Hollow Notch jct., 7.5 mi (12 km).

54 Mink Hollow Trail *(from Lake Hill, S of Devil's Path)*

Trails Illustrated Map 755: I16 / Map 141, NE Catskills: N6, trail MK

The Mink Hollow Trail runs N from the end of Mink Hollow Rd. in Lake Hill and crosses the Devil's Path through the col between Sugarloaf and Plateau mts., ascending 1090 ft. The old trail (trail 29) descended to Elka Park S of Tannersville and is still used, with a large parking area at the end of Mink Hollow Rd. It was an old road dating back to the 1790s; when Col. Edwards ran the leather tanning industry in Tannersville, the primary route for transporting hides from the Saugerties port on the Hudson was along this route. The same slope is a good cross-country ski route today.

    ▶Trailhead: Access from the S is from the end of Mink Hollow Rd., N of NY 212 in Lake Hill (W of Woodstock). (See Route Guide, p. 116.)◀

The route follows blue DEC trail markers along a woods road from the trailhead (0.0 mi). It forks R at 0.1 mi, near a trail register. The route narrows at 0.2 mi and crosses Mink Hollow Brook at 0.3 mi. The old road follows the E side of the cascading brook up a lush green hollow. At 1 mi, the trail again crosses Mink Hollow Brook. (This spot could be a problem for skiers if snowmelt has started.) The valley broadens and the route crosses a tributary at 1.4 mi. Footing is often rocky as the grade steepens, but it improves in gradual sections. At 1.7 mi, the route levels for a bit before resuming a steady grade. It passes boulders and soon begins leveling as it reaches the height of land at 2.3 mi; it remains level in attractive territory to the Mink Hollow Lean-to at 2.5 mi.

    A spur trail L leads 30 ft to the Mink Hollow Lean-to. A second path leads back to the trail, which reaches the Devil's Path jct. at 2.6 mi. in a col at 2600 ft. There is a spring 0.25 mi N on the old Mink Hollow Trail (trail 29), 50 yd L off-trail. A spring is 0.4 mi on the R on the Devil's Path, L, toward Plateau Mt. The new Mink Hollow Trail from the N (trail 28) is part of the Sugarloaf Mt. loop trail. It is 0.1 mi E of where trail 54 ends. (To Sugarloaf Mt. summit, 1.1 mi E on the Devil's Path [trail 30]; to Plateau Mt. summit, 1 mi W on the Devil's Path.)

    🕊 Distances: To first brook crossing, 0.3 mi; to second brook crossing, 1 mi; to first easing of grade, 1.7 mi; to height of land, 2.3 mi; to Mink Hollow Lean-to, 2.5 mi (4 km); to Devil's Path, 2.6 mi (4.2 km).

55 Overlook Mt. Trail

Trails Illustrated Map 755: H17 / Map 141, NE Catskills: O6, trail OS

The Overlook Mt. Trail follows the old carriage road to the summit of Overlook Mt. Pierre DeLabigarre, a French Revolutionist, was probably the first to write about the views from this mountain, after his climb in 1793. In 1833, James Booth built a temporary hotel there. It took until 1871 to establish a permanent hotel. It burned to the ground on April Fool's Day in 1874, when no one would believe a child who tried to convince staff that the smoke in the chimney was darker than usual. Rebuilt in 1878, the hotel burned down again in 1924. In the midst of rebuilding yet again, the struggle to keep it open ended with the stock market crash of 1929. Remnants of the half-finished foundations are still visible. The fire tower is renovated and open.

▶Trailhead: Access to the Overlook Mt. trailhead is from Woodstock. Travel 0.6 mi N on CR 33 (R of center village square) from Woodstock, passing the intersection of Glasco Turnpike and continuing 2.1 mi straight ahead up steep Meads Mountain Rd. to the DEC trailhead signpost and large parking area on the R side of the road. The building across the road from the trailhead, now a Tibetan Buddhist monastery, was once Mead's Mountain House, an early hotel.◀

The trail runs E from the trail register (0.0 mi) on a wide gravel road, following red DEC trail markers. There is a pipe with gushing water on the L at 0.35 mi. A less obvious spring is on the side of the road at 0.5 mi. A large flat boulder at 0.9 mi invites a break from steady climbing up the open road on a hot day.

At 1.2 mi, bear L at a fork. As the grade moderates at 1.5 mi, the huge ruins of the Overlook Mountain House appear ahead, at 1.75 mi. The trail circles L, passing a large antenna, several smaller buildings, and an old stone foundation. It reaches the Overlook Trail (trail 24) jct. at 1.9 mi. (The Overlook Trail runs 1.4 mi to Echo Lake Trail jct. [trail 25] and another 0.7 mi down to the lake. It also runs 4.7 mi to Platte Clove Rd.; see Platte Clove Section.)

The trail turns R and in 45 yd, a path diverges R from the road. (This path is the most scenic approach to the summit, not to be missed. It follows the edge of the drop-off for half a mile with two fine overlooks. At the largest rock cliff, the path heads away

Overlook Mountain House ruins. Mark Schaefer

Timber Rattlesnake in the Catskills. Cheryl Miller

from the edge and climbs to the summit in 200 yd., 0.5 mi from the jct. to the summit.)

The trail up the road gradually climbs, passing paths that lead down to viewing points. Nearing the summit, the route circles under scenic large ledges (which have rattlesnakes) to the fire observer's cabin at 2.3 mi. A fireplace and picnic table are across the road. Views are best from the renovated fire tower, which provides magnificent vistas in all directions. A fire tower interpreter is usually present in the summer to answer questions. Total ascent is 1425 ft.

The Hudson River stands out in the E; Ashokan Reservoir is S; Slide, Cornell, and Wittenberg mts. are W; Indian Head, Twin, Sugarloaf, Plateau, and Hunter mts. are N. On a clear day, several states can be seen from this summit. Rattlesnakes live in rocky terrain here.

🐾 Distances: To first spring, 0.35 mi; to second spring, 0.5 mi; to road fork, 1.2 mi; to Overlook Mountain House ruins, 1.75 mi; to Overlook Trail jct., 1.9 mi; to fire tower from jct. via road, 2.3 mi; via path, 2.4 mi (3.8 km). Summit elevation, 3140 ft (957 m).

56 Onteora Lake *(multiuse trails)*

Trails Illustrated Map 755: F18 / Map 146, Bluestone Wild Forest: O8

▶Trailhead: On NY 28 about 5 mi W of Thruway Exit 19, Kingston, a DEC sign "Bluestone Wild Forest: Onteora Lake" appears on N side of road at a strip mall. Follow entrance road to the end. There is accessible parking and a seasonal accessible port-a-john located in the parking lot.◀

From information kiosk (0.0 mi): The yellow-marked trail passes accessible paths toward the lake; at the second side path, continue straight ahead on the yellow-marked gravel trail. Designated campsites are located at 0.2 mi and a trail register is at 0.4 mi. Remnants of a quarry appear below a high ledge and the trail descends and passes the quarried area at 0.7 mi.

At 0.75 mi, the Y trail divides and can be followed in either direction around the lake loop. Continuing straight, at 0.9 mi a red-marked loop trail begins, L, and a blue loop trail diverges off the red trail. Continuing on the Y trail, in 1 mi a wrecked vehicle appears and just beyond this, the Y trail turns R. This turn is very easy to miss.

This is a pleasant walk through a shady hemlock forest, with a first view to a second lake appearing at 1.5 mi, and the trail follows close to shore for 0.1 mi. A beaver lodge can be seen across the lake. At 1.9 mi, a very steep, short ascent brings Onteora Lake into view and the route follows the edge of a steep bank. Large rock outcrops add interest to the landscape and at 2.5 mi, the trail climbs up through a cleft in the rock. At 2.6 mi, the trail returns to the loop junction. Turn L to return. A longer excursion can be had by including the red loop or the red and blue loops.

🐾 Distances: Y trail divides, 0.75 mi; to jct. of red trail, 0.9 mi; to lake view, 1.5 mi; to loop jct., 2.6 mi. (4.2 km); back to kiosk, 3.4 mi (5.4 km).

57 Jockey Hill *(multiuse trails)*

Trails Illustrated Map 755: F18 / Map 146, Bluestone Wild Forest: P8

▶Trailhead: From US 209 N of Kingston, access Sawkill Rd. (CR 31, then L on CR 30) past Sawkill to Jockey Hill Rd., L. The official DEC parking area is located 0.5 mi beyond the end of paved Jockey Hill Road. Bikers and others can park at the end of the paved road.◀

From the DEC trailhead (0.0 mi): At 0.1 mi, gullies crossing the road make driving farther impossible for many vehicles. This region is ideal for biking, with many trails heading off the main road, the first one R at 0.3 mi. The main trail swings 90 degrees L at 0.7 mi; watch for the next sharp turn L at 0.9 mi, leaving the road (which continues ahead on flat rock).

Entering an attractive section of trail with white pines and hemlock, a creek is crossed at 1 mi. At a fork with a cairn at 1.1 mi, the trail turns L into interesting terrain; a ravine drops steeply to the L, offering views to a hillside across. At 1.5 mi, the trail turns R uphill; this turn is easy to miss because it appears that the trail continues straight ahead—note the yellow marker where the trail goes uphill here. Remnants of a small quarry appear at 1.6 mi.

At 2.1 mi, a parallel trail appears to the R, with no apparent crossover path. Trail straight ahead curves around to this parallel trail. At 2.5 mi, a fork in the trail offers no immediate markers; turn R. A large rock outcrop soon appears L in the woods and a small foundation-shaped quarry is just off-trail.

At 3.1 mi, the trail turns 90 degrees L, reaching an attractive section with red pine at 3.3 mi. At 3.5 mi, the trail returns to the cairn jct.; turn L back to the road at 3.8 mi.

🐾 Distances: Trail leaves road, 0.9 mi; to R turn uphill, 1.5 mi; to R fork, 2.5 mi; return to cairn jct., 3.5 mi (5.6 km).

Ashokan High Point from Ashokan Reservoir. Mark Schaefer

Peekamoose Section

The southern border of the Catskills is somewhat isolated from the rest of the Catskill region. It is accessed along scenic narrow roads and one gets a glimpse of what it was like in yesteryear. In the eastern part, Ashokan Reservoir dominates the views from most peaks. Seven villages had to be moved so an old glacial lake bottom could be transformed into the reservoir. It takes 92 mi of tunnels to transport its water to New York City.

The ascents from the S side of the ridges in this section are often 1000 ft greater than ascents from the N sides, so some challenging climbs can be done. For example, the ascent to Table Mt. (3847 ft) from the Neversink River is about 1600 ft, compared to the ascent to nearby Peekamoose Mt. (3843 ft) from Peekamoose Rd., 2623 ft.

Buttermilk Falls is a beautiful waterfall along the N side of Peekamoose Rd., 1.6 mi from the trailhead to Peekamoose Mt. (See Route Guide, p. 132.) It is unusual in that it has a subterranean source that spouts out of a hole in a cliff. In a region with names like Bull Run, Sundown, Bangle Hill, Mombaccus, and Peekamoose, there is much history to interest the hiker.

❊ Trails in winter: From Peekamoose Rd., Peekamoose and Table are good winter snowshoe routes, in spite of having the greatest ascent in the Catskill Forest Preserve. Ashokan High Point's best viewing is in winter. Sections above the Mombaccus Mt.–High Point col are steep and crampons are recommended.

The trailless peaks over 3500 ft in this section, Balsam Cap and Friday mts., are potentially dangerous climbs because of the steep and often cliffy terrain. A fatality occurred on Friday's cliffs in April 2001. The cliffs on the E and NE side are near vertical and hazardous with ice, snow, or black ice. They require planning careful map routes. Most approaches to this pair are S of Friday, heading W toward the col between Balsam Cap and Friday, and even that route is very steep. Traveling these trailless peaks in a group is highly recommended and full crampons are essential.

This is an isolated area, so have plenty of gas and be sure your vehicle is in good condition.

Below is a list of suggested hikes in this region.

SHORT HIKES

Kanape Brook: approx. 3 mi (4.8 km) round-trip. Walk along a gurgling brook, ascending above it and crossing it into lovely hemlock woods.

The Blue Hole and Buttermilk Falls: From the Peekamoose Mt. trailhead, a short walk E along scenic Peekamoose Rd. by Rondout Creek leads to a beautiful deep pool called the Blue Hole below a waterfall; here there is great swimming for the hardy on a very hot day. Buttermilk Falls is 1.6 mi (2.6 km) E of the trailhead, with a short path approaching the falls.

MODERATE HIKES
Vernooy Falls: 3.6 mi (5.8 km) round-trip. Follow old woods roads to beautiful cascades and waterfalls, passing mountain laurel and old-growth white pine. Lots to explore in the falls area.

Peekamoose Mt. to lookout ledge at 3500 ft: moderate to strenuous 6 mi (9.6 km) round-trip; an ascent of 2330 ft. Alternating level sections with short, steep scrambles up scenic ledges make the climb seem like less. Passes Reconnoiter Rock, a great break at an interesting erratic.

HARDER HIKES
Ashokan High Point: 7.6 mi (12.2 km) round-trip. First a bubbling brook, then a stiff 2000 ft ascent to a mountain peak. Follow the red-marked trail NW from the summit to an open field for good viewing N, especially in winter; a 9 mi loop hike on the marked trail continues NW. A herd path off the main summit leads to a partially open knob at 120 degrees magnetic with interesting views; a loss of 325 ft must be re-climbed, but it's less strenuous than it sounds.

Peekamoose and Table mts.: 9.4 mi (15 km) round-trip. The highest vertical ascent in the Catskills, 2623 ft to the Peekamoose summit; a beautiful view at 3500 ft. Look for paths R to more views before reaching the now-wooded summit. Loss of 200 ft to Peekamoose-Table col. About 150 yd W of Table's wooded summit, slightly descending, look for paths L through evergreen to a small open ledge with outstanding views. Seek out the Blue Hole just E of the Peekamoose trailhead on Rondout Creek, for a brisk swim (see Short Hikes, above).

	Trail Described	*Total Miles (one way)*	*Page*
58	Samuels Point	trailless	133
59	Balsam Cap	trailless	135
60	Friday Mt.	trailless	135
61	Ashokan High Point Trail (3.8 mi, E route to summit; 5.2 mi, W route)	9.0 mi loop	137
62	Peekamoose-Table Trail (from Peekamoose Rd.)	4.7 (7.5 km)	138
63	Long Path (Upper Cherrytown Rd. to Peekamoose Rd.)	9.6 (15.4 km)	140

Route Guide for Peekamoose Rd. (see map p. 134)
This route guide runs from West Shokan to Claryville along what is collectively known as the Peekamoose Rd. Actually, under today's road number designations, the route involves several different roads. At times the pavement runs out for

short stretches. This is not a rapid-transit road. Plan to take your time, and have a full tank of gas.

Mileage E to W	Description	*Mileage* W to E
0.0	West Shokan. Jct. of NY 28A and CR 42 (Peekamoose Rd.); follow CR 42.	26.2
0.9	Moon Haw Rd., N side of road	25.3
3.9	Kanape Brook. Trailhead for Ashokan High Point; DEC parking area R side of road	22.3
8.3	DEC parking, N side of road; old Peekamoose Mt Trail. Trail no longer exists.	17.9
8.5	Parking, N side of road; Buttermilk Falls	17.7
10.1	DEC parking, N side of road; current Peekamoose Mt. maintained trail	16.1
10.3	DEC open campsite, N side of road; permit needed	15.9
10.6	Long Path trailhead, S side of road	15.6
10.7	Open campsite, N side of road	15.5
11.6	Parking area, N side of road	14.6
13.2	Sundown. CR 46 goes SW becoming CR 153; CR 42 goes N	13.0
16.4	Sugar Loaf Rd., N side of road	9.8
16.6	Lowes Corners. NY 55A goes SW; CR 153 goes N	9.6
16.8	N end of Rondout Reservoir	9.4
18.6	Jct. NY 55 goes W; NY 55A goes NW.	7.6
19.2	Grahamsville. NY 42 jct. to S; continue on NY 55.	7.0
21.6	Jct. CR 19 goes N; NY 55 goes E.	4.6
26.2	Claryville. Jct. CR 19 continues E to Denning; CR 157 goes N to Big Indian; CR 19 goes S towards Peekamoose.	0.0

58 Samuels Point *(bushwhack)*

Trails Illustrated Map 755: F14 / Map 143, Southern Catskills: L7

Samuels Point is a moderately high peak at the end of a ridge extending generally E from Wittenberg Mt. It offers a view of Ashokan Reservoir. For those interested in more strenuous exercise, follow the ridge of Cross Mt. and then climb Mt. Pleasant, when changes in the route of the Long Path occur, in 2013–2014.

▶Trailhead: Leave NY 28 at Boiceville and follow NY 28A, W and S, 0.9 mi to Traver Hollow Rd. Turn W and drive 0.7 mi on Traver Hollow Rd. to Bradken Rd. Follow Bradken Rd. 1 mi to where a stream crosses under the road. This can provide a starting point up the state land on the W side of the road. Vertical ascent from Bradken Rd. is 1985 ft.

Another approach is from West Shokan (see Route Guide, above). Turn W on CR 42, R on Moon Haw Rd., and R on Drybrook Rd. to state land. Bushwhack

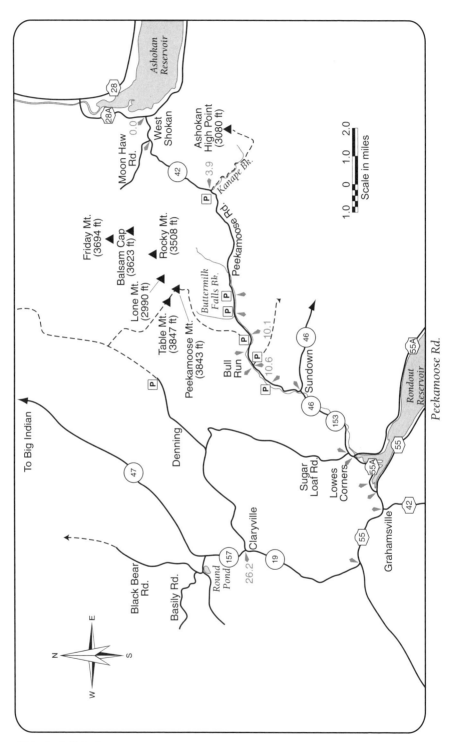

134 *Catskill Trails*

NE, crossing Dry Brook and staying on state land, to access the gradual S ridge. You will need a map and compass for both approaches. Vertical ascent from Drybrook Rd. is 1885 ft.◄

⩔ Samuels Point has a summit elevation of 2885 ft (879 m).

59 Balsam Cap (bushwhack)

Trails Illustrated Map 755: F13 / Map 143, Southern Catskills: K8

Balsam Cap, once called Balsam Top, is in that group of trailless mountains that also includes Friday, Rocky, and Lone mts. These are the hardest of the 3500 ft peaks to reach.

▶Trailhead: Travel to the end of Moon Haw Rd., which is public, until pillars at the end. There is plenty of parking here. It is necessary to go up on the L and around the private inholding. (There is no longer access from Shultis Rd. to Balsam Cap and Friday mts.)◄

Hikers should study maps well before starting on this trip, and refer often to a compass. There are cliffs to negotiate in the upper reaches. The more common approach to Balsam Cap is to combine it with Friday Mt. Following blazes, an old woods road is accessed in the lower reaches. In the upper reaches, angle toward the Balsam Cap–Friday col via herd paths. Just short of and below the col, the herd path to Friday heads up through the cliffs, while the paths (intermittent) toward Balsam Cap continue below the ridge.

Balsam Cap is also done from this side after an ascent of Friday. The walk along the ridge between the two peaks has its thicker spots, but is doable. The ridge between Rocky and Balsam Cap is negotiable but notably littered with blowdown.

On the W side of the ridge, Balsam Cap can be approached from the upper section of the East Branch of the Neversink via a herd path. The stream at 2.75 mi makes a reasonable ascent route. Approached from the W, grades are more gradual to the summit, but the overall trip in from Denning is much longer.

There is a good view 2 minutes N of the canister via a herd path.

⩔ Summit elevation is 3623 ft (1104 m).

60 Friday Mt. (bushwhack)

Trails Illustrated Map 755: F13 / Map 143, Southern Catskills: K8

Friday is a bushwhack peak just N of Balsam Cap Mt. It is generally done along with Balsam Cap, because climbing in this area is so rugged that hikers find one long trip preferable to two shorter ones.

▶Trailhead: Use the same approaches as those for Balsam Cap, above.◄

The most common approach from the E follows woods roads and herd paths

View to Ashokan Reservoir. Joanne Hihn

(upper portions can be tough to follow under snow or leaf litter) to a point a bit under the Balsam Cap–Friday ridge, short of the col. Here, well-defined herd paths follow natural faults in the cliffs and lead one very steeply (but safely) to the canister.

Another popular approach is via a large landslide on the N side of the E ridge. Follow the S branch of Wittenberg Brook for about a mile until the slide is apparent. The slide is loose gravel and dirt, so travel along the sides is generally easier. The slide, in three separated sections, brings one to about 3000 ft, at which point the steep but beautiful ascent of the ridge becomes necessary. There is a good view via a short bushwhack E of the canister.

The descent off the E side of Friday is very steep; this is not a good winter descent line (a man was killed in early spring 2001 here). One must search out the safest way down S of the summit area before heading E.

When hiking both Friday and Balsam Cap, hikers generally follow the ridge (which is the Delaware-Hudson watershed divide) between the mountains. For unsurpassed primeval grandeur, however, each mountain should be approached separately from the E.

𖢥 Summit elevation is 3694 ft (1126 m).

61 Ashokan High Point Trail

Trails Illustrated Map 755: E14 / Map 143, Southern Catskills: L9, trail AH

Ashokan High Point escaped having a hotel plunked on it in the 1800s. Its summit was never cleared for viewing, so it remains natural. Views E are excellent especially in winter, and following the trail W from the summit leads to an open meadow with good views to the Burroughs Range and Ashokan Reservoir in winter. A herd path off the main summit leads to a partially open knob at 120 degrees magnetic with interesting views, especially with leaves off; a loss of 325 ft is reclimbed.

▶Trailhead: Access to the trailhead is off the S side of Peekamoose Rd. at Kanape Brook. (See Route Guide, p. 132.) The Kanape Brook trailhead has a DEC signpost and is marked by a yellow metal barrier gate. A parking area is on the N side of the road.◀

From the yellow metal barrier gate (0.0 mi), the red-marked woods road drops down to Kanape Brook, which it crosses on a bridge, and soon reaches a trail register. The route at first stays next to the cascading brook, but soon begins to climb above the N bank. At a waterfall (not evident in drought) at 0.6 mi, the trail crosses a pair of stonework bridges. A woods road enters from the L at 0.9 mi. There is a spring L at 1.3 mi at an old cistern.

A bridge crosses a tributary at 1.5 mi, and another crosses Kanape Brook at 1.6 mi. The now-level trail enters a beautiful hemlock forest, following the S side of the waterway. An informal campsite can be seen in evergreens.

Leaving the hemlock forest, the route crosses wet areas impacted by Tropical Storm Irene, and begins a gradual to moderate ascent to the col between Mombaccus Mt. and Ashokan High Point at 2.7 mi. The trail turns L at an arrow. (Straight ahead, an attractive flat area is filled with mountain laurel and has a fire pit and places to sit. Nearby, an old cable is stretched between two trees, and the trees have enveloped the cable as they do with trail markers. This height of land, where a route descends to private land above Upper Samsonville Rd., might be mistaken for the trail. This is just a scenic resting spot.)

After the L turn marked by arrow, in 50 yd the trail comes to a jct. where a loop option is available. To the L, it is 2.5 mi to the summit. Straight ahead, the more direct trail climbs 1.1 mi to the summit, at first gradually from the jct. The trail is rerouted L at 2.9 mi, and from here the grade is steep. Shortly after passing a side road R at 3.15 mi, the woods road ends and a footpath ascends steeply in pitches, alternating with gradual areas. Mountain laurel is increasingly abundant, flowering in late June to early July, and the first blueberries whet your appetite.

The summit often seems imminent but remains elusive, finally topping out at 3.8 mi. Views E from the summit rock are very good, particularly when leaves are off. The ambitious can take a 25-minute bushwhack 325 ft down the E ridge to a partially open rocky knob at 120 degrees magnetic, where there are excellent views S and W, and, if foliage is off, E to the Ashokan Reservoir. Herd paths are developed along most of the way. (The route must be re-ascended.) Continuing NW past the summit, the red-marked trail passes a good view SW to Mombaccus Mt. in 100 ft. Note odd circular pools along the way to a large open area from 3.9 to 4 mi, with excellent viewing especially in winter on many feet of snow N to the Burroughs Range. In winter, the Ashokan Reservoir is best seen from here, but it is visible through trees as the trail leaves the open area at 4 mi, continuing NW, and descends below 2700 ft. The trail gains 100 ft of elevation again as it winds through the open woods.

At 4.8 mi, the trail turns 90 degrees L, to the S. (Ascending via this route, the turn R to the E is easily missed.) Views can be seen toward Table and Peekamoose and from a path, to Balsam Cap, Friday, Lone, and Slide mts. in the distance; views are best when foliage is off. Terrain is nearly level, and then pitches down briefly at 4.9 mi.

At 5.2 mi, the trail descends 50 yd very steeply, turning SW. It soon begins a gradual then steady descent down rocks that can be wet, to a low point at 5.9 mi.

Turning SE, the trail passes an impressive old-growth white pine and begins a gradual ascent back up to the jct. at 6.3 mi, regaining 150 ft of elevation. Turn R, reaching the flat col between Mombaccus Mt. and Ashokan High Point in 50 yd, where the trail turns R and descends as described in the first section, above.

⚐ Distances: To cistern, 1.3 mi; to bridge across Kanape Brook, 1.6 mi; to col and jct. to L, 2.7 mi; to summit (E route), 3.8 mi (6.1 km). Summit elevation, 3080 ft (939 m). Ascent from trailhead, 2070 ft.

Loop trail NW from summit (3.8 mi) to S turn, 4.8 mi; to steep descent, 5.2 mi; to low point, 5.9 mi; return to jct., 6.3 mi. Total round-trip using loop, 9 mi (14.4 km). From trailhead to summit via W route, 5.2 mi (8.3 km).

62 Peekamoose-Table Trail *(from Peekamoose Rd.)*

Trails Illustrated Map 755: E12 / Map 143, Southern Catskills: J9, trail PT

The lower part of the trail up Peekamoose Mt. was routed in the early 1970s by Ranger Peter Fish to replace the steeper trail then in use. It climbs the ridge between Bear Hole Creek and Buttermilk Brook from Gulf Hollow, where Rondout Creek flows close to the road. Enjoy Buttermilk Falls 1.6 mi E of the trailhead, and enjoy a bracing swim in the Blue Hole in Rondout Creek just E up the road from the trailhead.

▶Trailhead: The N side of Peekamoose Rd. (See Route Guide, p. 132.)◀

The blue-marked trail leaves a cable barrier (0.0 mi) and follows a moderate grade NE up an old woods road. At 0.15 mi, a trail register is in a clearing. The route continues its steady climb to 0.4 mi and then levels. The lower slopes up to 2025 ft were pasture until the 1920s, when the state purchased the land. Black birch, white ash, red oak, and big-toothed aspen predominate, since they typically

View from Cold Ledge, Table Mountain. James Appleyard

are pioneer species in areas where pastures are allowed to return naturally to forest.

Very gradual grades continue along the ridge. At 0.8 mi, the woods road diverges L, and shortly beyond, at 1725 ft elevation, there is a lovely red pine grove planted in the 1920s. The hiking trail continues as a footpath. Interesting sedimentary rock formations are near the trail.

More planted red pines can be seen, but hop hornbeam dominate. Beyond this zone, only selective logging was done, and there are far older trees here than on the lower slopes. A storm created 0.3 mi of blowdown and now berry bushes abound in more sunlight; more views were created.

Grades become moderately steep and then ease in a series of varying grades that take hikers up through rock outcrops. The climb becomes steep at 1.5 mi, passing through a cut in a rock ledge, and then nearly leveling to 1.8 mi, where rock "steps" ascend to another plateau. At 2.2 mi, the trail begins its steep ascent to Reconnoiter Rock, a large conglomerate boulder perched on a rock ledge at 2.3 mi, inviting a break.

After a level stretch, the route pitches steeply up ledges at 2.5 mi, where in winter good views NW are seen. The climb continues on moderate grades to the 3500 ft sign at 3 mi. A short, steep climb pitches up to a wide ledge with excellent views to Table Mt. near to the N and Doubletop and Balsam Lake mts. in the distance NW. The ascent to this point is 2300 ft.

This level plateau is where the old Peekamoose Trail entered, a short distance beyond the lookout ledge. (The red-blazed old route is not maintained and is fully grown in.) The trail swings L to the N and ascends very gradually to a spring, L, at 3.3 mi. The route ascends moderate and steep grades to a spur path R at 3.8 mi leading to good views; shortly beyond, another spur path R ends at a large rock atop which are views to Ashokan Reservoir and Ashokan High Point. Just before the summit, there is a final spur path R with the best views of all.

The summit is at 3.9 mi, in a clearing. There is a large sloping boulder that formerly offered views to the Burroughs Range, but trees now obscure the view. Summit elevation is 3843 ft; ascent from Peekamoose Rd. is 2623 ft.

Gradual downgrades lead toward Table Mt. At 4 mi, a blocked-off herd path leads R to limited views NE when leaves are off. The trail flattens out in an often wet or icy col at 4.1 mi and sharp spruces press in for a short distance. At 4.3 mi, just before the climb to Table Mt. begins, a herd path leads R to Lone Mt.

Moderate grades lead upward on good trailwork.

At 4.4 mi, the trail levels and crosses the nearly flat top of Table Mt. to the actual summit at 4.7 mi. There is no view from the true summit, but at 4.8 mi, two prominent herd paths head S (L) into evergreens. Look down, R, through trees for a small open ledge, where views are magnificent. Summit elevation is 3847 ft. Ascent from the col is 197 ft. (This trail continues 0.3 mi to the Bouton Memorial Lean-to and 3.95 mi from the Table summit to Denning parking area. See Peekamoose-Table Trail [trail 65], Big Indian–Pine Hill to Denning Section.)

🚶 Distances: To leveling of trail, 0.4 mi; to Reconnoiter Rock, 2.3 mi; to overlook ledge, 3 mi; to spring, 3.3 mi; to spur path views, 3.8 mi; to summit of Peekamoose Mt., 3.9 mi; to col, 4.1 mi; to summit of Table Mt., 4.7 mi (7.5 km); to spur paths to view, 4.8 mi (7.7 km).

63 Long Path (Upper Cherrytown Rd. to Peekamoose Rd.)

Trails Illustrated Map 755: C13 / Map 143, Southern Catskills: K9, trail LP and Map 146, Vernooy Kill

This is the southernmost section of the Long Path found within the Catskill Park. (For a complete sequence of the Long Path in the Catskills, refer to the Long Path in the chapter "Extended and Challenging Opportunities.") A short day trip to Vernooy Falls is an excellent hike and good choice if only one vehicle is available.

To hike this entire section, which passes through the Sundown Wild Forest, traveling in a S–N direction is recommended. A through trip requires extensive driving from Upper Cherrytown Rd. to place a return vehicle, but one can begin in Greenville, taking the snowmobile trail that leaves Dymond Rd. at its jct. with CR 46, which is a much shorter distance between trailheads. It is 1.9 mi from

Unnamed waterfall in the Catskills. James Appleyard

the snowmobile trailhead to Vernooy Falls.

▶Trailhead: Access is off US 209 onto CR 3 (Pataukunk Rd.), 0.7 mi E of the traffic light in Kerhonkson. Pass through the hamlets of Pataukunk and Mombaccus before turning L at an intersection 3.4 mi from US 209. After 0.2 mi, bear L at the fork with Ridgeview Rd. Drive another 0.6 mi, passing two more side roads. Stay L at each jct. Just after a small bridge crossing, there is a three-way jct. (A large concrete building marks the spot.) Turn R here on Upper Cherrytown Rd. and continue N another 3.1 mi to the DEC trailhead sign at the R side of the road. There is a large parking area on a side road opposite the trailhead sign. This is a total of 7.8 mi from US 209.◀

From the trailhead (0.0 mi), follow red trail markers into the woods. There are many trail sign changes along the way, but the blue paint blazes of the Long Path are seen at jcts. and sharp turns.

The route crosses a brook at 0.2 mi on a small bridge and continues along the woods road. Steady climbing proceeds over a ridgeline, after which the nearly level trail adorned with mountain laurel and white pine reaches a camping area before dropping to Vernooy Falls and a trail register at 1.8 mi.

There is a splendid view of Vernooy Falls from the bridge across the stream, but do not continue beyond unless you wish to take the snowmobile trail 1.9 mi to Greenville. This interesting waterfall has four cascades dropping a total of about 30 ft. Paths lead upstream to beautiful pools. Downstream are the remains of an old stone mill.

From the trail register, the Long Path makes a sharp R turn and heads NNE up a winding woods road, soon reaching the crest of a rise. Thereafter, the nearly level trail can be wet through very attractive deciduous woods.

At 2.7 mi, turn L off the road at a double-blazed jct. onto a path that easily climbs to the top of Pople Hill, where it levels and turns R at 3.1 mi, continuing N. The route alternates between a ferny path and a woods road.

The trail reaches another jct. at 4 mi, where it turns L on an old woods road. An informal hunters' camp is here. Ruts from their vehicles can make spring hiking muddy for the next couple of miles. (The R turn leads along Sapbush Creek to Riggsville.)

The route heads W on the level, crossing a gravel bridge with metal culverts over Vernooy Kill at 4.2 mi. At 4.4 mi, the first of three dirt roads leads away from the trail; there are places to camp. A nice stream approaches from the L at 4.55 mi and runs next to the trail.

A broken wood plank bridge crosses a tributary stream; vehicles can drive across in the stream. The often-wet trail passes through hemlock forest, and it is necessary to rock hop a stream at 4.8 mi. The route reaches a height of land and passes a house at 5.2 mi before crossing a stream on a metal pipe culvert at 5.3 mi. In 50 yd, a dirt road goes L (do not follow) to a beaver pond and camping spot.

At 5.6 mi, the Long Path leaves the woods road and climbs, often steeply, on a well-marked but primitive wilderness footpath. The unwary could walk past the turnoff, since the cairn is on the L and the woods trail, which is to the R, is not clearly indicated. (The woods road continues 0.8 mi to a paved road; Greenville is another 0.6 mi to the L on the paved road.)

At 5.9 mi, the path becomes even steeper up a rocky hillside through a section of blowdown; the route is hard to follow here. Keep a sharp eye for the trail signs as you ascend the lower slopes of Sampson Mt.

At 6 mi, at another woods road, the route turns L on level ground. At a small crest in the road at 6.1 mi, the trail turns R on a footpath, leaving the road and climbing through woods again over rough ground.

At 6.3 mi, the route turns L at a cairn onto a well-defined path that maintains

Ashokan Reservoir view. Henning Vahlenkamp

a fairly steady course WNW toward Bangle Hill. The pathway widens somewhat and provides enjoyable, nearly level walking. Yellow paint blazes indicating private property are encountered at two points. After crossing a stream at 6.8 mi and passing a higher point at 6.9 mi, the route loses elevation and crosses the scenic mossy headwaters of Sundown Creek at 7.25 mi.

Still another stream crossing is at 7.5 mi, after which the route regains elevation. At 8 mi, light through trees ahead with a drop to the R seems to indicate a hilltop, but the height of land on Bangle Hill (2350 ft) is not reached until 8.5 mi. At 8.55 mi, the trail drops through rocks and begins the very steep descent of 1150 ft to Peekamoose Rd. A view through trees can be seen.

At 8.75 mi, the trail turns L and slabs on contour through open woods, crossing the first of several small streams at 8.85 mi. The steep descent continues down a woods road; several other woods roads lead L off the Long Path. (Hikers walking this section from N-S have to be careful to watch trail signs. Some side trails make it easy to ascend the wrong route.) An interesting rock outcrop is next to the trail near the trailhead on Peekamoose Rd. at 9.6 mi.

The Long Path turns R and follows Peekamoose Rd. E 0.5 mi, where it ascends the Peekamoose–Table Mt. Trail (trail 62) N. There are DEC campsites in both directions along the road. Sundown is 2.6 mi W along Peekamoose Rd.

🥾 Distances: To Vernooy Falls, 1.8 mi; to jct. before Pople Hill, 2.7 mi; to jct. at hunter's camp, 4 mi; to Vernooy Kill bridge, 4.2 mi; to split from woods road, 5.6 mi; to cairn, 6.3 mi; to headwaters of Sundown Creek, 7.25 mi; to top of Bangle Hill, 8.5 mi; to Peekamoose Rd., 9.6 mi. (15.4 km). 🍃

Giant Ledge and Panther Mountain from Slide Mountain. Tony Versandi

Big Indian–Pine Hill to Denning Section

This section of the Catskills was long overshadowed by the Great Wall of Manitou rim hotels near Haines Falls, Tannersville, and Woodstock. After Professor Arnold Guyot of Princeton University showed that Slide Mt. was the highest peak in the Catskills, people began to take notice of places farther inland from the Hudson. When naturalist John Burroughs wrote about this region, the nation took interest. It was T. Morris Longstreth who said, "God made the Catskills; Irving put them on the map; but it is John Burroughs who brought them home." It is fitting that the United States Geological Survey now officially recognizes Slide, Cornell, and Wittenberg mts. as the Burroughs Range.

The southern part of this section is in the watershed of the Neversink River. Both its E and W branches rise on the shoulders of Slide Mt.

It was in the Neversink Valley that Gross Hardenbergh was shot in 1808, ending the Hardenbergh War. Wild pigeons came here in the thousands to eat beechnuts each fall, but commercial interests wiped them out by 1870. The low gradients of the stream channels resulted in many sandbars and other obstacles that made it difficult to get saw logs to market in the old days. These same factors created pools where great trout lurked.

Just as it was difficult to reach these branches in the 1800s, it is still a test of one's will to get to many trailheads today. For those who accept the challenge, some of the best wilderness in the Catskills awaits. Travelers in this region should have full gas tanks. In earlier days, county election results were often delayed a week or more because poor roads kept recorders from getting out the results.

Map aficionados notice the branch-like pattern of river systems in the Catskills. An exception to this is Esopus Creek. As it flows near Panther Mt., it begins a long, almost perfectly circular course around the mountain. Geophoto studies, supplemented by magnetic and gravitation field data, suggest that millions of years ago, a huge meteorite hit this spot. Later, ocean sediments filled in the region, and still later Panther Mt. formed. This caused the flow pattern of the Esopus and the "rosette" pattern of streams that run into it from Giant Ledge–Panther Mt. Ridge.

❋ Trails in winter: The climb to the Slide Mt. summit from the CR 47 trailhead, 0.9 mi SW of Winnisook Lake, is one of the easier Catskill ascents because the trailhead is at 2400 ft. However, the descent beyond the summit, via ladders in 0.2 mi and down two more cliffs to the col between Slide and Cornell mts., is very steep and should not be taken lightly. To do the whole Burroughs Range in one winter day is challenging and should be attempted only by experienced winter climbers.

Lone and Rocky mts. seem to be enjoyed more in winter than summer because it is possible to snowshoe over much of the blowdown and thick understory found on that terrain, and views are good in winter.

The Belleayre Trail from Pine Hill is an excellent snowshoe route with no steep sections or cliffs to negotiate. This trail is best in winter or when leaves are off the trees. Rochester Hollow is a good snowshoe or ski for intermediate skiers.

Below is a list of suggested hikes in this region.

SHORT HIKES

Rochester Hollow: A woods road to a John Burroughs Memorial at 1.7 mi; beyond, to remnants of an old estate at 2.3 mi and beyond to new lean-to. Ascent is 850 ft. Round-trip, 3.4 or 4.6 mi (5.4 or 7.4 km).

Red Hill: 2.8 mi (4.5 km) round-trip. A moderate hike up a small mountain in the southeast Catskill Forest Preserve to one of five renovated fire towers in the Catskills.

Giant Ledge: A series of overlooks to the Burroughs Range and E. Round-trip to first lookout is 3 mi (4.8 km); to last lookout, 3.8 mi (6.1 km). Ascent is 1000 ft.

MODERATE HIKES

Giant Ledge and Panther Mt.: 6.7 mi (10.7 km) round-trip. Some stiff climbing takes you to eight splendid vistas E along Giant Ledge and good viewing from two areas on Panther Mt., also E.

Slide Mt.–Curtis–Ormsbee Loop: 6.7 mi (10.7 km). Climb the highest mountain in the Catskills, a moderate ascent, and return by a scenic route created by two men who died on Mt. Washington on June 30, 1900, in a snowstorm.

HARDER HIKES

Slide-Cornell-Wittenberg Mt. Loop through Woodland Valley: 15 mi (24 km) loop over the Burroughs Range. This is a superb outing with many magnificent views for those in excellent shape, with several challenging areas to maneuver.

Table Mt.: 8 mi (12.8 km) round-trip from Denning trailhead. Cross the Deer Shanty/Neversink on a fine bridge, the crib of which was damaged in Tropical Storm Irene. For excellent viewing 150 yd before reaching the wooded summit, find small lookout ledge off-trail 40 yd to the R.

Pine Hill–West Branch Trail (Biscuit Brook–Pine Hill Trail): 14.2 mi (22.7 km) through trip from top of Woodchuck Hollow Rd. in Pine Hill to CR 47. A nice backpacking trail, but offering few views.

Trail Described		Total Miles (one way)		Page
64	Red Hill Trail	1.4	(2.2 km)	149
65	Peekamoose-Table Trail (from Phoenicia–East Branch Trail)	3.7	(5.9 km)	150
66	Lone Mt.	trailless		151
67	Rocky Mt.	trailless		152
68	Phoenicia–East Branch Trail (formerly Denning–Woodland Valley)	7.1	(11.4 km)	152
68Y	Winnisook Easement	1.5	(2.4 km)	155
69	Curtis-Ormsbee Trail	1.7	(2.7 km)	155
70	Slide-Cornell-Wittenberg Trail to Cornell	4.4	(7.0 km)	156
71	Giant Ledge–Panther Mt. Trail (Southern Section)	2.6	(4.2 km)	158
72	Pine Hill–West Branch Trail (Biscuit Brook–Pine Hill Trail)	12.0	(19.2 km)	160
73	Fir Mt.	trailless		162
74	Big Indian Mt.	trailless		163
75	McKinley Hollow Trail	1.9	(3.0 km)	163
76	Lost Clove Trail	1.3	(2.1 km)	164
77	Rochester Hollow Trail	2.8	(4.5 km)	165
78	Belleayre Mt. Trail	2.2	(3.5 km)	165
79	Belleayre Ridge Trail	1.0	(1.6 km)	166
80	Cathedral Glen Trail	1.7	(2.7 km)	167

Route Guide for Big Indian–Pine Hill to Denning (see map p. 148)
This route guide begins in the hamlet of Big Indian at the jct. of NY 28 and CR 47. It follows CR 47 S to Claryville. CR 47 becomes CR 157 N of Claryville, where it crosses from Ulster Co. to Sullivan Co. Local names for the road vary. Initially, it is Big Indian Hollow Rd., then it becomes Slide Mountain Rd., and finally, either West Branch Rd. or Frost Valley Rd.

At a T-intersection with CR 19, the route turns N to the end of the road beyond Denning.

The last four hikes above are accessed off NY 28, or from Pine Hill, or on Belleayre Mt.

Mileage E to W	Description	Mileage W to E
0.0	NY 28 and CR 47 jct. at hamlet of Big Indian; there is a general store here.	28.9
0.5	Lost Clove Rd.	28.4
2.9	Oliverea	26.0
3.0	McKinley Hollow Rd.	25.9
3.7	Burnham Hollow Rd./Association Rd.	25.2

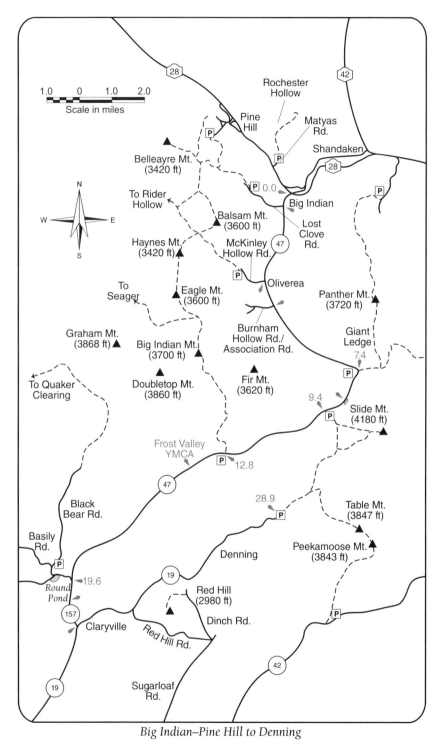

Big Indian–Pine Hill to Denning

	(Forest Preserve access parking at end)	
7.4	Hairpin turn; parking area for trail to Giant Ledge, Panther Mt.	21.5
8.5	Winnisook Lake	20.4
9.4	Slide Mt. parking area; Phoenicia–East Branch Trail (trail 68) passes through parking area to CR 47.	19.5
12.8	Biscuit Brook parking area. Pine Hill–West Branch Trail is 100 ft NE on road from parking area, opposite side.	16.1
14.0	Frost Valley YMCA Camp—some trails open to public	14.9
19.6	Round Pond Rd.	9.3
20.0	County line; CR 47 becomes CR 157	8.9
20.9	Claryville; jct. CR 157 and CR 19	8.0
28.9	Parking for Phoenicia–East Branch (formerly Denning–Woodland Valley) Trail	0.0

64 Red Hill Trail

Trails Illustrated Map 755: E11 / Map 143, Southern Catskills: H9, trail RH

This relatively new trail to the summit was created by members of the New York–New Jersey Trail Conference and DEC. A local group of volunteers in cooperation with the Catskill Center for Conservation and Development and DEC helped renovate Red Hill's fire tower. A fire tower interpreter is usually on site in the summer. Located in southern Ulster County, Red Hill was selected in 1920 as the southernmost Catskill site for a steel fire lookout station. It was staffed by a DEC observer until 1991, the last manned tower in the Forest Preserve. Adirondack hikers will be interested to learn that DEC forest rangers Pete Fish (retired) and Steve Ovitt served the Red Hill area before transfer to the Adirondacks.

▶Trailhead: From NY 28 in Big Indian, travel S on CR 47 for 21 mi to Claryville (CR 47 becomes CR 157). Turn L on CR 19, R up Red Hill Rd. for about 3 mi, L on Dinch/Coons Rd. over a height of land, descending on dirt road to a parking area, L. From the S, travel NY 55 to W of Grahamsville, to CR 19 N to Claryville.◀

A self-guided nature tour is now featured along the trail and an informational brochure is available at the trailhead. Follow yellow markers W over initially rocky ground, crossing an often-dry creek. The trail passes among attractive mature second-growth hardwoods of maple, beech, cherry, poplar, and ash.

At 0.2 mi, the trail climbs up through ledges on varying grades. It passes a small hemlock grove at 0.5 mi. At 0.7 mi, the route bears R where the trail merges with an old wagon road. Swinging S, the route ascends more steeply to a very gradual section around the hillside. Then the trail climbs quite steeply before leveling off at 1.3 mi, where the fire tower can be glimpsed ahead.

The restored observer's cabin is open to the public with pictures and information about Red Hill history. A smaller utility building and outhouse is L. The 60 ft tower is located in the middle of a clearing at 1.4 mi, surrounded by large maple and red spruce.

Views from the fire tower are impressive. Three bodies of water to the S are sections of Rondout Reservoir, part of the New York City water supply system. Water flows here from reservoirs on the East and West branches of the Delaware River and the Neversink River through underground aqueducts.

To the E (R to L) are Peekamoose Mt., Table Mt., Lone Mt., and farther distant, Balsam Cap Mt., Friday Mt., and Slide Mt., the Catskills' highest point. Looking N (R to L) are Doubletop Mt., Graham Mt., and Balsam Lake Mt., which also has a restored fire tower. Nearby Denman Mt. is SW.

🥾 Distances: To old road, 0.7 mi; to summit fire tower, 1.4 mi (2.2 km). Summit elevation, 2990 ft (911 m). Ascent, 890 ft (271 m).

65 Peekamoose-Table Trail *(from Phoenicia–East Branch Trail)*

Trails Illustrated Map 755: F12 / Map 143, Southern Catskills: J8, trail PT

From the Denning parking area, it is 3.95 mi to the summit of Table Mt. After 1.2 mi along the Phoenicia–East Branch Trail (trail 68), and descending to the Neversink Valley, the hiker ascends nearly 1700 ft to the summit of Table. Compare this to the 2600 ft ascent from trail 62, the Peekamoose-Table Trail from Peekamoose Rd., which is the greatest ascent in the Catskill Forest Preserve.

▶Trailhead: Access to the Peekamoose-Table Trail is at the jct. of the Phoenicia–East Branch Trail (trail 68), 1.2 mi from the Denning parking area.◀

From the jct. (0.0 mi), the blue-marked trail heads E, descending a slope to the Deer Shanty Brook–Neversink River flood plain, and turns sharply SW, crossing small brooks; at 0.3 mi Deer Shanty Brook and the East Branch of the Neversink River merge. The broad flood plain and shallow braided Neversink make this a wet, dangerous area in times of winter melt-water or heavy rain. In summer, it is mostly sandy soil and bare rock stream bottom.

The first main bridge over the East Branch of the Neversink survived Tropical Storm Irene, but its W bank abutment was undermined by flood waters so the bridge is twisted but easily passable; a new ramp onto the bridge was built. (This impressive new bridge is the first one to survive in this area.) A log bridge crosses another brook at 0.4 mi; at the top of the far bank, an informal path enters from the L. (This unofficial path to the Slide-Cornell Mt. col in 4.5 mi is used enough to be easily traveled, especially in the lower reaches. It crosses the Neversink beyond Donovan Brook in 1 mi, one of its many crossings. There is a good approach up Lone and Rocky mts. between two tributaries at 2.7 mi and 2.75 mi.)

On the blue-marked trail, rolling terrain becomes a moderate grade at 0.7 mi and ascends a series of pitches to 1 mi at 2800 ft elevation; a spur path R leads to a lookout S toward Van Wyck Mt. A gradual upgrade soon reaches height of land and descends pitches to a col at 1.2 mi, site of a huge rock outcrop. The route ascends again on varying grades.

The trail levels briefly at 1.45 mi at a lookout R. A steep pitch cuts through a large rock outcrop at 1.5 mi, followed by a second steep pitch. Three spur paths branch R beginning at 1.6 mi to a cliff edge, with excellent views S to Van Wyck Mt. and to the Tison Trust estate near the Denning clearing.

The trail dips slightly at 1.9 mi, levels, and then begins a long, steady gradual upgrade for the next half-mile. There is a spring to the L of the trail at 2.3 mi, and at 2.4 mi a path leads R 200 ft to the Bouton Memorial Lean-to.

The trail ascends steadily, passing the 3500 ft elevation marker at 2.5 mi. A steep ascent at 2.6 mi provides a good view N to Slide and Lone mts. A prominent herd path at 2.7 mi heads R; follow it through evergreens for 40 yd and look for a small ledge down to the R, a cliff top with room for two people, with magnificent views.

The blue-marked trail climbs easily from this herd path to the true summit of Table Mt. at 2.75 mi, set in conifers. Summit elevation is 3847 ft. How Table Mt. gained its name is apparent as the trail continues another 0.3 mi on the flat mountaintop.

Gradual downgrades on new trailwork begin at 3.1 mi, level out at the herd path L to Lone Mt. at 3.2 mi, and enter the dark col section, crossing wet stretches at 3.3 mi. Here the trail squeezes through tightly spaced conifers that nearly form a tunnel.

A gradual grade climbs to a less obvious unmarked herd path L at 3.55 mi, where views toward Slide Mt. can be seen in winter. (Bear R for the summit.) The summit clearing at 3.7 mi is completely surrounded by balsam fir and spruce. A tall person used to see views of the Burroughs Range by climbing the immense boulder at the clearing, but trees obscure former viewing. A new path L 100 yd farther offers fantastic views E and SE. Summit elevation is 3843 ft. The trail (as trail 62) continues 3.9 mi to Peekamoose Rd. near Bull Run.

🐾 Distances: To log bridge, 0.4 mi; to first lookout, 1 mi; to three lookouts, 1.6 mi; to Bouton Memorial Lean-to spur trail, 2.4 mi; to Table Mt. summit, 2.75 mi; to col, 3.3 mi; to Peekamoose Mt. summit, 3.5 mi (5.6 km); 4.75 mi from Denning parking area.

66 Lone Mt. *(bushwhack)*

Trails Illustrated Map 755: F13 / Map 143, Southern Catskills: J8

Lone Mt.'s summit canister is on a paper birch and fern covered mountaintop, indicative of a past forest fire. Time is gradually replacing this flora with balsam. Lone's ascent is often combined with ascents of Rocky Mt. or Table Mt. Accessed from the Phoenicia–East Branch Trail (trail 68), 1.2 mi NE of the Denning trailhead, and the Peekamoose-Table Trail (trail 65), the most common route is to follow the unmarked "Fisherman's Trail" up the East Branch of the Neversink, crossing the major tributary named Donovan Brook in a mile. From here, follow the ridge directly to the canister. Lone is also commonly reached via herd paths starting on the Table side of the Table-Peekamoose col. There is a good lunch spot on a ledge with a view, a little E of the canister.

The drop into the col between Lone Mt. and Rocky Mt. has some minor cliffs that are readily negotiable in summer, but they can be a problem in winter. The col itself has a dense thicket of balsam with some blowdown. The whole trek between Lone Mt. and Rocky Mt. is much easier if the hiker swings down the S slope of Lone Mt. and stays well below the balsam-covered col on the way to Rocky Mt. Less elevation need be lost dropping down the S side as opposed to staying below the col on the N side. Summit elevation, 3721 ft (1134 m).

67 Rocky Mt. (bushwhack)

Trails Illustrated Map 755: F13 / Map 143, Southern Catskills: K8

Rocky Mt. has gradual to moderate slopes but considerable blowdown. The thick growth surrounding the summit clearing has grown up considerably over the years and is somewhat less daunting. The route up the East Branch of the Neversink (see Lone Mt.), ascending the ridge between the two tributaries at 2.7 and 2.75 mi (see trail 65), is generally easy, especially if thicker spots are skirted to the N.

The direct ridge route between Rocky and Balsam Cap has also gotten easier over the years, and, with luck, can be negotiated without difficulty. As with Lone Mt., its long approach, from whatever direction the hiker chooses, necessitates an early start and careful planning by day-trippers.

Many hikers climb this peak in winter, when deep snow covers much of the blowdown. However, winter ascents pose their own problems and should not be attempted by poorly equipped or inexperienced people. Summit elevation, 3508 ft (1069 m).

68 Phoenicia–East Branch Trail
(formerly Denning–Woodland Valley Trail)
Trails Illustrated Map 755: F12 / Map 143, Southern Catskills: I8, trail PE

This trail provides the backpacker with a number of options. It crosses the divide from the East Branch to the West Branch of the Neversink River and then crosses another divide into the Esopus Creek watershed. The Giant Ledge–Panther Mt. Trail (trail 71), the Slide-Cornell-Wittenberg Trail (trail 70), and the Peekamoose–Table Trail (trail 65) can all be reached from this trail, as well as bushwhack peaks such as Lone and Rocky mts.

The Phoenicia–East Branch Trail continues on to Woodland Valley as trail 48; trail 48 is summarized from W to E on page 154.

▶Trailhead: The trail begins at the Denning Rd. parking area trailhead (see Route Guide, p. 147), 8 mi E on CR 19 from CR 157 in Claryville. There are few facilities to help the driver. The road bears R and becomes unpaved at 6.7 mi, 0.2 mi past Strauss Center. Pass the large Tison Trust estate 0.1 mi before reaching the trailhead. A trail register and an information board are at the N end of the parking area.◀

From the parking area (0.0 mi), the yellow-marked trail follows an old woods road NE up gradual grades. The route through hemlock forest is both comfortable and pleasant. A gradual downgrade at 1 mi leads to a bridge over a small stream. Lost elevation is slowly regained to a jct. at 1.2 mi. (The blue trail R, the Peekamoose-Table Trail [trail 65], leads 2.75 mi to the summit of Table Mt.)

Gradual to moderate climbing continues along the old woods road, which passes a spring L at 1.8 mi and crosses a brook at 2.1 mi. Level trail runs from 2.2 mi to 2.7 mi, where climbing resumes. Height of land occurs at 3 mi at 3050 ft elevation, 900 ft above the trailhead. The Curtis-Ormsbee Trail (trail 69) enters from the R; a monument to William Curtis and Allan Ormsbee is at this jct. (The Curtis-Ormsbee Trail ascends 1.7 mi up the shoulder of Slide Mt., joining the Slide-Cornell-Wittenberg Trail [trail 70] 0.7 mi from the summit of Slide Mt.)

The trail descends slightly, passing a spring R at 3.25 mi. Trail can be wet here. Footing becomes less rocky and more comfortable as the trail swings R downhill to a bridge over a large tributary of the West Branch at 3.5 mi. The route again levels and can be very wet before reaching the jct. of the Slide-Cornell-Wittenberg Trail (trail 70) at 3.8 mi. (This red-marked trail ascends 2 mi to the summit of Slide Mt. and continues across the Burroughs Range.)

The yellow-marked Phoenicia–East Branch Trail continues straight ahead, passing a pipe spring on the R at 3.9 mi. It leaves the old road at 4.1 mi, abruptly turning L at a trail sign arrow, descending stone steps. The trail descends at moderate grades over rocky terrain, improved by trailwork, before easing at 4.3 mi.

The path crosses the rocky West Branch of the Neversink River (sometimes dry and sometimes very challenging at high water), reaching the trail register at the Slide Mt. parking area at 4.5 mi. Here the trail turns R onto CR 47 and climbs uphill. The trail passes the Winnisook Club at 5.4 mi at the height of land between the West Branch and Esopus Creek watersheds.

At the end of Winnisook Lake, follow the unmarked former Denning–Woodland Valley Trail (trail 68Y) into the woods, which connects to the yellow-marked Phoenicia–East Branch Trail 20 yd W of the Giant Ledge–Panther Mt. Trail jct. (trail 71). The Winnisook Club provides an easement to hike this unmarked trail, thus avoiding road descent and saving a 500 ft re-ascent; they ask hikers to stay on the trail until state land is reached.

The marked trail (trail 68) continues down CR 47 and leaves the road at the Giant Ledge parking area on a hairpin turn at 6.4 mi, heading E at a DEC signpost, following yellow trail markers to a trail register. (Hikers climbing Giant Ledge and Panther Mt. use this section of the trail.) The route drops to a stream, which it crosses on a wide bridge at 6.5 mi.

The trail swings L up a moderate grade and then jags R before steeply climbing a short pitch at 6.6 mi. Varying grades sidle up the ridge to rock steps at 7 mi, as the trail curves R up steep rock cobble to a trail jct. Here, the old Denning–Woodland Valley Trail enters from the R. (This original trail, unmaintained [trail 68Y], can be used when hiking the loop from Woodland Valley to or from the Burroughs Range, to avoid road walking and losing 500 vertical ft to CR 47.)

Another 20 yd brings the hiker to a DEC signpost at a jct. at 7.1 mi. The blue-marked Giant Ledge–Panther Mt. Trail (trail 71) heads N. The yellow-marked Phoenicia–East Branch Trail continues E on flat terrain across the height of land to 7.15 mi. (Avoid R turn here at a woods road jct.)

A long, gradual descent to Woodland Valley commences, with the northern end of the trail identified as trail 48, the Woodland Valley Trail (see Woodstock-Shandaken Section).

For those continuing through, summary of the northern section of this trail from W to E (for the trail from E to W, see the Woodland Valley Trail, trail 48): The route, along a pleasant woods road through beech-birch forest, is most enjoyable. Following an undependable water flow L at 7.4 mi, the trail swings N. It narrows at 7.8 mi as the slope drops off steeply to the R and rises on the L.

At a waterfall and steady-flow spring L at 8 mi, a large rockslide creates an interesting section. Here the trail swings R to the E and the rate of descent increases. At 8.2 mi, the loose rock of a talus slope draws attention for 0.25 mi. When the talus slope ends, the grade becomes gradual in a forest of mostly beech.

At 8.6 mi a log barrier blocks travel on a woods road that leads to private property. The marked trail forks L into woods as a footpath, requiring the hiker to keep a sharp lookout for trail markers. Moderate grades descend into a ravine as the route switchbacks several times before bridging a stream on the valley floor.

Turning R from the bridge, the trail immediately swings L through a rocky area. At 8.8 mi, it very steeply climbs more than 100 stone steps and then continues steeply upward over large rocks.

The route turns R at 8.9 mi and reaches a broad shelf in the side of Fork Ridge. Nearly level terrain gives a much-needed respite. The shelf narrows at 9.1 mi, and a long, gradual downgrade to Woodland Valley begins. A trail register precedes a short steep pitch followed by wooden steps to the rear of the parking area of the Woodland Valley State campground at 9.8 mi. (The campground office is 500 yd R on the campground road; Phoenicia is 5.6 mi L on Woodland Valley Rd. and CR 28.)

Joanne Hihn

🐾 Distances: To Peekamoose-Table Trail jct., 1.2 mi; to Curtis-Ormsbee Trail jct., 3 mi; to Slide-Cornell-Wittenberg Trail jct., 3.8 mi; to Slide Mt. parking area, 4.5 mi; to Giant

Ledge parking area, 6.4 mi or via easement to height of land, 7 mi; to Giant Ledge–Panther Mt. Trail jct., 7.1 mi (11.4 km); to stone steps, 8.8 mi; to Woodland Valley State Campground, 9.8 mi (15.7 km).

68Y Winnisook Easement

Trails Illustrated Map 755: G12 / Map 143, Southern Catskills: J7

On Trail 68, elevation must be lost and regained because of rerouting around the private Winnisook Club, which forces the hiker down to CR 47 to avoid private property; however, this club has granted an easement to use the old Denning–Woodland Valley Trail that leaves CR 47 just N of Winnisook Lake (trail 68Y). This saves 500 ft of descent along the road and ascent to the Giant Ledge–Panther Mt. jct. (This is especially useful if hiking the 15 mi loop over the Burroughs Range through Woodland Valley.)

69 Curtis-Ormsbee Trail

Trails Illustrated Map 755: F12 / Map 143, Southern Catskills: J8, trail CO

This trail provides a very attractive and enjoyable route up Slide Mt., making a loop route combined with the Slide-Cornell-Wittenberg Trail (trail 70). It climbs 1.7 mi from its jct. with the Phoenicia–East Branch Trail (trail 68, at its 3 mi. point from Denning and 0.8 mi from the Slide-Cornell-Wittenberg Trail), to a jct. with trail 70. William Curtis and Allan Ormsbee, builders of the trail, died in a snowstorm on Mt. Washington on June 30, 1900. A monument commemorating them is at the trailhead.

▶Trailhead: The trail heads E from the Phoenicia–East Branch Trail jct. (0.0), following blue DEC trail markers.◀

After 0.1 mi of gradual climbing, the trail swings R steeply but easily up a great rock cut. From the cliff on top, an interesting view is seen down into the rock formation.

Gradual and moderate grades alternate, briefly becoming steep up ledges, where there is a view to Doubletop Mt. Beyond, the trail reaches the 3500 ft elevation marker at 0.5 mi. Gradual grades continue to 0.6 mi, where the trail again pitches steeply up rock ledges. On top at 0.65 mi where flat rocks cover the trail, an unmarked spur path leads R 25 yd to Paul's Lookout, with excellent views of Table and Lone mts. from a large rock shelf.

The trail soon levels, crossing 125 ft of wet area on log walkways. After gradual grades through attractive open woods and meadow, the trail resumes moderate climbing through shady hemlock woods. Log steps ascend a steep spot at 1.5 mi. The trail levels, passing over a high point, then very gradually descends to the Slide-Cornell-Wittenberg Trail jct. (trail 70) at 1.7 mi, 830 ft above the trailhead. Slide Mt. summit is 0.7 mi E.

🌀 Distances: To rock cut, 0.1 mi; to Paul's Lookout, 0.7 mi; to log steps, 1.5 mi; to jct., 1.7 mi (2.7 km).

70 Slide-Cornell-Wittenberg Trail to Cornell

Trails Illustrated Map 755: G12 / Map 143, Southern Catskills: J7, trail WS

This trail offers a wonderful diversity of terrain and forest. The route up Slide Mt. is surprisingly moderate, this peak being the Catskill's highest; the trailhead is at 2400 ft. The upper reaches are a beautiful walk through thick conifers, often on nearly level trail. Views to Ashokan Reservoir, Cornell, and Wittenberg are improved. In the next 0.9 mi below the summit, the trail drops 930 vertical feet. Four ladders scale a cliff, 0.2 mi from the summit, with magnificent views. The route to Cornell from Slide is challenging, down two steep rock areas. For scenic beauty throughout, it is hard to surpass. A deep V-cut in a 15 ft cliff E of the summit of Cornell lacks good footholds and handholds and requires care; a rope is winter is advised. The Slide-Cornell-Wittenberg Trail continues on as trail 49 to Wittenberg Mt. and Woodland Valley; trail 49 is summarized below from W to E for those wishing to continue on.

▶Trailhead: Access to the trail is from the Phoenicia–East Branch Trail (trail 68). The Slide Mt. parking area is on the S side of CR 47 (Slide Mountain Rd.). (See Route Guide, p. 147.)◀

Follow the yellow DEC trail markers of the Phoenicia–East Branch Trail past the trail register at the rear of the parking area. The trail crosses the West Branch of the Neversink River (sometimes dry, sometimes challenging) and heads E. The route climbs gradual grades to 0.2 mi, where it changes to a moderate grade up rocky trail, much improved by trailwork. The trail climbs stone steps at 0.4 mi to an old woods road, turning R and passing a pipe spring L at 0.6 mi. The route reaches the Slide-Cornell-Wittenberg Trail jct. at 0.7 mi. (The Phoenicia–East Branch Trail [trail 68] continues straight.)

Turn L at the jct. trailhead (0.0 mi) and follow red DEC trail markers E up a rocky old jeep road at varying grades. At 0.5 mi a sign points to a camping spot. The 3500 ft elevation sign is reached at 0.8 mi. When the trail turns N at 1 mi, the grade eases and becomes gradual or nearly level. As the trail swings E again, views N open up before reaching the Curtis-Ormsbee Trail (trail 69) jct. at 1.4 mi, which turns R. (This trail intersects the Phoenicia–East Branch Trail in 1.7 mi.)

The Slide-Cornell-Wittenberg Trail is beautiful, heading straight toward the summit through a thick conifer forest, often on level terrain. At 2 mi, a magnificent lookout N and E to Cornell and Wittenberg and many high peaks is seen from a rock ledge; Panther Mt. is L. At a clearing where the fire tower base support remains, the trail reaches the true Slide Mt. summit at 2.05 mi (4180 ft el-

Cornell Mt. view to Slide Mt. David White

evation and highest in the Catskills).

Continue to the open rock shelf that rewards the climber with a view over Friday and Balsam Cap to the Ashokan Reservoir and beyond—but unfortunately mainly in winter now, standing on many feet of snow. Tree growth increasingly obstructs this former vista, though at times it seems a bit improved. Walk to the base of the rock shelf to the John Burroughs Memorial Plaque.

The trail to Cornell leaves near the John Burroughs Memorial and rapidly descends, losing 930 ft in the next 0.9 mi. The route drops at grades varying from moderate to very steep, often at the edge of a cliff. Four ladders are at 2.3 mi; views are spectacular from this location. Near the base of the last ladder, blue markers lead L 25 ft to a marvelous spring that bursts out of the rock wall; red trail markers head R. Vistas are spectacular from this location.

Descent continues at a less precipitous rate from here, but there is a 15 ft vertical drop down a rock outcrop at 2.5 mi, followed by a 35 ft drop at another outcrop bluff. Descending below 3500 ft, the trail passes three designated campsites in scenic territory before reaching the col at 3250 ft between Slide Mt. and Cornell, at 2.9 mi.

Varying grades ascend about 600 ft to Cornell's summit. After three more designated campsites, water crosses the trail at 3.8 mi, where a spring is 130 yd R of the trail. At 4.1 mi, a spring is L of the trail. Before a lookout at 4.3 mi, there is a "lemon-squeezer," a narrow passage between rock ledges. The lookout provides a good view toward Slide Mt. A second viewing spot atop a rock ledge provides a sweeping 180-degree view from Table Mt. in the SW to the Devil's Path, N.

A blue-marked spur trail at 4.4 mi leads R 0.05 mi to the flat Cornell Mt. summit. Summit elevation is 3860 ft (1176 m). The view features a good profile of Wittenberg Mt.

Refer to the Wittenberg-Cornell-Slide Trail (trail 49) in the Woodstock-Shandaken Section for the description of this trail E to W from Woodland Valley to Cornell. Here is a W to E summary of trail 49: The trail descends easily to 4.5 mi, where Cornell's famous "V-cut" at the top of a vertical drop down a rock bluff requires great care. (Winter climbers may find a rope handy here.) After another steep drop down ledges, gradual grades continue to Wittenberg Mt. at 5.2 mi, 3780 ft (1152 m), where the trail breaks out onto a broad rock shelf with magnificent views.

After level trail, the route drops down many mossy ledges through scenic territory, reaching the first of two cliffs at 5.8 mi; descents require care in this N-facing section of trail, especially in winter. Nearing the Terrace Mt. Trail jct. (trail 50), a new section of the Long Path is R.

After ascending to a high point at 7.1, the route descends through mixed hemlock and deciduous woods to a cliff top. After descending rocky trail, at 8.1 mi the trail turns R on an old woods road to a beautiful shady hemlock area, and then descends interesting rugged terrain to a trail register at 8.9 mi. The descent continues steeply to the bridge across Woodland Creek at 9.1 mi, crossing the Woodland Valley State Campground and road to the parking area. Total distance from Slide Mt. parking area, 9.8 mi, including 0.7 mi on Phoenicia–East Branch Trail.

🐾 Distances: To Curtis-Ormsbee Trail, 1.4 mi; to Slide Mt. summit, 2.05 mi; to spring, 2.3 mi; to Slide-Cornell col, 2.9 mi; to Cornell Mt. summit spur trail, 4.4 mi (7 km). Summit elevations: Slide Mt., 4180 ft (1274 m), Cornell Mt., 3860 ft (1176 m).

71 Giant Ledge–Panther Mt. Trail *(Southern Section)*

Trails Illustrated Map 755: H13 / Map 142, Central Catskills: J7, trail GP

The Giant Ledge–Panther Mt. Trail runs 7.4 mi from a jct. on the Phoenicia–East Branch Trail (trail 68) N to Fox Hollow. This trail description covers only the southern portion of the trail, reached from CR 47 or Woodland Valley. (Through hikers can refer to the Panther Mt. Trail description [trail 47], Woodstock-Shandaken Section, for the northern part of this trail.)

▶ Trailhead: Trail access is from a DEC parking area at a hairpin turn on CR 47, 7.4 mi S of Big Indian. (See Route Guide, p. 147.) Crossing the road, follow yellow-marked Phoenicia–East Branch Trail E up to the jct. of the Giant Ledge–Panther Mt. Trail, 0.75 mi from the parking area and an ascent of 580 ft. A different access would be from Woodland Valley State Campground. Refer to trail 48 in the Woodstock-Shandaken Section. ◀

From the jct. (0.0 mi) the route goes N, following blue DEC trail markers. The route is almost level over wet areas with good trailwork and ascends gradually, passing inviting flat rocks. The route steepens to a spring 50 yd L on a yellow-marked spur trail at 0.6 mi. (The former Giant Ledge Lean-to was located just beyond the spur path.)

The slope increases to a moderate-to-steep grade through boulders and rock outcrops. The trail levels at 0.75 mi near 3200 ft elevation, the beginning of Giant Ledge. Eight outlooks in the next 0.4 mi provide excellent views of Woodland Valley, Wittenberg, Cornell, and eventually Slide Mt. The views E and NE are outstanding. An informal spur trail L at 0.95 mi leads to a lookout with views SW to Fir, Spruce, and Hemlock mts. Camping is allowed on Giant Ledge.

The trail then descends gradual to moderate grades into the long, flat col between Giant Ledge and Panther Mt. at 1.5 mi. (Hikers returning to the parking area from Panther Mt. could drop down the E side of the col at a large rock outcrop and bushwhack through open forest along the base of Giant Ledge, rather than re-climb the ridge, but there are wet areas and possibly difficult rock to negotiate back to the trail near the former lean-to site S of Giant Ledge. This alternative is attractive on snowshoes or skis.)

From the col to Panther Mt. summit is a vertical ascent of 725 ft. Moderate grades steepen as the trail switchbacks up to a fine lookout at 1.8 mi, 100 ft R of the trail. There is an undependable spring R at 2 mi in a level, wet area. The 3500 ft sign is passed at 2.1 mi. Areas of steep climbing precede level trail, characteristic of Catskill long, flat summits. A rock ledge marks the true summit of Panther Mt. at 2.6 mi. This cliff's edge offers a magnificent vista of the Burroughs Range of Wittenberg, Cornell, and Slide mts. and many Devil's Path peaks. A classic cirque formation gives proof of local mountain glaciers in the geological past.

Looking up towards the cliffs of Giant Ledge. Alan Via

(The trail continues another 4.9 mi down a scenic ridge to the trailhead at Fox Hollow. Refer to the Panther Mt. Trail description [trail 47], Woodstock-Shandaken Section.)

🥾 Distances: To spring spur path, 0.6 mi; to beginning of Giant Ledge, 0.75 mi; to spur to lookout, 0.95 mi; to col between Giant Ledge and Panther Mt., 1.5 mi; to lookout on Panther Mt., 1.8 mi; to Panther Mt. summit, 2.6 mi (4.2 km); total from parking area, 3.4 mi (5.4 km). Summit elevation, 3720 ft (1134 m). Ascent from parking area, 1545 ft.

72 Pine Hill–West Branch Trail *(Biscuit Brook–Pine Hill Trail)*

Trails Illustrated Map 755: F11 to I11 / Map 143, Southern Catskills: I7, trail PW and Map 142, Central Catskills: I7, trail PW

While few long views present themselves, the quality of the Pine Hill–West Branch Trail is excellent. Sections of the route as far as Belleayre Mt. are through virgin timber. The recreationist who wants to relax in beautiful surroundings will find this region most enjoyable. The long gradual upgrades to summits followed by steeper downgrades make hiking from S to N the easier direction of travel with heavy backpacks.

▶Trailhead: Access to the trail is off CR 47 at the Biscuit Brook parking area. (See Route Guide, p. 147.) The trailhead is across CR 47, 100 ft NE of the parking area.◀

The trail follows blue DEC trail markers generally N over a gradual upgrade as it hugs the Forest Preserve boundary. After several small brooks at 0.5 mi, the trail climbs a ridge at moderate grades. It swings L near the ridgeline, levels across the ridge and then swings R in a rerouted section to avoid blowdown. From here the route descends very gradually to the Biscuit Brook Lean-to.

At 2.1 mi, a yellow-marked spur trail leads L, 250 ft to the lean-to, which sits above a steep bank on Biscuit Brook. A tributary 0.05 mi farther along the main trail is also a water source. The lean-to is a good base camp for bushwhacking NNE to Fir Mt., N to Big Indian and Eagle mts. by trail, and for bushwhacking to Doubletop Mt. from the Big Indian Mt. height of land (see below; see also Fir Mt. [73], Big Indian Mt. [74], and Doubletop Mt. [88]).

The blue-marked trail swings R and upstream, soon crossing the tributary and then crossing Biscuit Brook at 2.3 mi. It follows the W bank of the creek to 2.6 mi; the gradual grade steepens at 2.7 mi and then becomes gradual again in 0.2 mi for another 0.25 mi. The route is well above the brook, but within sight of it for much of the way. The trail pulls away from the water and climbs on surprisingly moderate grades to a steep pitch at 3.9 mi, leveling again just before reaching the old Seager Trail jct. at 4 mi (barely discernible as a trail jct., but readily identified as where the trail makes a sharp turn from W to NE).

The route continues at gradual grade towards Big Indian Mt. Paint blazes mark boundary lines at two points before the trail reaches a small open area and lookout toward the W at the 3500 ft elevation marker. At 4.6 mi, a herd path heads 0.25 mi E to the canister on the wooded true summit of Big Indian Mt.

The trail remains on contour around Big Indian Mt., and then descends gradually with occasional moderate pitches. It passes the 3500 ft elevation marker at 5 mi. The trail levels in a col and, soon after beginning to climb again, reaches the Seager Trail (trail 87) jct. at 5.8 mi; see Arkville to Seager Section. (The Shandaken Lean-to is 0.9 mi down this trail; the Seager trailhead parking area is 3 mi.)

The trail climbs R around a rock wall at 6.2 mi, and then ascends easily to a pair of short pitches that bracket the 3500 ft elevation marker at 6.7 mi on Eagle Mt. It reaches the herd path to the wooded true summit at 6.9 mi, 90 yd L. (Summit elevation is 3600 ft.)

Ski-shoe up from Pine Hill and down Belleayre. Joan Dean

After some flat trail, the grade gradually descends in attractive terrain. The 3500 ft sign is reached at 7.2 mi. A pretty mossy opening dominates the minor col between Eagle and Haynes mts. at 7.6 mi. Gradual slopes predominate until a short steep pitch up ferny ledges alerts you that you are reaching the high point of Haynes Mt.'s long flat ridge at 8.3 mi. (Summit elevation is 3420 ft.)

Gradual slopes continue the descent through interesting forest to 8.95 mi, where the trail descends steeply to the four-way jct. with the McKinley Hollow Trail and Rider Hollow Trail (trails 75 and 85, named Oliverea-Mapledale Trail in Trail Conference maps) at 9 mi. Water is 40 yd L on the Rider Hollow Trail at the base of a rock wall. (Rider Hollow Lean-to is 1.25 mi, L, toward Rider Hollow trailhead at 1.75 mi; descent is steep for 0.5 mi. McKinley Hollow Lean-to is 1.15 mi, R, towards Oliverea trailhead at 1.9 mi; descent becomes very steep 0.1 mi to 0.5 mi from the jct.)

The trail up Balsam Mt. follows gradual and moderate grades to the 3500 ft sign at 9.6 mi, followed by a final pitch up through scenic ledges with overhangs, covered with moss and wood sorrel. The trail gently ascends through a fern-filled meadow to the balsam-covered summit (more a high point) at 9.8 mi on the S end of the 0.3 mi summit ridge. (Summit elevation is 3600 ft.) Posted property signs may help winter climbers identify it.

The trail drops down and continues a slight decrease in elevation to a lookout N at 10 mi. This is a good lookout in winter with a view directly E down to the hamlet of Big Indian, one of the few views on this trail and rapidly becoming obscured by tree growth.

The level trail reaches an open area with spruce trees at 10.15 mi. The trail descends down the ferny ridge to the 3500 ft sign at 10.3 mi, with a view N through trees. A steep rock cut is reached at 10.6 mi, and at the top, a short path R leads to a good view N to Belleayre Mt. Descending this N-facing area, often icy in winter, requires care.

Reaching nearly level terrain in deciduous woods, the trail reaches the low point between Balsam and Belleayre mts. at 11 mi, followed by a gradual climb to the Mine Hollow Trail (trail 86) jct. at 11.1 mi. (The Mine Hollow Trail descends 1 mi to a jct. near the Rider Hollow Lean-to; see Arkville to Seager Section.)

Climbing from the jct. to the E summit of Belleayre Mt. is excellent; the route is gradual and the forest is attractive, with unusually large maple and beech trees creating a cool, shady canopy. When the trail swings L at 11.7 mi, three short pitches climb steeply for 0.1 mi, then the route moderates to the E summit of Belleayre Mt. at 12 mi, known for Ski Belleayre. Its 3375-ft E summit no longer has a fire tower, but the hiker can obtain excellent views 1 mi NW from the jct. along the Belleayre Ridge Trail (trail 79) to the true summit (3420 ft) at Sunset Ski Lodge.

The Belleayre Mt. Trail (trail 78) from Pine Hill describes this final section of the trail in detail. Here is a summary: The trail turns R from the E summit, passing a pipe spring R at 12.3 mi and the Belleayre Lean-to at 12.4 mi. A jct. at 12.8 mi leads to Belleayre Beach, the Pine Hill Day Use Area.

The Lost Clove Trail (trail 76) jct. is shortly beyond at 12.9 mi. (It descends to a parking area 1.3 mi from CR 47 in Big Indian Hollow.) The trail leaves state land at 13.4 mi. A spring empties into a rock pool off-trail, L, at 13.7 mi, then passes a private road at 13.8 mi, and reaches a gate at 14.2 mi. A parking pullout beyond on state land is at the top of Woodchuck Hollow Rd., Pine Hill.

🦌 Distances: To Biscuit Brook Lean-to, 2.1 mi; to herd path to Big Indian Mt. summit, 4.6 mi; to Seager Trail jct., 5.8 mi; to Eagle Mt. spur path, 6.9 mi; to Haynes Mt., 8.3 mi; to McKinley Hollow Trail and Rider Hollow Trail (Oliverea-Mapledale Trail) jct., 9 mi; to Balsam Mt., 9.8 mi; to Mine Hollow Trail jct., 11.1 mi; to E summit of Belleayre Mt., 12 mi (19.2 km); to Belleayre Mt. Lean-to, 12.4 mi; to Lost Clove Trail jct., 12.9 mi; to gate at top of Woodchuck Hollow Rd., 14.2 mi (22.7 km).

73 Fir Mt. (bushwhack)

Trails Illustrated Map 755: G11 / Map 143, Southern Catskills: I7

Fir Mt. is NNE of Biscuit Brook Lean-to. There is some evidence that Arnold Guyot got mixed up when labeling Spruce and Fir mts. on his early Catskill map. It is likely that Spruce Mt. was the original name for this peak.

The usual approach is to take a compass bearing from Biscuit Brook Lean-to for a straight bushwhack to the summit. An interesting approach is to leave the Pine Hill–West Branch Trail (trail 72) as it begins swinging L, not far from the trailhead. Bushwhack NNE, skirting private property to the E, to 3000 ft where a long, nearly level ridge heads N to the Delaware–Hudson River Basin Divide and then NNW to Fir. Another approach is from Big Indian Mt. (see 74). Approaches from Big Indian Hollow or Maben Hollow require gaining permission from landowners before crossing private land. Summit elevation is 3620 ft (1103 m).

74 Big Indian Mt. *(bushwhack)*

Trails Illustrated Map 755: G11 / Map 142, Central Catskills: I7

Big Indian Mt. is a bushwhack peak, but just barely. Legend says Winnisook was the "Big Indian"—seven feet tall. All sorts of stories, ranging from his being killed by wolves to tales of romance and vengeance, were popular when the hotel business was brisk in the late 1800s.

The usual approach to the summit is from the Pine Hill–West Branch Trail (Biscuit Brook–Pine Hill Trail, trail 72). The canister is about 0.25 mi E on a herd path that leaves the main trail as it levels on the S end of Big Indian Mt., 2.5 mi from the lean-to.

Another approach is via the Seager Trail (trail 87, in the Arkville to Seager Section), to the Pine Hill–West Branch Trail (Biscuit Brook–Pine Hill Trail, trail 72), turning S 1.2 mi to the herd path, E, for 0.25 mi. Summit elevation is 3700 ft (1128 m).

75 McKinley Hollow Trail

Trails Illustrated Map 755: H11 / Map 142, Central Catskills: I6, trail OM

On other maps, this trail and trail 85 have been referred to as the Oliverea-Mapledale Trail. In this guide, the E side is referred to as McKinley Hollow Trail (trail 75) and the W side is Rider Hollow Trail (trail 85).

McKinley Hollow is an approach to Balsam Mt. and/or Eagle Mt. from Oliverea, but hikers should be ready to earn their spurs! This is the type of climb that stays in the memory, especially if done in winter. It is a good way to get off the Pine Hill–West Branch Trail (with good knees), but not a good way to get on it if toting a heavy backpack.

▶Trailhead: Access is via CR 47 at Oliverea. (See Route Guide, p. 147.) Drive 1 mi on McKinley Hollow Rd. to the DEC parking area L before the end of the (public) road.◀

Tropical Storm Irene washed out the former trail. A new high bridge was constructed over McKinley Brook at the parking area. Over the bridge, a new route goes up-slope past a trail register. The route connects to the existing trail across McKinley Brook. Follow red trail markers. The crossing to the N side of the brook is on rocks, possibly difficult in high water.

The trail continues upstream along a woods road to 0.65 mi, where informal camping areas are back in the woods, L. The McKinley Hollow Lean-to is located at 0.7 mi beside the creek at L. This site offers a low-profile fire pit in a lovely setting above the brook.

At 0.8 mi, the trail turns L down steps at a poorly marked spot, crossing a tributary of McKinley Hollow Brook. (Avoid path straight ahead.) The trail climbs above the brook and then becomes gradual, away from the brook. As the route climbs high above the brook, the ascent steepens as it sidles up the wall of the hollow. The brook is far below to the R. Passing an older-growth hemlock, the trail becomes steep.

The trail reaches a long series of rock steps at 1.4 mi, and climbs even more steeply upward to 1.5 mi. It then continues at a more moderate grade, swinging away from the brook. It becomes gradual at 1.8 mi, reaching the jct. of the Pine Hill–West Branch Trail (trail 72) at 1.9 mi. Ascent from McKinley Hollow Lean-to is 1375 ft.

The Pine Hill–West Branch Trail leads R to Balsam Mt. in 0.8 mi, and L for Haynes Mt. in 0.7 mi and a long ridge to the Eagle Mt. spur path in 2.15 mi. Water is located at the base of a rock outcrop, 65 ft ahead towards Rider Hollow; refer to Rider Hollow Trail (trail 85), in the Arkville to Seager Section.

🐾 Distances: To trail register, 0.2 mi; to McKinley Hollow Lean-to, 0.7 mi; to rock steps, 1.4 mi; to Pine Hill–West Branch Trail jct., 1.9 mi (3 km).

76 Lost Clove Trail

Trails Illustrated Map 755: I11 / Map 142, Central Catskills: I6, trail LC

The Lost Clove Trail provides access to Belleayre Mt. via a little-used woods road that presents the climber with some stiff climbing before intersecting the Pine Hill–West Branch Trail's N segment, referred to in this guide as the Belleayre Mt. Trail (trail 78). A loop hike can be made by spotting a car here and ascending via McKinley Hollow to climb Balsam and Belleayre mts.

▶Trailhead: Access is off CR 47 in Big Indian Hollow, via Lost Clove Rd. (See Route Guide, p. 147.) Drive 1.4 mi up Lost Clove Rd. to a parking area on the R. ◀

The trail leaves the rear of the parking area (0.0 mi), crosses a small brook, and enters an open field at 0.05 mi. Turn L and climb a steep grade on a woods road. Grades are steep or moderate for most of the next mile. Avoid side trails and bear L at a jct. at 0.4 mi. Go straight through the jct. at 0.6 mi. Bear L at another jct. at 0.85 mi. There are occasional gradual grades in the upper reaches. The trail enters state land at 1.2 mi, before the jct. with the Belleayre Mt. Trail (trail 78; this is also the northern end of the Pine Hill–West Branch Trail [trail 72]) at 1.3 mi, having ascended 780 ft. (Turn L for Belleayre Mt. summit and R for Pine Hill.)

🐾 Distances: To first jct. bearing L, 0.4 mi; to second jct. bearing L, 0.85 mi; to jct. with Belleayre Mt. Trail, 1.3 mi (2.1 km).

77 Rochester Hollow Trail

Trails Illustrated Map 755: 112 / Map 142, Central Catskills: I5

Rochester Hollow is part of the Shandaken Wild Forest, offering a couple of camping spots and a lean-to. It is an excellent ski route.

▶Trailhead: Access is at the end of Matyas Rd., which leaves NY 28 1.05 mi W of the NY 28/CR 47 intersection at Big Indian. Drive 0.1 mi N on Matyas Rd. to a pair of stone columns, where state land begins. A parking area is 100 yd beyond the columns.◀

The trail parallels a stream for 1.7 mi as it climbs at first gradually up a woods road on state land. It reaches a designated campsite at 0.14 mi and a second one at 0.3 mi. The route enters a shady hemlock forest at 0.6 mi as it climbs into the hollow. Stream banks steepen on the other side.

It reaches a gateway at 1.4 mi and the way becomes steeper to a culvert where the trail swings L at 1.7 mi. A yellow trail goes R here; beyond the Burroughs Memorial a red trail goes L. From here, the grade becomes more gradual, in 200 ft reaching a path up stone steps, R, to a memorial to naturalist John Burroughs, a prolific author who wrote about the streams and mountains of the Catskills.

The trail ascends gently and nearly levels, arriving at the remnants of an old estate at 2.3 mi. A great curved stone wall adorns the trailside, across from a foundation of concrete and stone.

Shortly beyond, there is a new lean-to set back on the R, complete with wheelchair-accessible privy. The public trail ends at 2.8 mi, where a yellow barrier gate and "Do Not Enter" sign mark the limit of state land; the route proceeds onto private land that is not open to the public.

🐾 Distances: To designated campsites, 0.14 and 0.3 mi; to gateway, 1.4 mi; to John Burroughs Memorial, 1.7 mi; to old estate, 2.3 mi; to lean-to, 2.4 mi; to barrier at end of state land, 2.8 mi (4.5 km). Ascent, 850 ft.

78 Belleayre Mt. Trail (Pine Hill–West Branch Trail)

Trails Illustrated Map 755: 111 / Map 142, Central Catskills: I6, trail PW

In the heyday of hotels in the Catskills, Pine Hill was a railroad stop and had many small hotels. Guests climbed to the fire tower on Belleayre's E summit for a marvelous view of the region. Today, the fire tower is gone and so is that summit view. However, an extension of the trip along Belleayre Ridge to Sunset Lodge and the true summit at the Belleayre Ski Area provides excellent views. The Belleayre Mt. Trail is the first part of the Pine Hill–West Branch Trail (trail 72), from the N.

▶Trailhead: From NY 28 in Pine Hill, proceed S on Elm St., turning R on Main St. Turn L on Bonnie View Ave. and L on Depot Rd., crossing the open area to Woodchuck Hollow Rd. above the railroad bed. Travel 0.55 mi up Woodchuck Hollow Rd. to a parking clearing on the R. The trail begins beyond the gate.◀

The trail enters a shady hollow past the gate and soon makes a sharp turn E on nearly level terrain. An enormous boulder with overhangs adorns the trailside; the trail ascends gradually through deciduous forest to 0.4 mi, where arrow signs at a jct. with a private road indicate a R turn.

The trail begins to climb a moderate grade and enters state land. At 0.5 mi, the route passes a rock wall off-trail to the R, where a spring emerges and fills a rock pool. After passing runoff along the trail, the climb moderates a bit; footing is good on the grassy route.

The Lost Clove Trail (trail 76) enters from the L at 1.3 mi. (It leads 1.3 mi down moderate to steep grades to a parking area on Lost Clove Rd.) The Belleayre Beach trail jct. is 1.4 mi. (It leads to the Pine Hill Day Use Area, an improved descent for 1.9 mi.)

The trail steadily climbs to Belleayre Lean-to at 1.7 mi. Beyond the lean-to, the grade becomes moderate to steep, curving past a pipe spring on the L at 1.8 mi. At 1.9 mi, the grade becomes gradual as it passes scenic mossy terrain on this N-facing section. The grassy clearing of the E summit of Belleayre Mt., originally the site of a fire tower, is reached at 2.2 mi. (The Pine Hill–West Branch Trail [trail 72] continues, L, 2.2 mi to the summit of Balsam Mt., and terminates at CR 47 at 14.2 mi.)

The Belleayre Ridge Trail (trail 79) heads W from the tower clearing to the Belleayre Mt. Ski Area and Sunset Lodge, near the true summit of Belleayre Mt. It is well worth walking the 1 mi, with some ascent and descent, to that area for excellent views (see next trail).

🐾 Distances: To private road and turn, 0.4 mi; to Lost Clove Trail jct., 1.3 mi; to Belleayre Lean-to, 1.7 mi; to Belleayre Mt. E summit, 2.2 mi (3.5 km). Summit elevation, 3375 ft (1029 m). Ascent from Pine Hill village, 1475 ft.

79 Belleayre Ridge Trail

Trails Illustrated Map 755: I11 / Map 142, Central Catskills: H6, trail BR

The Belleayre Ridge Trail is a short connector trail between the Pine Hill–West Branch Trail (trail 72) and the Belleayre Ski Area. Principal use of the trail is for hikers heading from Belleayre's viewless E summit to the ski area, where excellent views N and S are found at Sunset Lodge. The route is a grass-covered jeep trail with minor ascent and descent. Views gained at the ski area are well worth the short time it takes to travel the ridge.

▶Trailhead: The trail leaves Belleayre's E summit (at the jct. of trail 72 and trail 78, 0.0 mi), the site of the old fire tower, following red DEC trail markers W. ◀

A slight decrease in elevation occurs before the Cathedral Glen Trail (trail 80) intersects the trail from the R at 0.3 mi. The grade becomes gradually uphill, reaching the Hirschland Lean-to at 0.45 mi. (A spur trail R leads a few ft to the lean-to, which sits at the top of a ski slope where a narrow view N is available.)

The trail continues W to a jct. at 0.8 mi, with a DEC sign: "Highmount Train Station, 2.9 mi" and "Belleayre Beach, 3.6 mi" (Pine Hill Day Use Area). The red-marked Ridge Trail continues to an open field at Chairlift 1 and Sunset Lodge at 1 mi, elevation 3420 ft. The best views are N from the chairlift. Immediately below in the valley is small Monka Hill, with Halcott Mt. behind it in the distance. Rose Mt. is R of Monka Hill, with Balsam, Sherrill, and North Dome mts. behind. Still farther R, West Kill Mt. blocks the view of Hunter Mt.'s fire tower.

Cooling off on Belleayre. Alan Via

From the deck of the lodge, Balsam Lake Mt. with its visible fire tower is due S. Graham Mt. to its E is viewed best when leaves are off.

🐾 Distances: To Cathedral Glen Trail jct., 0.25 mi; to Hirschland Lean-to, 0.45 mi; to Chairlift 1 and Sunset Lodge, 1 mi (1.6 km).

80 Cathedral Glen Trail

Trails Illustrated Map 755: I11 / Map 142, Central Catskills: I5, trail CG

The Cathedral Glen Trail is unique. The upper half of the trail descends steeply down Belleayre Mt.'s easternmost ski slope, providing good views of the distant landscape to the N. The lower half of the trail passes through older-growth hemlock.

▶Access: Trail access to the first 0.6 mi of the Cathedral Glen Trail (down a ski slope) is from the top of Belleayre Mt., off the Belleayre Ridge Trail (trail 79). Legal access from the railroad bed in Pine Hill is not available (in spite of signs and markers). However, the beautiful lower mile of the trail, through older-growth hemlock forest to Belleayre Mt.'s snowmaking reservoir, can be accessed from Belleayre's Overlook Lodge or Discovery Lodge, making a nice loop trip.

From Overlook Lodge, walk E on a service road below the fenced pond, cross a ski slope to signs "Roaring Brook" and "Super Chief," and access a woods road leading in 0.2 mi to the base of the Cathedral Glen ski slope; across is the start of Cathedral Glen's lower half. (See last two paragraphs of trail description below.) This loop is described in detail in *Catskill Day Hikes for All Seasons*.

To access the lower Cathedral Glen section from Discovery Lodge, pass lifts 1 and 2 and follow a path E into the woods and then bear L on the HH trail, following the service road down to the reservoir. From both approaches, avoid the railroad bed and cross on the embankment.◀

Ski Run Road. *Mark Schaefer*

From Belleayre Mt. Ridge Trail, the Cathedral Glen Trail jct. is 0.7 mi E of Sunset Lodge on the summit and 0.3 mi W of Belleayre Mt.'s E summit (site of a former fire tower). Turn N at this jct. on the blue-marked Cathedral Glen Trail (0.0 mi). The trail descends moderately through woods on slippery rocks and emerges onto a fern-covered ski slope at 0.2 mi. Turning R and continuing downward steeply, the trail levels off at times and reaches the base of the ski slope at 0.6 mi. At the far R corner, the second half of Cathedral Glen Trail descends at first moderately and then gradually through an increasingly magnificent older-growth hemlock forest. At 1.35 mi (0.75 mi from base of ski slope), an overgrown informal path L leads to Cathedral Brook.

The grade is gradual or level now through the shady hemlock. At 1.7 mi (1.1 mi from base of ski slope), passing Belleayre Mt.'s snowmaking reservoir, the trail descends and terminates at the railroad bed. Although there are signs and markers, legally the railroad bed is not available for public use. The hiker should leave the trail before the final pitch down to the railroad bed, bushwhack to the embankment below the reservoir, cross here, and ascend via service roads and ski trails to Discovery or Overlook lodges, or cross tracks to a path leading to the end of Bonnie View Ave.

🐾 Distances: To ski slope, 0.2 mi; to base of ski slope, 0.6 mi; to railroad bed, 1.7 mi (2.7 km).

Prattsville to Arkville Section

The northwest Catskills, described in this section, is outside the Blue Line border of the Catskill Park, but there are two peaks over 3500 ft that are required peaks for membership in the Catskill 3500 Club. It is perplexing that Roxbury is not in the Catskill Park, because the northwest Catskills nourished naturalist and writer John Burroughs, who was born in Roxbury and attended a one-room schoolhouse there. He developed acute observational skills exploring the mountains, streams, and woods of the region; special editions of some of his twenty-seven books about nature were required reading in schools across the United States.

It was in this region that Zadock Pratt later built one of the great tanneries of the Catskills. Visit the Zadock Pratt museum in Prattsville and Pratt Rock for the history of this unique personality who served the nation in Washington, D.C., in the mid-nineteenth century. He was an environmentalist who moved the main street of the village away from the Schoharie Creek. Although Prattsville was devastated by Tropical Storm Irene, perhaps Pratt's initiative saved lives and property.

The nearby Gilboa Museum features tree fossils from the Devonian Period. Combined with a view of the Gilboa Dam at the Schoharie Reservoir, this makes an interesting side trip from Prattsville.

South of Grand Gorge, the headwaters of the East Branch of the Delaware River parallel the road; the old Delaware and Ulster railroad bed can be discerned across. The DURR rail ride from Arkville terminates in Roxbury. The Catskill Center for Conservation and Development is just E of NY 28/CR 38, with the Erpf Art Gallery.

❈ Trails in winter: Bearpen via Ski Run Rd. is easy for snowshoers and excellent for skiers of intermediate skills.

SUGGESTED HIKES

Pratt Rock: 1 mi (1.6 km) round-trip. Short, steep ascent through a twenty-acre park devoted to Zadock Pratt. An information board offers his interesting personal and social history, and above the picnic area, many fascinating whitewashed figures are carved on the escarpment.

Bearpen Mt.: 9 mi (14.4 km) round-trip. Although long, this climb is never more than moderate up an old ski road; the second half is nearly level terrain. Summit views N and NE are excellent, especially in winter when leaves are off the trees.

Prattsville to Arkville

Trail Described		Total Miles (one way)	Page
81	Bearpen Mt.	old woods road	171
82	Vly Mt.	trailless	172
83	Pratt Rock Park	0.5 (0.8 km)	173
84	John Burroughs Memorial State Historic Site		174

Route Guide for Prattsville to Arkville (see map p. 170)

Mileage N to S	Description	Mileage S to N
0.0	Jct. NY 23 and NY 23A	24.2
0.4	Pratt Rock Park	23.8
1.5	Schoharie Creek bridge, N end of Prattsville	22.7
6.2	Jct. NY 30 in Grand Gorge	18.0
12.1	Hardscrabble Rd.	12.1
12.8	Roxbury	11.4
23.2	CR 38 to Arkville	1.0
24.2	Jct. NY 28 in Arkville	0.0

81 Bearpen Mt. (*old woods road*)

Trails Illustrated Map 755: L11 / Map 145, Bearpen Mt.: I3

Bearpen Mt. has no marked trail to its summit, but from the N an old woods road, Ski Run Rd., leads to the summit area on this state reforestation area, acquired in 1999. No canister has been placed at the summit, although Bearpen is technically a bushwhack. Ski Run Rd. is a pleasant hardscrabble route to the abandoned Bearpen Mt. Ski Area, a moderate steady climb, then level to a final short steep grade to the summit. This route is easy for snowshoers and excellent for skiers of intermediate to expert skills.

▶Trailhead: Access to Ski Run Rd. is off NY 23 immediately N of the Schoharie Creek Bridge in Prattsville. Turn S on CR 2, up to a height of land past Harry Peckham Rd. at 1.9 mi. Unidentified Ski Run Rd. is on the R at 2.1 mi at a fine vista toward Bearpen Mt. Park at the beginning of Ski Run Rd. In winter, since Ski Run Rd. is not plowed, care must be taken in locating it.◀

The route is unmarked but easy to follow. Gradual grades of a tree-lined lane take you generally W, passing old stone walls. Avoid side trails. At 0.5 mi is a sign, Bearpen Mt. State Forest.

The road curves L at 1 mi and again at 2.1 mi, steepening along the way. It passes a road, R, at 2.3 mi, and at 2.4 mi reaches a clearing. *Turn L here.* (Avoid the level R fork across the clearing, which leads to the Roxbury Ski Area; a bushwhack N leads to the viewless summit of 3440 ft Roundtop Mt. in about 0.5 mi.)

After a few more pitches up, the old road levels off and has a few large wet areas. (Watch carefully for the unmarked route as it eventually swings slightly L; it may circumvent an old embankment.) At 4.2 mi, it passes a pond on the R and drops down a small grade to the site of the former ski lodge.

Turn R here and bushwhack up an obscured path, passing an old lane and climbing steeply to the summit at 4.5 mi; this route passes a side path R to a good viewing spot W on a ledge with a sharp drop. Continue to the open area facing N, with excellent views. Roundtop Mt. is NW and the ridge that Ski Run Rd. ascends is directly across the valley. Hunter Mt., Windham High Peak, and Kaaterskill High Peak stand out on the horizon to the NE. Pratt Rock is barely discernible in Prattsville.

A summit path goes to a second clearing and good N view; an old truck is in the woods beyond. A woods road descends from this end of the summit and leads back to the ascent route—the woods road can be taken to this summit area first. In either direction, avoid old routes that descend the mountain. Look for the slight rise to the pond, L, on the return.

Another approach is from the high point of Halcott Mountain Rd.—the col between Vly Mt. and Bearpen. It presents an opportunity to climb both Bearpen and Vly mts. Halcott Mountain Rd. can be accessed from the N or S. (See Vly Mt., below.) To Bearpen, follow the dirt road past the front of a small hunters' cabin on alternating steep and moderate grades. (The dirt road is a public right-of-way to state land, which starts just past this cabin.) At a fork bear L and at a hairpin curve L continue up almost to where the road levels. A snowmobile trail is marked to the R; follow a ways to a possible herd path L up the slope. The herd path eventually connects to an old road leading R to the summit. There is a view before reaching the summit. Look for an old truck in the woods, R, just before the summit.

🐾 Distances: To clearing, 2.4 mi; to pond, 4.2 mi; to summit, 4.5 mi (7.2 km). Ascent from Ski Run Rd., 1600 ft. Ascent from col on Halcott Mountain Rd., 790 ft; total ascent from end of pavement on Halcott Mountain Rd. (N approach), 1940 ft. Summit elevation, 3600 ft (1097 m).

82 Vly Mt. (*bushwhack*)

Trails Illustrated Map 755: L12 / Map 145, Vly Mt.: I4

The ascent of Vly Mt. is best made from Halcott Mountain Rd. (See directions below.)

The word vly (vlei) is a Dutch term for marsh or swamp. Vly Valley is S of the peak and Vly Creek originates high on the shoulder of Vly Mt., but there are no marshes in the immediate area.

▶Trailhead: From NY 23 in Prattsville—just N of the Schoharie Creek Bridge, proceed S on CR 2 for 2.7 mi, passing Ski Run Rd. parking clearing, down a steep hill to a T-jct. Turn L on CR 2 for 2 mi to a jct.; turn R on CR 3 (Halcott Mountain

Rd.) and immediately bear L. (Jaeger Rd. is passed at 0.2 mi.) Park off the road across from the last house or up at a clearing (not a DEC parking area); avoid blocking the way.

From NY 42 in Shandaken—travel 7.4 mi to West Kill; turn L up South Beech Ridge Rd., pass Beech Ridge Rd. on the R (this road returns to NY 42) and continue on North Beech Ridge Rd. until it reaches the T intersection at the Schoharie Creek near Mosquito Point Bridge. Turn L (W) along the creek; fork L onto CR 2 to the jct. with CR 3 (Halcott Mountain Rd), bear L (twice), passing Jaeger Rd. at 0.2 mi to road end at 0.5 mi. See parking advice above.

From NY 28 in Fleischmanns—take Delaware CR 37 (Lake St.) from Main St. at the fire station; this road becomes Greene CR 3. Follow CR 3, Halcott Mountain Rd., which is paved to a fork; turn R on a dirt road for a mile. There is a small parking area on the left; a red highway sign states "no parking; snowplow turnaround." Park here if snow is not an issue, but leave room for vehicles to continue up the unmaintained, but public, road to the col (a hunter cabin here). It is legal to park alongside the road on the shoulder. There is a homemade sign before the last house, stating private property, but it is legal to drive the Halcott Mountain Rd. to the N side, where it is again marked CR 3. (If snowing or just after a storm, parking may be a problem.) A high-clearance vehicle is essential. ◀

Hiking from the N begins at the end of pavement (0.0 mi). Hardscrabble Halcott Mountain Rd., bounded by private lands on each side, ascends steeply for 1.3 mi to a col, where there is a hunting camp. Just N of the camp, on the opposite side of the road, is an indistinct herd path that follows the boundary of the new Bearpen Mt. State Forest to the wooded Vly summit. Descending in winter, a view to Bearpen is seen.

From Fleischmanns, hike up the woods road to the hunting camp. Across is the herd path to Vly; see detailed description (in trail 81) to access the Bearpen herd path. The dirt road is a public right-of-way to state land, which starts just past the cabin.

🀅 Summit elevation, 3529 ft (1076 m).

83 Pratt Rock Park

Trails Illustrated Map 755: M12

The short climb around Pratt Rock, created by Zadock Pratt to memorialize his life, includes a climb above the cliff for excellent views. This park provides a fascinating glimpse into another era. One soon learns why Pratt's employees revered him and changed the name of their little settlement, Schoharieskill, to Prattsville. It is particularly remarkable because Pratt was a tanner baron—a breed of businessmen not often regarded with fondness. Prattsville was called "the Gem of the Catskills," because it was a "planned community" in the early 1800s. The main road was rerouted from the riverfront to avoid pollution, hundreds of trees were planted, and the settlement burgeoned into the largest tannery in the world with many hotels, schools, churches, textile factories, gristmills, stores, sidewalks, and homes.

In 1825, Pratt's tannery worked 60,000 hides, burned 1500 cords of wood, and extracted tannin for tanning from 6000 cords of hemlock bark. In time, he became a U.S. Congressman, founded the National Bureau of Statistics, pushed for the completion of the Washington Monument, and introduced the Postage Act that reduced rates from a quarter to a nickel. After the great hemlock forests were gone, the Pratt Tannery closed in 1846 and farming became the chief industry.

The rerouting of the main street may have saved life and property in 2011, because Prattsville was among the villages hardest hit by Tropical Storm Irene. Located just downstream from the confluence of the Schoharie Creek and the Batavia Kill, many homes and businesses were destroyed.

▶Trailhead: Pratt Rock, listed in the State Register of Historic Places, is on the E side of Prattsville on NY 23, 0.4 mi W of the jct. of NY 23 and NY 23A.◀

From the parking area, steps lead up to a covered exhibit area, where interesting information and photos are located. Beyond, a path parallels the highway, passing picnic tables and a monument commemorating one of Pratt's favorite horses. Pratt owned over 1000 horses during his life and he also had five wives. A small shelter cut into a boulder was originally intended to be Pratt's grave.

A branch path ascends the hill toward Pratt Rock, which is reached after 5 to 10 minutes of climbing. Pratt Rock is a high cliff into which is sculptured whitewashed figures and writings that symbolize Zadock Pratt's life: an arm representing the working person, whom Pratt held in great regard; a hemlock, necessary for tanning; the family motto and shield; a horse; Pratt's face; and his son, who died in the Civil War.

Do not go farther along this trail; a better path to the cliff top was created that avoids very steep ascents and barbed wire. Retrace to a side path that climbs R under the horse symbol to ascend to the top of the cliff face. This lookout offers a splendid view down the Schoharie valley toward Deep Notch (CR 42) and Halcott Mt.

🐾 Distances: Round-trip approximately 1 mi (1.6 km) if all sections are walked. Vertical ascent is about 200 ft. Elevation, 1500 ft (457 m).

84 John Burroughs Memorial State Historic Site and Woodchuck Lodge

Trails Illustrated Map 755: M9

▶Access location: From Roxbury, drive 0.7 mi N on NY 30 to Hardscrabble Rd. From the N, the turn is just before the Hubbells Corner sign (on the outskirts of Roxbury). Turn W for 0.9 mi to Burroughs Memorial Rd. Turn L and drive 1.1 mi to Woodchuck Lodge and 1.3 mi to the John Burroughs Memorial State

John Burroughs Forest sign (now repaired). Alan Via

Historic Site. ◀

No one represents the essence of nature in the Catskills as much as John Burroughs. The John Burroughs Memorial State Historic Site is just 0.2 mi up Burroughs Memorial Rd. from his Woodchuck Lodge, and the tranquility of another age permeates the very air here. A pictorial display commemorates his youth, long marriage, many friendships with "movers and shakers" of his era, and writings about the everyday miracles of the natural world. Walk back on the path to Boyhood Rock, where he is buried; look out to the mountains from these slopes high above Roxbury.

His restored Woodchuck Lodge is open for tours the first weekend of each month, May through October from 11 AM to 3 PM. Thomas Edison, Henry Ford, and other friends visited Burroughs at Woodchuck Lodge when he spent summers there from 1910 to 1920, where he continued to write. He expressed increasing concern about the modern world: "One cannot but reflect what a sucked orange the earth will be…our civilization is terribly expensive to all its natural resources. One hundred years of modern life exhausts its stores more than a millennium of the life of antiquity."

An early member of the conservation movement with John Muir, with whom he explored the coast of Alaska in the famed Harriman Expedition, Burroughs's hiking companions also included President Theodore Roosevelt, Andrew Carnegie, Walt Whitman, Thomas Edison, and Henry Ford. Burroughs believed that regular retreat to the natural world is essential for spiritual renewal and physical health: "The most precious things of life are near at hand, without money and without price. Each of you has the whole wealth of the universe at your very door," said Burroughs. "We can use our scientific knowledge to poison the air, corrupt the waters, blacken the face of the country, and harass our souls with loud and discordant noises, or we can mitigate and abolish all these things." Does this sound like a contemporary environmentalist? This was Burroughs in 1913.

Walk up behind Woodchuck Lodge and find an old pathway, L. At an old shed, a marker facing the opposite direction says "8." Continue in either direction around an indistinct path behind Woodchuck Lodge.

The United States Geological Survey officially recognizes as the Burroughs Range the imposing three-peak mountain range with the Catskills' highest peak, 4180 ft Slide Mt.

Dry Brook Ridge Trail. Joanne Hihn

Arkville to Seager Section

This region is a popular destination, with many resorts, fine restaurants, winter sports, and a train excursion. The Catskill Center for Conservation and Development is in Arkville, and New York State's Belleayre ski complex, now a year-round attraction, is in Highmount. The trailheads in this region are not easily found unless one has a guidebook, since they are often at the end of long hollows, well beyond heavily traveled roads. Nevertheless, for those who seek them out, there are very nice hikes throughout this section.

❉ Trails in winter: The trails in this section are all good winter snowshoe trips. If one is hiking the Rider Hollow–Balsam Mt.–Mine Hollow loop, steep sections N of Balsam Mt. require care; crampons are recommended. An old woods road (a section of the Dry Brook Ridge Trail from Mill Brook Rd. to the Balsam Lake Mt. jct.) is a fine route for skiing. The trails are excellent for snowshoeing, with no precipitous cliffs to negotiate.

Dry Brook Ridge and the Huckleberry Brook Trail are best when leaves are off, because open viewing is minimal.

Below is a list of suggested hikes in this region.

SHORT HIKES
Rider Hollow: 2.4 mi (3.8 km) round-trip. Walk through a scenic glen with rippling waters and beautiful trees. Turn back when the route becomes steep beyond the last stream crossing. (At 0.2 mi, the trail is rerouted above the brook after Tropical Storm Irene.)

Kelly Hollow: 1.7 mi (2.7 km) short loop; 3.6 mi (5.8 km) long loop; crossover, 0.2 mi (0.3 km). Hike past waterfalls and conifer forests to a pretty pond and idyllic lean-to setting. Include the crossover trail on your ascent and again on the descent to enjoy all the trails and to see the rushing brooks up close.

MODERATE HIKES
Balsam Mt. Loop: 5.2 mi (8.3 km) loop. Follow the Rider Hollow or Mine Hollow Trail to the Pine Hill–West Branch Trail. A view atop Balsam Mt. is largely treed-in now and is best in winter; a view to Belleayre Mt. on the N side is good.

Dry Brook Ridge viewpoints: 6.6 mi (10.6 km) round-trip. Huckleberry Loop Trail (trail 92) from Hill Rd. in Margaretville to the Dry Brook Ridge Trail; continue S from jct. to excellent views in 1 mi from 3200 ft across a broad valley and to Pepacton Reservoir.

Pakatakan Mt.: 4.2 mi (6.7 km) through trip. Ascend the German Hollow Trail and descend Pakatakan Mt. to Margaretville on the Dry Brook Ridge Trail (or in

Arkville to Seager

178 *Catskill Trails*

reverse). Beautiful scenery in spite of wooded high points. Spot car or road-walk 2.1 mi.

HARDER HIKES
Dry Brook Ridge Trail: 9.4 mi (15 km) through trip from Margaretville to Mill Brook Rd. (Spot cars.)

Huckleberry Loop and Dry Brook Ridge Trail circuit: 12.9 mi (20.6 km). Trails wind up and down the Dry Brook and Huckleberry ridges for a long ramble. Beautiful spruce forest begins 0.5 mi up Huckleberry Loop Trail W from Ploutz Rd.; a stately red pine forest from Hill Rd. is especially notable. No views on the Huckleberry Ridge section of the circuit. Pick a cool day and bring plenty of water.

	Trail Described	Total Miles (one way)	Page
85	Rider Hollow Trail	1.8 (2.9 km)	180
86	Mine Hollow Trail	1.0 (1.6 km)	181
87	Seager Trail	3.0 (4.8 km)	181
88	Doubletop Mt.	trailless	183
89	Graham Mt.	trailless	183
90	Dry Brook Ridge Trail	13.7 (21.9 km)	183
91	German Hollow Trail	1.7 (2.7 km)	186
92	Huckleberry Loop Trail	12.9 (20.6 km)	187
93	Balsam Lake Mt. Trail	1.6 (2.6 km)	188
94	Kelly Hollow Ski Trail	3.5 (5.6 km)	190

Route Guide for Arkville to Seager (see map p. 178)
This guide begins at Arkville. It follows the Dry Brook Rd. to its end in Seager. Dry Brook Rd. is CR 49.

Mileage N to S	Description	Mileage S to N
0.0	Arkville. Jct. of NY 28 and Dry Brook Rd. Immediately W of Dry Brook bridge on NY 28, follow Dry Brook Rd. (CR 49).	9.5
0.4	Jct. Chris Long Rd. on S side	9.1
3.5	Cemetery	6.0
4.3	Delaware/Ulster Co. line	5.2
4.7	Jct. after Mapledale Bridge, CR 49A on E side (turn L 0.5 mi to Rider Hollow Rd., R).	4.8
6.1	Jct. Stewarts Turn; Mill Brook Rd. on W side of jct.; Dry Brook Rd. continues straight.	3.4
8.9	Jct. Prior Rd. on E side of road	0.6
9.5	Parking area. End of road.	0.0

85 Rider Hollow Trail

Trails Illustrated Map 755: I11   /   Map 142, Central Catskills: H6, trail OM

This is the W side of what the New York–New Jersey Trail Conference maps call the Oliverea-Mapledale Trail. (The McKinley Hollow Trail [trail 75] is the E side.)

The first mile and a quarter of the trail is a very nice short trek. The trail connects to the Pine Hill–West Branch Trail (trail 72), and, combined with the Mine Hollow Trail (trail 86), makes a fine loop hike over Balsam Mt.

▶Trailhead: Access to the Rider Hollow Trail is from Mapledale on Dry Brook Rd., CR 49. (See Route Guide p. 179.) The L turn, immediately after a church and bridge, is unmarked CR 49A. In 0.5 mi, turn R on Rider Hollow Rd. You may notice red trail markers as you drive to the trailhead. It becomes a dirt road at 2.2 mi and narrows to a large DEC parking area at the end of the road at 2.6 mi.◀

A gate and trail register are at the far end of the parking area. The level trail leaves the gate (0.0 mi) and follows red trail markers along the S side of Rider Hollow Brook; an information board shows designated campsites, R. In 120 yd, the trail crosses the brook on a new bridge. At 0.2 mi, a new route bypasses serious trail damage caused by Tropical Storm Irene; it ascends well above the brook. A fork R then descends to a bridge over Rider Hollow Brook at 0.3 mi. (The fork L climbs to access the Mine Hollow Trail [trail 86] past all storm washouts.)

The red-marked Rider Hollow Trail crosses to the S side of the stream on the bridge and turns L. A designated campsite is off-trail at 0.4 mi. The Rider Hollow Lean-to with privy is at 0.5 mi.

At 0.6 mi, the trail recrosses the stream on rocks (easy in summer, but can be difficult at high water). It follows a wide woods road up a gradual grade until it is high above the water, out of sight of the stream except when leaves are off. Crossing a mossy steep drainage, the route descends again and crosses on rocks (more easily here) at 1 mi.

Where a tributary joins the stream, the trail crosses again at 1.1 mi and starts to climb next to the rocky stream rushing below. After a final crossing at 1.2 mi, the trail moves up the slope away from streams and its character changes from an idyllic glen walk to a tough climb. Long pants are a good idea to protect oneself from nettles.

The route now gains a total of 750 ft elevation to the jct. with the Pine Hill–West Branch Trail (trail 72). A notable old-growth hemlock is passed, a large flat boulder offers a resting spot, and the slope finally eases at 1.7 mi. It then pitches up and reaches a side trail, R, to a spring at the base of the rock massif. The four-way jct. with the Pine Hill–West Branch Trail is at 1.8 mi.

(The McKinley Hollow Trail [trail 75] continues straight with red trail markers, descending steeply 1.2 mi to the McKinley Hollow Lean-to and 1.9 mi to the trailhead in McKinley Hollow. On the blue-marked Pine Hill–West Branch

Trail, Balsam Mt. is L 0.8 mi and Eagle Mt. is R 2.15 mi.)

🐾 Distances: To Mine Hollow jct., 0.3 mi; to Rider Hollow Lean-to, 0.5 mi; to final stream crossing, 1.2 mi; to spur to spring, 1.7 mi; to Pine Hill–West Branch Trail jct., 1.8 mi (2.9 km). Ridge elevation, 3050 ft; ascent, 1060 ft.

86 Mine Hollow Trail

Trails Illustrated Map 755: I11 / Map 142, Central Catskills: H6, trail MN

Mine Hollow Trail is a connector trail from the Rider Hollow Trail to the Pine Hill–West Branch Trail (trail 72). It makes possible an excellent loop with the Rider Hollow Trail (see above) over Balsam Mt. for day-hikers. The trail also gives backpackers from Rider Hollow a way to bypass Balsam Mt. if heading N.

▶Trailhead: Access is from a jct. at the 0.3 mi point of the Rider Hollow Trail (trail 85), 0.2 mi W of Rider Hollow Lean-to.◀

Washouts from Tropical Storm Irene required relocation of the Rider Hollow Trail (trail 85) and the lower portion of this trail. The new route climbs above Rider Hollow Brook at 0.2 mi from the trailhead and reaches a fork at 0.3 mi. Turn L on the new Mine Hollow Trail (0.0) and continue for another 0.2 mi to the original Mine Hollow Trail.

The route bears L along Mine Hollow Brook. Gradual and then steepening grades take the trail higher and higher above the brook. The route is well designed, though strenuous with a backpack. It slabs higher, pulling away from the brook at 0.5 mi and swinging N through a magnificent hemlock grove. A small boulder at 0.65 mi invites a rest; a brief respite in the grade provides welcome relief.

The grade becomes moderate again at 0.9 mi. The trail bears R around an interesting rock outcrop at 0.95 mi, pitching up to the level jct. with the Pine Hill–West Branch Trail (trail 72) at 1 mi. (Balsam Mt. is S [R] 1.3 mi, and Belleayre Mt. is N [L], 0.9 mi.)

🐾 Distances: Rerouted trail joins original trail, 0.2 mi; to Pine Hill–West Branch Trail jct., 1 mi (1.6 km). Ascent from Rider Hollow jct., 800 ft.

87 Seager Trail

Trails Illustrated Map 755: H10 / Map 142, Central Catskills: H7, trail SE

The Seager Trail follows Dry Brook and its tributary, Shandaken Brook, up to a jct. with the Pine Hill–West Branch (trail 72), between Eagle and Big Indian mts. It provides several hiking options in conjunction with other trails, and is a good winter ascent route. However, it entails several brook crossings without bridges.

▶Trailhead: Access to the trailhead is at the end of the Dry Brook Rd. from Arkville. (See Route Guide p. 179.) Park at the DEC parking area at the road's end in Seager.◀

The trail leaves the parking area and trail register (0.0 mi), and heads SE on private land along a woods road with yellow trail markers. The grassy lane parallels the W side of Dry Brook, making a wide bend R at 0.1 mi in a shady hemlock woods. The trail sidles along the bank for a short distance at 0.25 mi, where there is a washout, and crosses a rocky tributary from Drury Hollow. Take care descending to the crossing. The trail soon reaches a wide, flat section and rejoins the old woods road as it goes through the attractive woods by the brook.

At 0.7 mi the trail leaves the road at a ford and climbs R up a small mound to another woods road. The trail crosses Flatiron Brook as it flows into Dry Brook at 0.9 mi and a very attractive waterfall and pool are seen upstream on Dry Brook. Then the route curves next to it.

The trail levels and reaches a jct. with DEC distance signs at 1 mi. Here, a private road crosses Dry Brook on a wooden bridge. Beautiful waterfalls cascade above and under the bridge. This is the place where many hikers begin the bushwhack, R, up Doubletop Mt. The hiking trail stays on the W side of Dry Brook and soon passes an interesting section of flat rock.

Tropical Storm Irene wreaked havoc here, as on many other trails near streams. Currently, yellow trail markers would have you cross the brook and recross almost immediately before coming to a third crossing at 1.2 mi. (This is doable in dry weather but difficult during high-water.) The brook and the banks are full of cobblestones and a road crosses and recrosses the brook also. There is a DEC sign on the far bank. Do not follow the woods road by the sign, but rather head E up the slope to a second woods road that follows above the N bank of Shandaken Brook. (Be careful not to pass this spot on the return trip.)

The grade is gradual and provides comfortable hiking. At 1.5 mi, the route forks L above the brook, and at 1.6 mi it drops down and crosses to the S side of Shandaken Brook. The woods road climbs a curving grade to 1.65 mi, where it forks R on cobble. The route becomes grassy again and enters state land at 2 mi, where it passes through an open birch, beech, and maple forest.

The trail returns to Shandaken Brook at 2 mi and crosses it. Shandaken Lean-to is on the opposite bank in an open wooded flat area above the water. A pipe with spring water comes out of the far side of the brook bank.

The trail leaves at the R rear of the lean-to and starts a diagonal ascent, edging away from the water. Soon it is a steady, moderate upgrade, working its way up the ridge to the E. The ascent eases at 2.4 mi, actually drops a little, and then becomes steep again. At 2.7 mi, the trail finally levels and becomes an enjoyable rolling path with a few short pitches to the Pine Hill–West Branch Trail (trail 72) jct. at 3 mi. (Big Indian Mt. herd path is 1.2 mi. S on the blue-marked trail; Eagle Mt. is 1.1 mi N. One might be able to locate a faint old trail that drops down to Burnham Rd. to the E.)

🐾 Distances: To Flatiron Brook, 0.9 mi; to Shandaken Lean-to, 2 mi; to Pine Hill–West Branch Trail jct., 3 mi (4.8 km). Jct. elevation, 3110 ft; ascent from trailhead, 1110 ft.

88 Doubletop Mt. *(bushwhack)*

Trails Illustrated Map 755: G10 / Map 142, Central Catskills: H7

Doubletop Mt., once called Roundtop Mt., is a bushwhack peak. For many years, the usual way up Doubletop was from the Frost Valley YMCA. Use of this property by the general hiking public has not been permitted since 1993.

A good way up the mountain is from the Pine Hill–West Branch Trail (trail 72; see Big Indian–Pine Hill to Denning Section). One can walk to the top of the first ridge, at 0.7 mi from CR 47, and then follow the Forest Preserve boundary line NW to Pigeon Brook. A tributary of Pigeon Brook, just upstream from the state boundary line, runs NW up to the ridgeline of Doubletop. Here an informal trail can be followed to the N end of the ridge. There is one good lookout near the flat summit, but the canister is past it in the conifers. You may have to search a bit to find it.

A second approach is from the Seager Trail (trail 87). The easiest route is to hike S up the ridge from the Seager Trail, leaving the marked trail where a bridge spans waterfalls. If you are also climbing Big Indian Mt., take the Seager Trail up to the Pine Hill–West Branch Trail, turning S for 1.2 mi to the Big Indian Mt. herd path (its true summit is 0.25 mi E off-trail); continue to the sharp turn where the original Seager Trail intersection was located. (If you go too far S, a steep descent down the Pine Hill–West Branch Trail soon begins.) From this turn, bushwhack down the ridge directly W into the col leading to Doubletop Mt. A third and popular approach to Doubletop Mt. is combining it with a climb of Graham Mt. Summit elevation of Doubletop is 3860 ft (1176 m).

89 Graham Mt. *(unmaintained trail)*

Trails Illustrated Map 755: G10 / Map 142, Central Catskills: H7

The informal route to Graham Mt. begins at a jct. at a height of land at the 11.7 mi point of the Dry Brook Ridge Trail (trail 90), 2.1 mi S of Mill Brook Rd. or 2 mi N of the S trailhead of the Dry Brook Ridge Trail from Balsam Lake Mt. parking area. It is entirely on private land; hikers must gain permission before hiking it. The usual route is to travel 0.4 mi E on an informal trail, the old Trappen Rd., which descends to a fork, and then bear R on a good herd path for the mountain.

90 Dry Brook Ridge Trail

Trails Illustrated Map 755: J8 / Map 142, Central Catskills: F5, trail DB

The Dry Brook Ridge Trail starts near Margaretville and climbs Pakatakan Mt., which has no discernible or open summit. The trail proceeds generally S along Dry Brook Ridge to the Beaverkill Valley. A good backpack trail, it also provides side trips to Graham and Balsam Lake mts. The name Dry Brook is a corruption of *drei brucke*, which is "three bridges" in German. At one time, three covered bridges spanned Dry Brook, which parallels the ridge to the E.

▶Trailhead: Access to the trailhead is from Margaretville. From the bridge over the E Branch of the Delaware River in Margaretville, turn W on NY 28/30 for about 0.3 mi to Fair St. Turn L uphill for 0.1 mi and L again on South Side Spur for 0.2 mi to a pull-off past the DEC sign marking the trailhead.◀

From the trailhead (0.0 mi), follow blue trail markers steeply up a hillside to join an old logging road at an enormous, scenic rock overhang and small cave L. The woods road was widened by the Civilian Conservation Corps in the 1930s to make a ski trail. Soon entering state land, the trail gains elevation steadily on moderate grades, passing beautiful mossy ledges and overhangs. At 0.6, the grade levels as the route heads S, passing a camping area well off-trail R. A broad swing E begins at 1 mi, and the trail passes a small spring at the base of a bank at 1.1 mi. The ascent becomes very steep to 1.25 mi and begins a series of climbs mixed with level "breathers."

The route continues to ascend to 1.7 mi, where the trail levels at the "summit" of Pakatakan Mt. (2500 ft), more of a change in grade reaching a ridgetop than a peak. Occasional short rises continue to 2.4 mi, where a very steep ascent begins to higher terrain on Dry Brook Ridge. New rock stairs facilitate this steep climb, which levels before the jct. of the German Hollow Trail (trail 91) at 2.6 mi. (Water is found 0.45 mi down this trail and another spring at 1 mi, after much elevation loss. A lean-to here was destroyed by a falling tree.)

At 2.8 mi, the trail swings L through ledges, not continuing straight ahead as it might appear. At 3.15 mi, a downgrade begins and does not reach a low point until 3.4 mi, after which the trail regains this loss of elevation very steeply to the Huckleberry Loop Trail jct. at 3.5 mi (see trail 92). (To avoid this elevation loss, after a steep pitch up at 3 mi and past ledges [walking N to S], when significantly higher terrain appears R, bushwhack for up to 0.1 mi to access the Huckleberry Loop Trail, turning L, where the route is easy to the jct. Likewise, going N on the Dry Brook Ridge Trail, at this jct. stay L on the Huckleberry Loop Trail for about 0.3 mi and then bushwhack R for 0.1 mi, turning L on the Dry Brook Ridge Trail.)

Beyond the Huckleberry Loop Trail jct., the trail begins to circle a small pond off-trail L that is often dry. The trail meanders around the ridge and begins to ascend at 4.4 mi, reaching the first of excellent lookouts at 3200 ft toward Pepacton Reservoir at 4.6 mi; large ledges just below the trail offer beautiful views.

Dry Brook Ridge Trail. ADK Archives

Pepacton Reservoir is W. Shortly beyond, the trail passes next to a sheer drop and then reaches another large open area. After moving away from the edge, the trail again runs next to beautiful lookouts to 5.2 mi, where it swings away from the edge and climbs to its high point above 3400 ft, before reaching the next jct. at 6.1 mi at a marsh; here the other end of the Huckleberry Loop Trail enters (see trail 92).

The trail very gradually loses elevation to a spot at 6.8 mi that affords partial views SW, and climbs to the top of a cliff-like ledge. The climb continues briefly and then the route traverses mostly level terrain before ascending to another small summit at 7.1 mi. At 7.2 mi, moderate pitches downward continue to 7.5 mi, where varying gradual grades continue the descent to 7.8 mi. The trail passes interesting ledges and begins a steady descent to an area with private property marks L of the trail at 8.1 mi. Continue on the blue-marked trail (in winter this area can be confusing). Descent continues on easier grades to the Dry Brook Ridge Lean-to at 8.25 mi; the trail loses about 750 ft of elevation in the last mi. There is a spring here, and a tributary of Mill Brook.

From the lean-to, the trail continues on the level to 8.4 mi, then gains 350 ft of elevation to a high point at 8.8 mi. The forest is very attractive as the small summit draws near, with wood sorrel and club moss and attractive ledge walls. The trail pitches down steeply to 8.9 mi, then begins its gradual descent to Mill Brook Rd. through fields of ferns, passing scenic ledges adorned with peeling paint fungus at 9.1 mi. At 9.45 mi, new steps are built through mossy ledges. The trail enters the rear of a large parking area on the N side of Mill Brook Rd. at 9.6 mi.

(Dry Brook Rd. is 2.2 mi NE down Mill Brook Rd.; Arkville is 6.1 mi N on Dry Brook Rd. To the R, 0.9 mi on Mill Brook Rd., is the trailhead that leads 0.25 mi N to the Mill Brook Lean-to.)

The blue-marked Dry Brook Ridge Trail continues across Mill Brook Rd., about 50 ft SW. The trail turns L off the road and ascends a moderate grade S along an old woods road. (This section provides a quick route into Balsam Lake Mt. and Graham Mt., and makes an outstanding ski-shoe route in winter. Because of heavy use by hunters, it is wise to avoid this trail in deer season. Camping is not permitted here.)

The upgrade passes an interesting boulder, swings R, and ascends gently to a trail register at 9.9 mi, where the road levels for quite a distance. Swinging L, it climbs moderately and becomes more gradual after swinging R. A spring, not indicated by a sign, may be visible down in the woods, R, at 10.7 mi. Alternating short climbs and long level sections pass an old road, L, which is not the herd path to Graham Mt. After more climbing, the trail levels at a height of land at 3250 ft and the trail swings slightly R at 11.7 mi; here is the herd path to Graham Mt., doubling back above the main trail.

The trail continues on nearly level terrain to the Balsam Lake Mt. Trail jct. (trail 93) at 11.8 mi. (This trail leads 0.75 mi to the summit of Balsam Lake Mt.; 1 mi to the Mill Brook Ridge Trail [trail 95]; and 1.2 mi down to the Balsam Lake Mt. Lean-to, before returning to the Dry Brook Ridge Trail.)

The blue-marked trail bears L from the jct. and descends in gradual and moderate grades to a view E at 12.5 mi. It reaches a jct. at the other end of the Balsam Lake Mt. Trail at 12.8 mi. (It is 0.4 mi and a 500 ft ascent to the lean-to.) The trail continues to lose elevation slowly, crossing drainages at 13.2 mi. It leaves the woods at 13.4 mi and skirts an open meadow before reaching a trail register at 13.6 mi. The DEC parking area is at 13.7 mi at the end of Beaver Kill Rd.

Distances: To Pakatakan Mt. summit, 1.7 mi; to German Hollow Trail jct., 2.6 mi; to Huckleberry Loop Trail jct., 3.5 mi; to first lookout, 4.6 mi; to second Huckleberry Loop Trail jct., 6.1 mi; to Dry Brook Ridge Lean-to, 8.25 mi; to Mill Brook Rd., 9.6 mi; to spring, 10.7 mi; to Graham Mt. herd path, 11.7 mi; to first Balsam Lake Mt. Trail jct., 11.8 mi; to second Balsam Lake Mt. Trail jct., 12.8 mi; to Beaver Kill Rd. parking area trailhead, 13.7 mi (21.9 km).

91 German Hollow Trail

Trails Illustrated Map 755: I9 / Map 142, Central Catskills: G5, trail GH

The German Hollow Trail is an access route to the Dry Brook Ridge Trail (trail 90) from the N.

▶Trailhead: Trail access is off Dry Brook Rd. (See Route Guide, p. 179.) Turn S onto unmarked Chris Long Rd. 0.4 mi along Dry Brook Rd. from NY 28. The dirt road climbs a grade 0.3 mi to a private turnabout and DEC signpost. Parking is tight. Please do not block private driveways.◀

From the DEC signpost (0.0 mi), the yellow-marked trail crosses a small brook and begins to ascend a gradual grade on a woods road to a trail register. From here to state land, about 150 yd, is a target-practice area, so note that the yellow-marked DEC trail forks R. The route enters attractive stands of hemlock forest to 0.4 mi. Very steep pitches upward culminate at a privy on the R when the grade finally levels at 0.6 mi.

The trail leaves the woods road and bears L to where the former lean-to stood at 0.7 mi. (Avoid a trail that heads E from the site, which leads 0.15 mi to water at Rensselaer Creek.) Follow yellow markers and continue on level terrain to 0.8 mi. The trail switchbacks L and climbs a moderate-steep grade with a brief respite. Moderate and gradual grades alternate up the ridge.

At 1 mi, the route swings back R and passes a spring at 1.2 mi. A very large rock cairn marks the spot. A metal pipe has a good flow of water. In the logging days of the past, considerable work was done to develop this old spring.

One last steep grade leads to a height of land at 1.4 mi. A gradual slope loses a little elevation as the route swings NW and soon levels. This is an attractive section. At 1.5 mi, the route swings W again and steadily climbs until leveling just before reaching the Dry Brook Ridge Trail (trail 90) at 1.7 mi after a total climb of 1280 ft. (It is 2.6 mi NW to the trailhead of the Dry Brook Ridge Trail in Margaretville, and 5.65 mi SE to the Dry Brook Ridge Lean-to.)

👣 Distances: To privy, 0.6 mi; to spring, 1.2 mi; to Dry Brook Ridge Trail jct., 1.7 mi (2.7 km).

92 Huckleberry Loop Trail

Trails Illustrated Map 755: I8 / Map 142, Central Catskills: F6, trail HL

The Huckleberry Loop Trail is 10.3 mi long and, when combined with 2.6 mi of the Dry Brook Ridge Trail (trail 90), makes a loop of 12.9 mi through the Dry Brook Ridge Wild Forest. (It is described as a loop because both ends of the Huckleberry Loop Trail are on top of Dry Brook Ridge.) Frequent elevation changes make the trek strenuous, so carry plenty of water and food and expect a full day.

▶ Trailhead: From the bridge over the E Branch of the Delaware River in Margaretville, turn W on NY 28/30 for 2.2 mi. Turn L off NY 28/30 onto an unmarked road that promptly reaches a T-intersection. Turn L again and drive 0.3 mi to Huckleberry Brook Rd. Turn R for another 0.3 mi. At a fork, bear L up Hill Rd. for 1.3 mi to a DEC parking area; or bear R 0.6 mi to a parking area up a rise, L, on Huckleberry Rd., just beyond a bridge over Huckleberry Brook. The final section of the Huckleberry Loop Trail descends 1000 ft to this bridge parking area.

A second parking area on Huckleberry Brook Rd. is 1.2 mi from the Hill Rd./Huckleberry Brook Rd. fork (0.6 mi beyond the first); the second parking area is L just before the Huckleberry Brook Storage Area vehicle bridge at a yellow barrier. Across the bridge and R past the building (signs may not reflect current mileages), the red-marked trail climbs 300 ft in 0.4 mi from Huckleberry Brook Rd. to Hill Rd. From the Hill Rd. parking area to the Dry Brook Ridge Trail is 2.3 mi and a climb of 1150 ft. ◀

Starting at the Hill Rd. parking area, the first 0.3 mi is a steady climb through a magnificent red pine forest. The ascent moderates through a variety of deciduous woods and evergreen stands until the trail turns R on an old woods road at 1.5 mi. Then it climbs steadily to 3100 ft, gaining the ridgetop at 1.9 mi. Now on nearly level terrain, the trail reaches a jct. with the blue-marked Dry Brook Ridge Trail (trail 90) at 2.3 mi.

The route now turns R on the Dry Brook Ridge Trail. It passes a small pond (sometimes dried up), meanders along the middle of the ridge, and at 3.2 mi (0.9 mi from the jct.) begins to ascend and swings R toward the edge. At 3.3 mi, there is a good view, and 130 yd farther, large ledges below the trail offer splendid views over the valley to the Pepacton Reservoir.

Soon the trail passes another excellent lookout next to a sheer drop and then reaches a large open area. The trail soon runs next to the drop, and passes two more open viewing areas at 3.8 and 4 mi. From here, the trail heads up toward the middle of the ridge, reaching a high point of 3460 ft and staying mostly at 3400 ft. Passing through a marshy area, the route leaves the Dry Brook Trail at 4.9 mi.

The red-marked Huckleberry Loop Trail turns R and very gradually descends before reaching a series of rocky ledges of varying grades. The trail is well marked, but can become obscure in places, so watch for markers.

After descending through open deciduous woods, the trail enters an attractive spruce and red pine forest at 6 mi and reaches the parking area on Ploutz Rd. at 6.3 mi. The red-marked trail continues across the road, turning L and descending to a small stream.

The trail follows an old woods road, regaining 250 vertical ft to Huckleberry Brook Ridge. An inviting cool, dense spruce forest at 6.8 mi (0.5 mi from the Ploutz Rd. parking area) offers shade for 0.3 mi, a great destination for a short hike. The trail enters deciduous woods and meanders W along the ridge, gaining and losing elevation between 2600 ft and 2800 ft, often through prickly berry bushes.

At nearly 9.3 mi, the trail enters a second spruce forest, and at 10.3 mi enters a large meadow. The trail climbs briefly, descends and slabs the hillside briefly, and enters a dark hemlock forest at 10.7 mi. Now heading N, the trail switchbacks down the steep 1000 ft descent to Huckleberry Brook, crosses the brook on a bridge at 11.8 mi, and turns R along the road.

Passing the road up to the first parking area, a vehicle bridge at 12.5 mi at the Huckleberry Brook Storage Area is marked by a red marker. Across the bridge and R past the building, the red-marked trail climbs to Hill Rd. The trail ascends moderately to Hill Rd., reaching the parking area at 12.9 mi (6.6 mi from the Ploutz Rd. parking area).

🐾 Distances: To woods road, 1.5 mi; to Dry Brook Trail jct., 2.3 mi; to lookout, 3.3 mi; to second Dry Brook Trail jct., 4.9 mi; to Ploutz Rd., 6.3 mi; to first spruce forest, 6.8 mi; to second spruce forest, 9.3 mi; to meadow, 10.3 mi; to Huckleberry Brook, 11.8 mi; to storage area, 12.5 mi; to Hill Rd., 12.9 mi (20.6 km).

93 Balsam Lake Mt. Trail

Trails Illustrated Map 755: G9 / Map 142, Central Catskills: G7, trail BL

The 1.6 mi Balsam Lake Mt. Trail, combined with the Dry Brook Ridge Trail (trail 90), is a fine loop hike from Beaver Kill Rd. Balsam Lake Mt. can be done in conjunction with Graham Mt. to make a full day's outing. A renovated fire tower affords spectacular views.

▶Trailhead: Trailhead access is from the Balsam Lake Mt. DEC parking area at the end of Beaver Kill Rd. (near Quaker Clearing; see Route Guide map, pp. 216–217.)

The Balsam Lake Trail is 0.9 mi N up the Dry Brook Ridge Trail, at that trail's 12.8 mi point from Margaretville. The trail is also accessed 2.2 mi S from the Dry Brook Ridge trailhead on Mill Brook Rd. (2.2 mi SW off Dry Brook Rd.). At the 11.8 mi point of the Dry Brook Trail from Margaretville, the Balsam Lake Mt. Trail goes W.◀

Detail in nature along the Balsam Lake Mountain Trail. Joanne Hihn

From the S trailhead (trail 90) at Quaker Clearing, turn L at 0.9 mi at the jct. of the Balsam Lake Mt. Trail and the Dry Brook Ridge Trail (0.0 mi). Follow red trail markers NW up moderately steep terrain. The new Balsam Lake Mt. Lean-to spur path jct. is at 0.4 mi; the lean-to is 0.1 mi L from the spur jct. A spring comes from the base of a rock ledge in 100 yd on the main trail. New trailwork ascends the ledge and a path R goes to the spring source.

The trail passes an old spur trail, R, to two former lean-tos and then the 3500 ft sign at 0.5 mi. The trail becomes nearly level and reaches the Mill Brook Ridge Trail jct. (trail 95) at 0.6 mi.

The climbing is easy through shady woods to the summit at 0.85 mi. In a large clearing surrounded by evergreen trees, there is a picnic table. The renovated fire tower affords spectacular views above the treetops. Graham and Doubletop mts. rise to the E. Summit elevation, 3720 ft. Ascent, 1193 ft. A privy is in the woods behind the tower.

The trail now heads E from the clearing, passing the fire observer's cabin. In summer, a summit tower interpreter is present and the cabin is open, full of interesting historical photos. Continuing E, at first on the level, the trail is surrounded by evergreens. This area is beautiful in winter. Alternating level sections and short pitches down lead to a fine view E at 1.25 mi, before the 3500-ft sign. From here, moderately steep grades alternate with more level sections as the old jeep road curves down the slope. The descent eases before a barrier gate and second jct. with the Dry Brook Ridge Trail (trail 90) at 1.6 mi. (The blue-marked Dry Brook Ridge Trail goes S 1.9 mi to Beaver Kill Rd. and 2.2 mi N to Mill Brook

Rd. The unmarked jct. for the old woods road to Graham Mt. is 0.1 mi toward Mill Brook Rd. from here.)

🏕 Distances: To spur path jct. for new Balsam Lake Mt. Lean-to, 0.4 mi; to spring, 0.5 mi; to Mill Brook Ridge Trail jct., 0.6 mi; to Balsam Lake Mt. summit, 0.85 mi; to Dry Brook Ridge Trail jct., 1.6 mi (2.6 km).

94 Kelly Hollow Ski Trail

Trails Illustrated Map 755: H8 / Map 142, Central Catskills: F6

The Kelly Hollow Ski Trail is in a very attractive hiking area. Its lean-to makes it a good short overnight backpack trip. The trail, which has been marked as a cross-country ski trail, is interestingly laid out. The Long Loop is 3.5 mi, the Short Loop is 1.7 mi, and the crossover trail is 0.2 mi; the hiker experiencing all sections of trail at Kelly Hollow by hiking the crossover twice will cover 4 mi.

▶Trailhead: Trail access is off Mill Brook Rd. (See Route Guide, p. 179.) From Arkville, travel S 6.1 mi on Dry Brook Rd. (CR 49), turn R up Mill Brook Rd. for 2.2 mi to the Dry Brook Ridge parking area at a height of land and continue about 5 mi more to Kelly Hollow (passing Grants Mill covered bridge). Kelly Hollow has two access/parking areas on Mill Brook Rd.; a second access is 0.2 mi W of the first and has several car camping sites. The E access road has a trail register (a privy may be rebuilt).

Kelly Hollow is also reached from Margaretville, following variously named roads on the S side of Pepacton Reservoir to Jim Alton Rd., L, which becomes Mill Brook Rd., for 5.5 mi.◀

From the E access: Leave the rear of the parking area through the beautiful conifer forest to the trailhead (0.0 mi) at a barrier located L on a hardscrabble road. The E route climbs gradually S past apple trees and old stone walls. There is a trail register at 0.25 mi.

The gradually ascending route passes a woods road jct. at 0.3 mi. On the R, the slope drops off into a deep ravine. The grassy lane reaches the crossover short loop option at 0.5 mi. (The crossover trail descends above a scenic brook with waterfalls and crosses a large wooden bridge. Halfway across, the footing can be wet. At 0.15 mi, a second cascading stream is crossed and the trail ascends steeply to the W Long Loop trail at 0.2 mi.)

Continuing straight ahead on the E Long Loop trail, a lovely spruce forest is L. At 0.8 mi, a deep foundation is R, off-trail. The trail crosses a bridge at 1.05 mi, skirts a bog, and enters an attractive pine forest.

The far point of the trek is at 1.2 mi as the trail crosses another bridge, switchbacks, and ascends a hillside. Terrain drops off to the R and the trail swings L into shady hemlock woods, passing a spring at 1.8 mi. The Kelly Hollow Lean-to at 2 mi is in a beautiful setting amidst large conifers, complete with picnic table, fireplace, and privy. Beaver Pond is nearby. This is 450 ft in elevation above

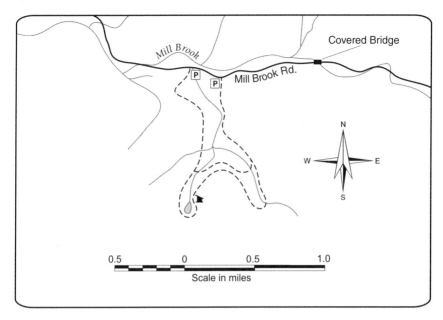

Kelly Hollow Ski Trail

the trailhead; Mill Brook Ridge rises above.

The trail continues L around Beaver Pond, crossing its inlet at 2.1 mi and then beginning the descent on the W trail. This route reaches the W jct. of the crossover trail (see above) at 2.5 mi and, continuing straight, descends steeply to a bridge at 2.6 mi. It again descends steeply, leveling at 3 mi and swinging NW past stone walls at 3.1 mi. It reaches a barrier and passes a small cemetery at 3.2 mi, worth exploring. There are several nice campsites beneath large evergreens along the W access road. Continue to Mill Brook Rd. at the brook crossing at 3.3 mi. The trail returns to the E access parking area at 3.5 mi through an attractive conifer forest.

🀣 Distances: To Short Loop jct. (E side), 0.5 mi; to bridge crossing at far point, 1.2 mi; to Kelly Hollow Lean-to, 2 mi; to Short Loop jct. (W side), 2.5 mi; to Mill Brook Rd., 3.3 mi; to E parking area, 3.5 mi (5.6 km). If hiking entire "figure 8" trail layout, 4 mi (6.4 km). 🍃

Coykendall Lodge at Alder Lake, the estate of Edward and Frederick Coykendall, who headed the Cornell Steamboat Company. Only some pillars survive today.
David White

Delaware Wild Forest Section

Most of the individual trails in the Delaware Wild Forest area of the western Catskills connect and are collectively known as the Delaware Ridge Trail. Extending from Balsam Lake Mt. to Trout Pond/Mud Pond, these trails are not heavily used, and thus may not be maintained as well as might be desired. However, they are well marked and provide the hiker with a wilderness experience not often found on other trails that have more hiking pressure. For the experienced backpacker, they provide a rugged and thoroughly interesting network of trails.

Delaware Ridge Trail Sections, E-W	*Miles*
Mill Brook Ridge Trail	5.9
Alder Lake Loop (N side)	0.7
Alder Lake to next trailhead	0.4
Alder Lake to Big Pond Trail	3.1
Connecting road section	0.15
Big Pond to Touchmenot Trail	1.1
Touchmenot Trail to Beech Hill Rd.	2.5
Connecting road section on Beech Hill Rd.	0.2
Middle Mt. Trail	2.3
Mary Smith Hill Trail	4.4
Pelnor Hollow (connecting section only)	1.3
Campbell Mt. Trail	6.3
Trout Pond Trail	5.1
TOTAL	33.45 (53.2 km)

This is a beautiful land and a wild part of the Catskills, whose road network wanders from county to county, the roads changing names and numbers at each border. Hikers should study their maps well, use the Route Guides provided in this book, and have a full tank of gas. Many of the best hikes are through trips requiring two vehicles. The trails often cross ridgelines from valley to valley; the trailheads are generally much farther apart by connecting roads than by trail.

That understood, there are many excellent trails where few other hikers will disturb your solitude. Extensive backpack trips are possible on connecting short trails. One has to work a little harder to reach many of these trailheads, but the rewards are commensurate with the efforts.

❈ Trails in winter: These trails are somewhat isolated and thus not as utilized in winter as they might be otherwise. The trail around Alder Lake is especially good for skiing. The western trails are also snowmobile trails or connect to them. This can provide a packed trail but can also diminish the wilderness experience.

Below is a list of suggested hikes in this region.

SHORT HIKES

Little Pond: 2.8 mi (4.5 km) round-trip, from trailhead at bathhouse to good viewing from open fields beyond an old foundation near a pond; turn back at view, or complete a 3.3 mi loop over Touchmenot Mt. (no view) back to campground.

Alder Lake: 1.5 mi (2.4 km). Clockwise, walk along the shoreline path past several designated campsites and loop past the Mill Brook Ridge Trail (trail 95), climbing gently uphill through forest away from the lake for the return trip. Trail begins at the remnants of the old Coykendall Lodge.

MODERATE HIKES

Little Spring Brook Trail and Pelnor Hollow Trail to Split Rock Lookout: 3.6 mi (5.8 km) round-trip. This hike passes a beaver meadow and traverses a beautiful red pine forest, uphill to Split Rock for views from a ledge that has split away from the cliff. The first 0.5 mi await repair following Tropical Storm Irene.

Trout Pond–Mud Pond Loop: 3.9 mi (6.2 km) loop. Visit nice ponds via old woods roads, climbing 450 ft over Cherry Ridge. Take a fishing pole or a camera.

HARDER HIKES

Mill Brook Ridge to Balsam Lake Mt. fire tower: 13.6 mi (21.8 km) round-trip. Hike halfway around Alder Lake and on significant ups and downs along Mill Brook Ridge to a renovated fire tower atop Balsam Lake Mt. (Or spot vehicle at Alder Lake and hike up Balsam Lake Mt. Trail [trail 93] from the end of Beaver Kill Rd. and across Mill Brook Ridge back to lake, 8 mi.)

	Trail Described	Total Miles (one way)		Page
95	Mill Brook Ridge Trail	5.9	(9.4 km)	196
96	Alder Lake Loop	1.6	(2.6 km)	198
97	Alder Lake to Big Pond (Touchmenot Trail)	3.1	(5 km)	199
98	Big Pond to Beech Hill Rd. (Touchmenot Trail)	3.6	(5.8 km)	201
99	Campground Trail from Little Pond Campground to Big Pond jct.	1.1	(1.8 km)	202
100	Little Pond Trail	1.65	(2.6 km)	203
101	Middle Mt. Trail	2.3	(3.7 km)	204
102	Mary Smith Hill Trail	4.5	(7.2 km)	204
103	Huggins Lake Trail	1.7	(2.7 km)	206
104	Pelnor Hollow Trail	4.45	(7.1 km)	206

105	Campbell Mt. Trail	6.3	(10.1 km)	208
106	Little Spring Brook Trail	0.7	(1.1 km)	210
107	Trout Pond Trail	5.1	(8.2 km)	211
108	Mud Pond Trail	3.9	(6.2 km)	213

Route Guide for Margaretville–NY 206 (see map pp. 216–217)

Mileage E to W	Description	Mileage W to E
0.0	Parking area and kiosk in Margaretville. Turn R out of parking area.	23.8
0.1	At traffic light at jct. of NY 28/30, turn R if driving W; turn R on NY 30 to parking area if driving E.	23.7
2.0	Turn L then immediate R off NY 28/30 on Old NY 30 if traveling W; turn L then R onto NY 28/30 if driving E.	21.8
5.7	Reach Jim Alton/Mill Brook Rd.	18.1
10.2	Reach Barkaboom Rd.	13.6
12.1	Jct. with NY 30 bridge across Pepacton Reservoir. NY 30 continues past the bridge on S side of reservoir.	11.7
14.4	Beech Hill Rd.	9.4
19.0	Holliday and Berry Brook Rd.	4.8
20.9	Miller Hollow Rd.	2.9
23.8	Jct. NY 30/206 (CR 7) turns S. (Downsville is 3.2 mi W on NY 30/206.)	0.0

Route Guide for Beaver Kill Rd.–Quaker Clearing (see map pp. 216–217)
Unmarked Beaver Kill Rd. runs E from a jct. with NY 206 (CR 7) 2.8 mi N of the village of Roscoe traffic light and 4 mi N of the bridge over Beaver Kill Creek. It is also 3.2 mi S of the Little Spring Rd. jct. on NY 206. Beaver Kill Rd. runs through parts of three counties to Quaker Clearing and the parking area at the Balsam Lake Mt. trailhead.

Mileage W to E	Description	Mileage E to W
0.0	Beaver Kill Rd. and NY 206 (CR 7) jct	22.3
0.5	Delaware/Sullivan Co. line	21.8
2.1	Jct.—do not cross bridge. Continue straight ahead; Prince Hall Masonic Home is here.	20.2
3.1	Jct. Unmarked Pelnor Hollow Rd. turns N and climbs hill on dirt road.	19.2
4.3	Jct. Holliday and Berry Brook Rd. goes N, straight ahead. Beaver Kill Rd. makes a hard turn R if driving E, a hard turn L if driving W.	18.0
5.3	Beaver Kill Public Campground is on S side of road.	17.0
5.5	Beaverkill village. Pass through covered bridge and turn R if going E; turn L and go through covered bridge and bear L if going W.	16.8

5.7	Jct. Turn L if going E; turn R if going W.	16.6
6.2	Jct. CR 152. Turn L if going E; turn R, towards Beaverkill, if going E.	16.1
6.3	Jct. Continue past Elm Hollow Rd.	16.0
9.2	Jct., Lew Beach; Mary Smith Hill Rd. goes N, from E side of Shin Creek bridge; Beaver Kill Rd. goes straight past intersection.	13.1
10.1	Sullivan/Ulster Co. line	12.2
10.8	Jct. Beech Hill Rd. goes N.	11.5
12.9	Jct. Barkaboom Rd. goes N. Little Pond Public Campground's entrance road is 0.2 mi up Barkaboom Rd.	9.4
14.3	Jct. at Turnwood; CR 54 N goes 2.6 mi to Alder Lake.	8.0
16.0	Road unpaved to E; paved to W	6.3
17.4	Hardenburgh hamlet	4.9
18.3	Huge estate, S side of road	4.0
19.3	Zen Studies Society International building, N side of road	3.0
20.3	Mongaup–Hardenburgh Pond trailhead and DEC parking area, S side road	2.0
22.3	DEC Balsam Lake Mt. trailhead parking area	0.0

95 Mill Brook Ridge Trail

Trails Illustrated Map 755: G8 / Map 142, Central Catskills: F7, trail MB

Constructed in 1997, this trail links Alder Lake with Balsam Lake Mt., providing an ambitious day hike over Mill Brook Ridge. A new lean-to along the route lends this trail to an enjoyable overnight experience as well. This trail can also be hiked E-W from the Balsam Lake Mt. Trail (trail 93) at its 0.6 mi point.

▶Trailhead: Follow the trail access directions for the Alder Lake Loop (trail 96). Follow the red-marked Alder Lake Loop, L, around Alder Lake to its jct. with the Mill Brook Ridge Trail, 0.7 mi E of the Alder Lake trailhead parking area. To hike the Mill Brook Ridge Trail E–W, drive to the end of Beaver Kill Rd. (See Route Guide for Beaver Kill Rd.–Quaker Clearing, p. 195.)◀

From the trailhead (0.0 mi) on the E side of Alder Lake, yellow foot trail markers lead E up a short grade along an old woods road. At 0.15 mi the trail crests a hill and briefly descends before resuming its gradual ascent at 0.25 mi. The trail crosses a small stream at 0.4 mi and then passes through an old log landing. At 0.5 mi the trail begins a short, steep climb after which the grade moderates.

A herd path forks R at 0.9 mi, leading to the first of three beaver meadows that the trail passes. The woods road that the trail has been following ends at a stream crossing at 1 mi; the hiking trail turns L and continues as a footpath. (Stinging nettles grow here, so wear long pants or avoid brushing against them.)

At 1.1 mi the trail crosses another stream by way of a single log, hewed flat. It turns L at 1.2 mi and begins a moderate ascent, following a brook to the R. At 1.3 mi the grade eases. The brook is now at the bottom of a steep ravine on the R. At 1.4 mi the trail turns L as it reaches a second beaver meadow.

The trail skirts around the N side of the meadow and reaches a jct. with two paths at 1.5 mi. The path L leads 100 ft to a pipe spring. The path R leads 80 ft to a lean-to overlooking the beaver meadow. This lean-to is 2.25 mi E of the Alder Lake trailhead (1.5 mi from start of Mill Brook Ridge Trail), and 4.4 mi W of Balsam Lake Mt. Trail (trail 93).

After leaving the lean-to, the trail turns N, climbing to a beaver pond and crossing its outlet on large rocks at 1.6 mi. (Long sections here have nettles.) After crossing a seasonal watercourse, the trail begins to climb moderately, following a drainage up Mill Brook Ridge. After a rather steep ascent near the top of the drainage, the trail reaches the top of the ridge at 2.1 mi and turns E. It soon passes a rock ledge on the L and swings ESE, passing a modest view W over trees at 2.5 mi.

At 2.6 mi, the trail climbs steeply with a switchback before reaching the top of ledges where a chair is built from the flat rock, L. This is a good spot to enjoy the views and take a break. Just beyond, the trail crosses over the highest point on the ridge (3480 ft) at 2.8 mi, and then begins a long, moderate descent.

At 3.3 mi the trail begins to climb again as it swings SE, turning L at 3.6 mi and passing through a rocky ledge before switching back S. The grade eases to gradual at 3.7 mi with a first view of Beecher Lake through trees. At 4 mi, the trail reaches an opening with a good view of Beecher Lake and the Beaver Kill Range to the S.

Leaving the vista, the trail easily climbs over another high point on the ridge (3420 ft) in 100 yd and then gradually descends, crossing a very small seasonal drainage at 4.4 mi. Continuing E now on a nearly level traverse, the trail reaches a vista of Balsam Lake Mt., including the fire tower, at 4.7 mi.

Turning sharply N, the trail descends at first steeply and then more moderately as the route swings gradually E. Reaching the col at 4.8 mi, the trail turns ESE, climbing gradually until reaching a short but steep ascent at 5 mi. After turning sharply R and ascending a ledge, the trail turns E again and follows along the top of the ledge. A long ledge shelf provides nice views of the mature hardwood forest. The trail turns S and passes a vista of a pair of beaver ponds in the Balsam Lake drainage at 5.15 mi.

Continuing S along the shelf, the trail crosses a seasonal spring at 5.4 mi. Passing interesting ledges, the trail swings R up rock steps and begins a moderate ascent of Balsam Lake Mt. After two switchbacks and occasional steep climbs, the trail reaches the 3500 ft sign at 5.7 mi. At a turn N in a final switchback, a short path straight ahead through ferns at 5.8 mi offers a scenic vista W and NW to Mill Brook and Dry Brook ridges.

The trail turns sharply R and heads E over level ground to join the red-marked Balsam Lake Mt. Trail (trail 93) at 5.9 mi (6.6 mi from the trailhead). Turn L to reach the summit of Balsam Lake Mt. at 6.15 mi. A path to a spring under a rock ledge is just S, and the spur trail to the Balsam Lake Mt. Lean-to is 0.2 mi S. The Balsam Lake Mt. trailhead parking lot at the end of Beaver Kill Rd. is 1.5 mi S.

🎎 Distances: To lean-to spur at Beaver Meadow, 1.5 mi; to high point on Mill Brook Ridge, 2.8 mi; to vista, 4 mi; to Balsam Lake Mt. Trail, 5.9 mi (9.4 km); to summit of Balsam Lake Mt., 6.15 mi (9.8 km). Summit elevation, 3720 ft (1134 m). Ascent from Alder Lake, 1520 ft.

96 Alder Lake Loop

Trails Illustrated Map 755: G8 / Map 142, Central Catskills: F7

Alder Lake is a lovely place for an afternoon walk, a swim and picnic, or modest canoeing. It has several designated campsites that are well spaced to provide a degree of privacy. Fishing is allowed with worms or artificial lures only.

▶Trailhead: Using the Route Guide for Beaver Kill Rd.–Quaker Clearing, p. 195, turn N onto CR 54 at the jct. at Turnwood. This is at the 14.3 mi (W to E) point of the route guide. Drive 2.6 mi to the Cross Mt. camp entrance road (Old Edwards Rd.). Bear R at this curve. A second jct. immediately confronts you. Do not go up the hill; bear R instead. The next 0.4 mi is gravel road that terminates at the large Alder Lake trailhead parking area.

Beyond the barrier gate is a sign and a trail register. Follow the roadway past the barrier a short distance to the remains of the old Coykendall Lodge. Turn R and follow a path down a grade to the lakeshore, a dam, and a DEC signpost 0.1 mi from the barrier gate. This is the trailhead of the Alder Lake Loop Trail.◀

From the DEC signpost (0.0 mi), turn N away from the dam and follow the shoreline path around the lake. At just over 0.1 mi, the first of three well-spaced designated campsite side trails branches off. Soon after, red trail markers begin; these should be followed on this trail. The attractive trail continues past some high bushes to another designated campsite at 0.2 mi, and a third at 0.45 mi before crossing a bridge shortly beyond. After a second bridge 50 yd farther along, the trail edges away from the lake and gradually climbs.

Bear L at a narrow fork at 0.6 mi, where a spring can be found at stone steps; bear R 20 ft farther onto a broad woods road. This road gradually ascends a grade and reaches a jct. with the Mill Brook Ridge Trail (trail 95) at 0.7 mi. (This yellow-marked trail ascends 1.5 mi to a lean-to and then continues over Mill Brook Ridge to the Balsam Lake Mt. Trail [trail 93], 5.9 mi E.)

Just beyond, the trail drops down to a large bridge that crosses the major lake inlet. Though hard to spot unless one is looking for it, there is a pleasant designated campsite 100 ft along the trail from the bridge, 250 ft toward the lake.

The level trail begins to climb gradually again at 0.8 mi, briefly levels, and then gradually ascends to a height of land at 1 mi. The route is now well above the lake and 250 ft from the shore, though the lake is easily viewed through the trees. The trail gradually descends to a small bridge at 1.2 mi, then a slight upgrade leads to a side path R and another designated campsite. Soon the route passes through a small woods opening and joins another woods road. Bear R, following arrow signs.

The woods road curves down to an open field and heads back to the lake's outlet dam. Across the field a path leads into the woods to two more designated campsites. The route crosses the dam on a wide walkway and returns to the DEC trailhead signpost at 1.6 mi.

🦌 Distances: To first designated campsite side trail, 0.1 mi; to jct. with Mill Brook Ridge Trail, 0.7 mi; to height of land, 1 mi; return to trailhead, 1.6 mi (2.6 km).

97 Alder Lake to Big Pond Section of Touchmenot Trail

Trails Illustrated Map 755: H8 / Map 142, Central Catskills: F7 and Map 144, Western Catskills: E7, trail TO

This trail connects Alder Lake to Big Pond, providing a complete route from Alder Lake to Trout Pond, permitting a backpacker to hike across Delaware County. It originally followed old woods roads across ridges, but now seems more like a hiking trail much of the way. Scenic in places, ascents make it more rigorous than it looks.

▶Trailhead: Follow directions for the Alder Lake Loop (trail 96) to the 2.6 mi point on CR 54, at the Cross Mt. camp entrance road. The trail begins 75 ft S of this entrance road. A few vehicles can be parked on a wide shoulder, just around the curve from the trailhead.◀

From the trailhead (0.0 mi) on the W side of CR 54, red trail markers lead down a short grade and across Alder Creek to a flat path that heads downstream. At 0.1 mi, the path zigzags and begins a moderate ascent up a wide old woods road. It soon makes a sweeping curve NW, becoming a gradual upgrade generally to the W.

The route levels at 0.4 mi, running roughly parallel to the ridge, having gained about 250 ft elevation from the trailhead. Posted signs come into view on the uphill side of the trail at 0.5 mi, where there are 10 to 15 ft cliffs.

Bear L (W) at 0.6 mi, where arrow signs at a three-way jct. point the way. At 0.65 mi, the nearly level height of land drops down a short moderate grade. The trail passes through a small field and, with more arrow signs, makes an abrupt L turn S in woods at 0.7 mi.

The route soon swings SSW and back to the S again, beginning a long gradual downgrade through fern-filled deciduous woods. Another small clearing is R at 0.9 mi as the route continues its descent to an arrow sign very near the bottom of the grade in a tributary valley of Alder Creek. The sign points R (avoid going straight ahead here) and the trail crosses a brook at 1.15 mi on a bridge made of immense rock slabs.

Another grassy, wider woods road leads WSW up a gradual and then moderate grade. Having lost over 200 ft elevation in the descent, the trail now regains it, and more, until it nearly levels out at about 1.5 mi. Several stone walls and foundations visible during the ascent suggest an agricultural past here.

The SW route curves slightly R at 1.7 mi, where the unobservant hiker may unwittingly follow a fork road L and head back downhill. AVOID THIS.

The trail becomes a path again and begins to swing from SW to NW at 1.9 mi. Ascending a gentle grade, it reaches another height of land at 2 mi and 2550 ft elevation. The trail begins the downgrade toward Big Pond in a WNW direction, becoming moderate in grade.

The remainder of the trail is unusual in two respects. First, there are two small groves of spruces, which are relatively rare in Delaware County. Second, the person who designed the trail took advantage of the even slope and built a series of long switchbacks. Such lengthy switchbacks are common on trails in the western United States but are quite rare in the East. This excellent design makes a stubborn grade a pleasant stroll to Big Pond.

The trail winds N and then W before heading NW through a spruce grove at 2.2 mi. It then heads N through open deciduous forest, where the hiker must keep the trail markers in sight. Passing through another spruce grove at 2.3 mi, the route swings W, NW, and finally SW. At 2.5 mi, the route joins a woods road, makes an acute turn R and gradually descends to the N.

At 2.6 mi, the trail curves to the SW and descends a moderate grade along a deeply worn rocky woods road. (If traveling in the opposite direction, be careful to avoid going onto a narrow path NE at this curve.)

At the bottom of the grade the trail turns R, crosses a small creek valley floor, and climbs quickly to an open field. The level trail now follows the L edge of the field to another field and then goes down a small grade to the rear of a large parking area at 2.9 mi. Big Pond can be seen through the trees to the N. Two faint trails lead from the NE corner of the parking area, near the yellow metal barrier gate, to designated campsites above Big Pond.

A gravel road descends to Barkaboom Rd. at 3 mi. There is a second parking area 165 yd N on the road at the shore of Big Pond. The Big Pond to Beech Hill Rd. Trail (trail 98) begins along Barkaboom Rd., 100 ft N of the trail register at this parking area.

🥾 Distances: To first arrow jct., 0.6 mi; to rock bridge, 1.15 mi; to second height of land, 2 mi; to woods road, 2.5 mi; to Barkaboom Rd., 3 mi; to parking area near Big Pond, 3.1 mi (5 km).

98 Big Pond to Beech Hill Rd. Section of Touchmenot Trail

Trails Illustrated Map 755: H7 / Map 144, Western Catskills: E7, trail TO

This trail ascends the shoulder of Touchmenot Mt., intersecting with the Campground Trail (trail 99) that heads S over Touchmenot Mt. to Little Pond State Campground. The trail continues N beyond the jct. of Little Pond Trail and ascends Cabot Mt. to Beech Hill Rd.

▶Trailhead: Follow the Route Guide for Beaver Kill Rd.–Quaker Clearing (p. 195) to the Barkaboom Rd. jct. at 12.9 mi, traveling W to E. Turn N and travel 0.9 mi to a large parking area at Big Pond. There is a trail register and exhibit board at this parking area. The trailhead is 100 ft farther N on the W side of Barkaboom Rd. (A gravel road 0.1 mi S on Barkaboom Rd. leads 100 yd up to a second parking area for the Alder Lake to Big Pond Trail [trail 97] trailhead.)

From the N, follow Route Guide for Margaretville–NY 206 (p. 195). Turn L off NY 28/30 2 mi W of Margaretville to a T-jct., turning R. Travel 8.2 mi on old NY 30 (S of Pepacton Reservoir) to the Barkaboom Rd. jct.◀

From the trailhead (0.0 mi), the route climbs 175 ft up a steep slope with red trail markers. The trail is mostly NW and the climbing is continuous, alternating from gradual to moderate in slope. At 0.4 mi, the open trail narrows to a path and the hiker must pay more attention to trail markers.

At 0.6 mi, the route heads W for a short distance and becomes steep. From this point to 1 mi, climbing is moderate to the ridge crest. Heading NW from the crest, the path gradually descends and reaches the Campground Trail jct. (trail 99) at 1.1 mi. (The tree-covered summit of Touchmenot Mt. is 0.3 mi S from this jct.)

Turning N (R), the Touchmenot Trail (trail 98) descends through mossy, narrow ledges at 1.2 mi; take care to watch trail markers in this section. The trail drops over another ledge and continues to descend to 2450 ft before climbing over a small rise to the Little Pond Trail jct. at 1.5 mi. (The Little Pond Trail [trail 100] leads in 0.25 mi to an expansive view S from an open field; in 1.15 mi to Little Pond; and in 1.3 mi to the campground.)

The Touchmenot Trail continues the slight descent after the jct., and then ascends toward Cabot Mt. At 1.8 mi, the ascent becomes steep, assisted by stairs, and at 1.9 mi a very steep ascent passes under a ledge overhang and climbs more stairs. A view S through trees is at 2.15 mi (best when leaves are off), and the Cabot Mt. summit (more of a high point) is at 2.3 mi. The wide trail curves around the mountaintop to the NW, and rolling terrain continues on a slow descent. Another limited view appears atop a ledge on a gradual descent to 2.9 mi, where the trail drops steeply into the Beech Hill Rd. valley.

The trail moderates at 3.5 mi in very wet, rocky terrain briefly, and then enters a narrow public land corridor that is posted on each side. The lane climbs gradually to Beech Hill Rd. at 3.6 mi. There is a wide spot here where cars can be parked. NY 30 is 3.7 mi N; Beaver Kill Rd. is 2.6 mi S. The Middle Mt. (trail 101) trailhead is 0.2 mi N on Beech Hill Rd.

🥾 Distances: To steep section, 0.6 mi; to Campground Trail jct., 1.1 mi; to Little Pond Trail jct., 1.5 mi; to first stairs, 1.8 mi; to Cabot Mt. summit, 2.3 mi; to steep descent, 2.9 mi; to Beech Hill Rd., 3.6 mi (5.8 km).

99 Campground Trail from Little Pond Campground to Big Pond Jct.

Trails Illustrated Map 755: G7 / Map 144, Western Catskills: E7, trail CG

This is a steep connector trail from Little Pond State Campground parking area, which, when combined with the Little Pond Trail (trail 100), makes a loop route to and from the campground. It climbs viewless Touchmenot Mt. and descends through an interesting section of narrow ledges to connect with the trail coming up from Little Pond. A swim and a picnic can be a climax to the day.

▶Trailhead: Trail access is at the Little Pond Public Campground, 0.2 mi N of Beaver Kill Rd. The campground is 0.9 mi off Barkaboom Rd. (See Route Guides for this chapter.) Beyond the campground tollbooth is a parking area. From the N end of the parking area, walk along the macadam path between the showers and the bathhouse to a trail register.◀

From the trail register (0.0 mi), go R 30 ft to a blue-marked trail that enters the woods. The trail immediately climbs a moderate grade to the NE. The slope continues for 0.3 mi, where a big rock slab adorns the trail. The route becomes very steep, assisted with new trailwork at 0.7 mi, then ascends on natural steps up the rock through great mossy cuts in rock outcrops.

The way suddenly flattens out at 0.8 mi on the 2760 ft summit of Touchmenot Mt. Viewing is minimal if leaves are off, nonexistent otherwise. The trail continues along the summit ridge and begins a gentle descent, passing a ledge high above the forest, reaching a jct. where the Touchmenot Trail from Big Pond (trail 98) enters at 1.1 mi. (A loop hike can be made by continuing on the Touchmenot Trail to the Little Pond Trail [trail 100] jct. in another 0.4 mi, returning to the campground on the Little Pond Trail.)

🥾 Distances: To summit of Touchmenot Mt., 0.8 mi; to jct. of Touchmenot Trail to Big Pond, 1.1 mi (1.8 km).

Joanne Hihn

100 Little Pond Trail

Trails Illustrated Map 755: G7 / Map 144, Western Catskills: E7, trail LT

The first part of the Little Pond Trail is a lovely woods road walk through an abandoned farm, by fields that have yet to turn back into woods. The many ferns to enjoy, stone walls to admire, berries to pick, and excellent views of Touchmenot Mt. enhance your day. A myriad of different flowers and trees welcome the hiker.

Many hikers travel only to the vista. Those seeking more rugged climbing can continue up the last section of this trail and return to the campgrounds via part of the Touchmenot Trail (trail 98) and Campground Trail (trail 99). This description begins with a path around the E side of Little Pond, joining the Little Pond Trail at its 0.2 mi point.

▶Trailhead: For access to the trailhead, use the same directions given for the Campground Trail (trail 99). From the trail register (0.0 mi) at the rear of the bathhouse noted in that trail description, walk L, following yellow trail markers.◀

The trail follows the E side of Little Pond, passing near campsites. It avoids wet spots by moving away from the shoreline when necessary. At the N end of the pond, the trail crosses the inlet of Little Pond on a bridge. At a jct. at 0.5 mi, yellow arrow signs point R. (Yellow trail markers also go L, 0.2 mi to the official start of the Little Pond Trail at the NW corner of the pond.)

A short pitch up quickly becomes a gradual grade along the W side of the inlet stream, still following yellow trail markers. An old beaver pond R at 0.75 mi is evidence of past beaver activity.

The trail continues uphill to beautiful dark tree plantations of red pine and spruce. Becoming grassy, the roadway runs N along the W side of a meadow whose side is bordered by spruce.

The route climbs a gentle slope, now with a pine plantation L. The route turns R at 1.1 mi and passes a stone wall near 1.2 mi. Paths lead L to a pond at 1.3 mi, and past an old foundation. Just beyond, the trail enters a large meadow where fine viewing greets the hiker.

At 1.4 mi, the trail curves NE into a fern-filled woods and ascends gradually to the jct. of the Touchmenot Trail (trail 98) at 1.65 mi. (Turning R, the Touchmenot Trail climbs 0.4 mi to the jct., L, to Big Pond; the Campground Trail [trail 99] continues R [straight ahead] up Touchmenot Mt. Very steep grades descend to the register where your trip began. Turning L, the Touchmenot Trail [trail 98] ascends Cabot Mt. and reaches Beech Hill Rd. in 2.1 mi. Though short, these sections of the Touchmenot Trail are rugged, with steep ascents and descents.)

🐾 Distances: To jct. and R turn at end of pond, 0.5 mi; to old beaver pond, 0.75 mi; to lookout vista, 1.3 mi; to Touchmenot Trail jct., 1.65 mi (2.6 km). Ascent, 540 ft.

101 Middle Mt. Trail

Trails Illustrated Map 755: G6 / Map 144, Western Catskills: D7, trail MM

This short section of the connecting Delaware Ridge trails gains and loses ascent along the way and is thus a greater workout than it appears. At 1.1 mi, a good view may be available even in summer. (It is a nice viewing spot when leaves are off.)

▶Trailhead: The trailhead is at the jct. of a dirt road on the W side of Beech Hill Rd. From NY 30, it is S 3.5 mi (partially unpaved) along Beech Hill Rd.; from Beaver Kill Rd., it is N 2.8 mi. (See Route Guides for this chapter.) There is room to park on the shoulder of the road at this jct., or you can drive 0.1 mi W on the trailhead dirt road to park. The Middle Mt. trailhead is 0.2 mi N of the Touch-menot Trail to Cabot Mt. (trail 98) trailhead.◀

From the Beech Hill Rd. trailhead (0.0 mi) walk W, following red trail markers. Follow the dirt road, Hay Barn Hill Lane, for 0.1 mi. The trail turns L and begins climbing the mountain, soon steeply, to 0.3 mi. The ascent becomes gradual to the summit of Beech Hill (2884 ft) at 0.5 mi. Ascent from the trailhead is 594 ft. A gradual downgrade leads to a low point at 0.8 mi. Level terrain pitches up at 0.9 mi and reaches a lookout S, becoming obscured by tree growth, at 1.1 mi. The grade eases from there to the summit of Middle Mt. (2975 ft) at 1.3 mi. Ascent from the col is 200 ft.

The summit is typical level terrain, covered with berry patches, to 1.55 mi, where the trail bears R and pitches downward. At 1.7 mi it reaches an interesting area along the top of a rock outcrop, then turns and descends a small cliff. Descent resumes at a more moderate rate on loose rock.

Leveling out at 2 mi, the trail heads SW through an open deciduous woods by a hillside. It reaches the parking area and trailhead on Mary Smith Hill Rd. at 2.3 mi. Across the road, the Mary Smith Trail (trail 102) heads W. NY 30 is N, 2.2 mi on partially unpaved Mary Smith Hill Rd. and then L for 1.1 mi on Beech Hill Rd. Beaver Kill Rd. is S, 3.2 mi on Mary Smith Hill Rd. (See Route Guides for this chapter.)

👣 Distances: To Beech Hill, 0.5 mi; to Middle Mt. summit, 1.3 mi; to Mary Smith Hill Rd., 2.3 mi (3.7 km).

102 Mary Smith Hill Trail

Trails Illustrated Map 755: G5 / Map 144, Western Catskills: D7, trail MS

This trail runs E-W from the Middle Mt. Trail (trail 101) to the Pelnor Hollow Trail (trail 104). It crosses Holliday and Berry Brook Rd. and leads to Split Rock Lookout via a short section of the Pelnor Hollow Trail in 1.4 mi.

▶Trailhead: From NY 30, travel 1.1 mi up Beech Hill Rd., then fork R onto Mary Smith Hill Rd. for another 2.2 mi on partially unpaved surface to the trailhead. From Beaver Kill Rd., it is 3.2 mi N on Mary Smith Hill Rd. (See Route Guides for this chapter.) The parking area is on the E side of the road. (The Middle Mt. Trail leaves the rear of this parking area.)◄

The Mary Smith Hill Trail is on the W side of the road across from the parking area. Leave the trailhead (0.0 mi) and head W, following red trail markers through evergreen forest.

The trail soon turns L and begins a steep upgrade. Switchbacks climb to 0.3 mi, where the trail makes a sharp R. It moderates and reaches a good view S at 0.5 mi from a rock in a fern-covered flat area. Ascent to this lookout is 300 ft. A series of alternating pitches and level zones lead to a height of land at 0.9 mi, 600 ft above the trailhead.

The path loses elevation gradually and heads NW along level terrain. The trail is on the W edge of the ridge and presents views of surrounding hills through the trees if leaves are off. At 1.4 mi, the trail pitches down. There is evidence of rock work at 1.6 mi. The route gradually descends nearly 150 ft and makes a sharp L. Minor upgrades take it to the S side of the summit of Mary Smith Hill.

A short path L next to a boulder at 2.1 mi leads to a rock overlook with good views S toward the Beaver Kill Valley. The route becomes nearly flat through berry brambles to a slight upgrade at 2.3 mi, reaching the top of a large cliff-like ledge. (Slightly R off-trail leads to a view down into the ledges.) The trail then pitches down between the rocks and begins sections of gentle descent combined with pitches down scenic mossy ledges. Switchbacks L and R lead to the top of a ledge at 2.8 mi, and the path drops down a rocky area with loose rock. The rate of descent moderates at 2.9 mi, but becomes very steep again (take care) before leveling at 3.2 mi.

Holliday and Berry Brook Rd. intersects the trail at 3.3 mi, at the high point of the pass. There is a large parking area and trail register on the E side of the road. NY 30 is 3 mi N; Beaver Kill Rd. is 3.6 mi S. (See the Route Guides for this chapter.)

The trail continues SW across the road. It crosses under a high power line at 3.4 mi; the hiker is also walking over the East Delaware Aqueduct, which is far under the ground surface.

The trail reenters the Forest Preserve at the woods line. The route bears R on a grassy road at 3.5 mi and begins a gradual ascent that pitches upward at 3.6 mi. It levels at 3.7 mi and passes through a young woods filled with berry brambles.

An arrow sign points R at 4 mi, and the route climbs again. The terrain becomes more hilly at 4.3 mi and remains steep to a jct. with the Pelnor Hollow Trail (trail 104) at 4.5 mi. Pelnor Hollow Rd. is 3.2 mi S. A three-way jct. with the Little Spring Brook Trail (trail 106) and the Campbell Mt. Trail (trail 105) is 1.25 mi NW.

🀄 Distances: To view, 0.5 mi; to height of land, 0.9 mi; to lookout, 2.1 mi; to Holliday and Berry Brook Rd., 3.3 mi; to Pelnor Hollow jct., 4.5 mi (7.2 km).

103 Huggins Lake Trail *(unmaintained trail)*

Trails Illustrated Map 755: G5 / Map 144, Western Catskills: C7

The woods road to Huggins Lake makes a pleasant afternoon's walk to an attractive body of water. It is also a good cross-country ski trail.
▶ Trailhead: The trailhead is on the E side of Holliday and Berry Brook Rd. 4.5 mi S of NY 30 and 1.8 mi N of Beaver Kill Rd. (See the Route Guides for this chapter.) Huggins Lake parking area is up a dirt road on the E side of Holliday and Berry Brook Rd. Posted signs refer to land bordering the trail near the beginning; the corridor to the lake and the lake itself are state-owned. ◀

The unmarked woods road leaves the trailhead (0.0 mi) and gradually climbs 100 yd to a gate in an open spot. Passing through the opening in the gate, continue along the grassy lane, which swings L at 0.1 mi. The young hardwood forest has many ferns.
  The trail ascends gradually. At 0.4 mi a woods road comes in from the L and the hiking route also bears L. Leveling off at 0.7 mi, it has curved SE. It reaches a grassy height of land at 1.15 mi after easier climbing.
  Beyond, the woods road is a gently rolling route from which Huggins Lake can be seen below to the L. The road swings sharply N at 1.5 mi and descends to the S end of the lake. There is a dam (1993) at R and a bridge across Huggins Hollow Brook at 1.7 mi. A woods road runs along the W side of the brook. There are grassy areas beside the lake on the other side of the bridge, and informal campsites around the shoreline. Another road runs around the E side of the lake and continues N. (In time, proposals may result in a trail along this road to connect with the Mary Smith Hill Trail [trail 102].)
  ᨂ Distances: To woods road, 0.4 mi; to height of land, 1.15 mi; to descent to lake, 1.5 mi; to bridge and Huggins Lake, 1.7 mi (2.7 km).

104 Pelnor Hollow Trail

Trails Illustrated Map 755: G5 / Map 144, Western Catskills: C8, trail PH

The Pelnor Hollow Trail is little used except by hunters in autumn. This is unfortunate, because much of the route is attractive and Pelnor Hollow Lean-to is one of the best in the Catskills.
  ▶ Trailhead: Trailhead access is off the N side of Beaver Kill Rd. (See Route Guide for Beaver Kill Rd.–Quaker Clearing, p. 195.) Unmarked and unpaved Pelnor Hollow Rd. climbs N at a fairly steep grade before nearly leveling. About 1.1 mi from Beaver Kill Rd., beyond a small farmhouse and large barn, an obscure route is passable only with a high-clearance vehicle. (The landowners do not allow parking on their property.) The remaining 0.4 mi to the trailhead is very overgrown over loose rock and then up a rough grade. The trailhead signpost and state land are 1.5 mi from Beaver Kill Rd. ◀

Split Rock, on the Pelnor Hollow Trail. David White

From the trailhead (0.0 mi) a grassy lane leads N, following blue trail markers. The level roadway reaches a small clearing at 0.35 mi, where a barrier gate blocks further advance. (A cabin is down the road.) The trail bears L up a slope from a DEC sign and enters the woods. The route soon levels again, ascending only occasionally on very easy grades. The open sugar maple forest is most attractive.

Two stone cairns at 0.8 mi mark a side trail R that leads downslope to a very large pond (not shown on most maps). The trail continues N, passing stone walls at 0.95 mi, and reaches the Pelnor Hollow Lean-to at 1 mi. Located in open woods, with the pond visible about 0.1 mi downslope, this is a very pleasant spot. A trail leads E from the lean-to to a spring.

The trail beyond the rear of the lean-to is less maintained, but is still easy to follow. It ascends a short, moderate slope that soon becomes a gradual grade.

At 1.3 mi, the trail makes abrupt L and R turns. A rocky area with possible caves is L at 1.4 mi. The footpath climbs a short steep pitch up a hill to a ridge at 1.7 mi and reaches a height of land at 1.8 mi on an unnamed hill of 2672 ft elevation.

At 2.1 mi, the trail loops back R and descends a moderate grade to 2.45 mi. The route becomes a rocky woods road and soon levels in an area with large oak trees. The hiker needs to watch trail markers at a brief blowdown section at 2.6 mi.

Widely varying grades gain elevation to a height of land at 3.15 mi before the trail reaches the Mary Smith Hill Trail (trail 102) jct. at 3.2 mi. (The Mary Smith Hill Trail heads NE, 1.2 mi to Holliday and Berry Brook Rd.)

The trail turns NW, soon losing elevation on a moderately steep grade. At 3.4 mi it makes a sharp R turn and is again level. At this turn a very good lookout W is offered from an interesting rock outcrop called Split Rock. (Take care at deep drops where the rock has split off from the cliff.)

The trail continues N on nearly level terrain above the cliffs. (Old markers may be noted where the old trail descended steeply and ran through a wet section; avoid this route.) The new trail gradually descends as it curves W and then S. Turning W again, the route pitches down and enters a beautiful pine and spruce plantation at 4.1 mi.

Watch the trail markers for a sharp L turn halfway through the conifer forest. The route crosses a brook at 4.4 mi just before reaching a clearing with a three-way jct. at 4.45 mi. Little Spring Brook Trail (trail 106) enters from the S; the Campbell Mt. Trail (trail 105) heads N toward NY 206 (see below). This large, open clearing sprinkled with apple trees is a good place to take a break and enjoy watching butterflies and birds.

※ Distances: To clearing, 0.35 mi; to lean-to, 1 mi; to height of land, 1.8 mi; to Mary Smith Trail jct., 3.2 mi; to Split Rock, 3.4 mi; to three-way jct., 4.45 mi (7.1 km).

105 Campbell Mt. Trail

Trails Illustrated Map 755: G4 / Map 144, Western Catskills: B7, trail CM

The Campbell Mt. Trail runs from valley to valley, climbing over Brock and Campbell mts. It is good hiking on a fairly rugged but well-maintained trail.

▶Trailhead: The trail starts at a three-way jct. with the Little Spring Brook and Pelnor Hollow trails. The easiest approach to the trailhead is N via the 0.7 mi. Little Spring Brook Trail (trail 106).◀

The trail heads N from the DEC signpost (0.0 mi), following blue trail markers. The nearly level grassy road soon begins a gradual descent, with fine stone walls bordering each side of the roadway. Don't miss the abrupt L-turn arrow sign at 0.25 mi, where the trail cuts through an opening in the stone wall and enters a conifer plantation.

The route climbs NW through attractive conifer forest at varying but comfortable grades on good footing. It levels at 0.55 mi and then climbs again to 0.8 mi, where it turns S. At a high point at 1.2 mi, Buck Mt. Club signs are affixed to trees.

The footpath now turns WNW, entering state land at 1.4 mi and reaching an intersection with a snowmobile trail from Miller Hollow at 1.6 mi. After a sharp turn L on a woods road, the trail soon turns R, leaving the road and climbing a moderate grade.

The ascent of Brock Mt. continues steeply, with short level stretches, to 1.7 mi. The trail then bears L through a flat wet spot, where the top of Brock Mt. can be seen. Take care to watch trail markers in this section. Bearing R again, the route soon becomes very steep. Leveling off at a high point at 2.15 mi, 50 ft below the wooded top of Brock Mt. (2760 ft), the trail passes through a thorny berry patch.

A moderate and then gradual grade drops down to a col and unmarked jct. at 2.7 mi. (The side trail L descends to NY 206.) The blue trail swings N and heads toward the lower summit of Brock Mt., which it reaches by easy grades at 2.9 mi.

After a turn L at a woods road jct. at 2.95 mi (an old quarry is straight ahead), at 3 mi a sign points to a downgrade that is gradual at the start but soon becomes steep. There are fewer trail markers but more orange paint blazes. At 3.35 mi, after a steep descent for 100 yd, the trail swings R. The path angles down a slope for the last 200 ft to NY 206, at 3.9 mi. (This path is difficult to spot from the highway.) Across the road at a small signpost there is enough room for several vehicles to park, well off the road.

This trailhead is on the N side of a height of land on NY 206 (CR 7). From NY 30 it is S, 2.2 mi on NY 206. (See Route Guide for Margaretville–NY 206, p. 195.) It is 3 mi N of Little Spring Brook Rd. on NY 206. On some maps, NY 206 is called Cat Hollow Rd.

From the small trailhead post marker (3.9 mi) on the W side of NY 206, the trail goes L down a woods road to a gate with a stop sign on it. Blue trail markers show the way as the descent continues to a stream crossing at 4.2 mi. Many stone foundations and orchards appear in this area, evidence of an old settlement.

After a second stream, the trail becomes grassy as it turns NW. A dark spruce forest precedes a log bridge at 4.35 mi, followed by another attractive forest of red pine. The route passes a rock wall at 4.7 mi and reaches an unmarked trail jct. at 4.8 mi. An unmarked trail continues N, but the marked trail swings W, beginning a gradual climb. Depending on the season and weather, many cascading drainages from the hillside cross the trail, which passes three small streams with 10 ft cascades in the next short stretch.

The trail turns S. At 5.05 mi the roadway divides, with the marked trail bearing R. Easy to moderate grades bring you to the Campbell Mt. Lean-to at 5.1 mi. (The divided trail rejoins the marked trail here.) The lean-to is in an attractive setting near a mossy cascading brook with waterfalls and wood fern. Litter has been a problem: "If you carry it in, carry it out."

Beyond the lean-to, elevation continues to increase as the trail gradually swings from SW to NW and back to W. The height of land (2430 ft) on Campbell Mt. is at 5.6 mi, after a gain of 680 ft elevation from the first creek W of NY 206.

The trail is relatively flat to 5.9 mi and then descends. After making a sharp L, the roadway swings SE on moderate downgrades. It passes a cabled gate at 6.1 mi. After the route swings R, drainage causes muddy footing to the Campbell Mt. trailhead on Campbell Mt. Rd. at 6.3 mi.

The quickest way to this trailhead, if roads are dry, is via Jug Tavern Rd. Turn W on this road 0.8 mi S of the Campbell Mt. trailhead on NY 206 (CR 7). Drive 1.6 mi to Campbell Mt. Rd. Turn R for 0.7 mi to the parking area at the trailhead on the E side of the road.

The trailhead can also be reached from Downsville by driving S 3.6 mi on NY 30 to Campbell Brook Rd. Turn E, drive through Corbett and at 2.3 mi turn L and then R onto Campbell Mt. Rd. Drive 2.9 mi to the trailhead. The Trout Pond Trail (trail 107) is on the opposite side of the road from the Campbell Mt. Trail.

🥾 Distances: To stone wall turn, 0.25 mi; to state land, 1.4 mi; to Miller Hollow snowmobile trail, 1.6 mi; to high point on Brock Mt., 2.15 mi; to lower summit of Brock Mt., 2.9 mi; to NY 206, 3.9 mi; to Campbell Mt. Lean-to, 5.1 mi; to height of land on Campbell Mt., 5.6 mi; to Campbell Mt. Rd., 6.3 mi (10.1 km).

106 Little Spring Brook Trail

Trails Illustrated Map 755: G5 / Map 144, Western Catskills: B7, trail LS

Little Spring Brook Trail is a short connector trail that meets the ends of both the Pelnor Hollow and Campbell Mt. trails (trails 104 and 105) at a three-way jct. It allows the hiker to modify the length of hikes on these trails. The Little Spring Brook and Pelnor Hollow trails lead to Split Rock Lookout in 1.65 mi.

Tropical Storm Irene destroyed the first 0.5 mi of the Little Spring Brook Trail. The damage will be repaired in the future.

▶Trailhead: Trailhead access is off the E side of NY 206 (CR 7) at the end of Little Spring Brook Rd., which is 6.2 mi N of the traffic light in Roscoe and 5.2 mi S of the NY 30 jct. (See Route Guides for this chapter.) Park at the turnout 1.1 mi down Little Spring Brook Rd.◀

Head N from the unmarked trailhead (0.0 mi), passing a camp on the R. At 100 ft, there is a spring with a pipe. A trail sign is another 50 ft along the way, where state land begins. Yellow trail markers guide you up a gradual grade beside the bank of Little Spring Brook, which the trail crosses at 0.3 mi.

The trail reaches the L side of a pond at 0.4 mi and stays between it and a stone fence on the L. The trail footing improves markedly on a wide lane as it passes a beautiful forest of mixed conifers at 0.55 mi. It swings NE and reaches a three-way jct. with Pelnor Hollow Trail (trail 104) and Campbell Mt. Trail (trail 105) at 0.7 mi. This clearing has nice old apple trees on one side and red pine on the other. (The Campbell Mt. Trail runs 2.4 mi W to NY 206 and beyond; the

Pelnor Hollow Trail runs 4 mi S to Pelnor Hollow Rd.)
👣 Distances: To pond, 0.4 mi; to three-way jct., 0.7 mi (1.1 km).

107 Trout Pond Trail

Trails Illustrated Map 755: G3 / Map 144, Western Catskills: A7, trail TP

The Trout Pond Trail, combined with the Mud Pond Trail (trail 108), offers a route to two ponds or a loop hike over Cherry Ridge. The trail offers a good overnight backpack trip, especially for the angler. Unfortunately, heavy use of the area has resulted in a large amount of litter. Please do not add to the problem. If you carry it in full, please carry it out empty.

▶Trailhead: From the S, the Russell Brook Rd. trailhead is reached from NY 206 (CR 7). From the traffic light in Roscoe, it is 2.4 mi N on NY 206 to Morton Hill Rd., immediately past the Beaver Kill bridge. Turn W onto Morton Hill Rd., bear R at 0.2 mi, and drive to a jct. 3.2 mi from NY 206. Turn L onto unmarked Russell Brook Rd. and drive 0.5 mi to the trailhead parking area. Russell Brook Rd. can also be reached off I-86 or old NY 17 at Cooks Falls/Butternut Grove. The parking area at the S end of Russell Brook Rd. has a barrier so there is a road walk to any of the trailheads. The barrier at the N end is close to the Trout Pond trailhead. The Trout Pond trailhead is 1.4 mi N of the Mud Pond trailhead (trail 108) on Russell Brook Rd.

To reach the northern trailhead on Campbell Mt. Rd., refer to the access directions in the Campbell Mt. Trail description (trail 105). From the trailhead (0.0 mi) on the S side of Campbell Mt. Rd., follow blue trail markers S. (The Campbell Mt. Trail, on the N side of this road, also has blue trail markers.)◀

The trail descends past a gate and crosses a bridge over Russell Brook. There is a magnificent large waterfall on Russell Brook just upstream beyond remnants of an old stone dam, off the trail. Don't miss this cooling-off spot.

At 0.1 mi at a snowmobile trail jct. to Mud Pond, there is a trail register. Campsites and a privy are available in this area. The blue-marked Trout Pond Trail continues straight (N) to Trout Pond, ascending on gradual and then moderate grades. Signs for campsites are posted to the L between the trail and the outlet stream. At 0.9 mi, the trail reaches the S end of Trout Pond, also called Cables Lake.

Shortly after passing a spawning box and spring, the trail reaches a jct. at 1.4 mi. A relocated lean-to is 50 yd N and a second one is 0.15 mi W from this jct. on a spur path off the Mud Pond Trail (trail 108), which continues 1.85 mi to the snowmobile trail jct. (The Mud Pond spur trail is 0.1 mi W of that jct.)

The trail continues N and climbs nearly 500 ft before passing between two high points at 2500 ft, where a trail sign at 2.1 mi indicates a snowmobile trail, R, heading to Campbell Brook Rd. The trail soon begins a 400 ft descent on moderate to steep grades, crossing a brook on a bridge and then a second bridge over the S Branch of Campbell Brook at 2.85 mi. A gradual ascent passes a snowmobile

Trout Pond from the lean-to. Joan Dean

trail, R, and leads to Campbell Brook Rd. at 3.1 mi, beyond a gate. The trail turns L and runs E 175 yd along the road, then turns R off the road at 3.2 mi at a trailhead marked by a DEC sign.

(This trailhead can be reached from NY 206 3.3 mi S of NY 30, between Roscoe and the Pepacton Reservoir via Jug Tavern Rd. Turn W for 1.6 mi to Campbell Mt. Rd., L for 0.4 mi to Campbell Brook Rd., then R 0.55 mi to the trailhead. From the W, the trailhead is reached by driving S for 3.6 mi on NY 30 to Campbell Brook Rd. Turn E 4.9 mi to the trailhead, which is on a dirt road.)

Heading N, the trail is muddy for several yards and then veers L; footing improves. The route ascends 350 ft, passing a herd path R leading to an open field full of berries, before reaching its high point of 2525 ft at 3.7 mi. Heading NW, gradual grades begin a descent of 475 ft to the N branch of Campbell Brook. An old road crosses the trail at 4 mi and a snowmobile trail branches L at 4.2 mi. The hiker needs to be sure to follow small blue DEC trail markers rather than the larger snowmobile trail markers, since snowmobile trails cross the hiking trail occasionally.

As the trail swings about 180 degrees to the E, over 200 ft are lost before it levels off and then descends again to the wooden bridge across the S branch of Campbell Brook at 4.8 mi. A pipe from a sometimes-flowing spring protrudes from the bank nearby. The trail ascends to Campbell Mt. Rd. at 5.1 mi.

🅰 Distances: To register and jct. to Mud Pond Trail, 0.1 mi; to S end of Trout Pond, 0.9 mi; to Mud Pond jct. and lean-to spurs, 1.4 mi; to snowmobile jct., 2.1 mi; to Campbell Brook Rd., 3.1 mi; to trailhead and turn from Campbell

Brook Rd., 3.2 mi; to high point, 3.7 mi; to S branch Campbell Brook, 4.8 mi; to Campbell Mt. Rd., 5.1 mi (8.2 km).

108 Mud Pond Trail

Trails Illustrated Map 755: G3 / Map 144, Western Catskills: A7, trail MP

The Mud Pond Trail provides the hiker of the Trout Pond Trail (trail 107) with a loop option.

▶Trailhead: The Mud Pond Trail description begins at the jct. of the trail and the Trout Pond Trail at the N end of Trout Pond (1.4 mi point of Trout Pond Trail). For trailhead access to this location, see the trailhead directions for the Trout Pond Trail (trail 107).◀

The blue-marked Mud Pond Trail heads generally W from the trail jct. at the N end of Trout Pond (0.0 mi). It crosses the inlet of Trout Pond and passes the former lean-to site. A spur path L beyond the inlet bridge leads 0.1 mi to the relocated lean-to. Red snowmobile trail markers are also present on the main trail, which ascends about 450 ft to the top of Cherry Ridge, swinging S and reaching a height of land at 0.8 mi. The trail now descends on moderate to gradual grades, swinging W through a young hardwood forest to a three-way jct. at 1.9 mi near Mud Pond.

To the L (E), the blue-marked snowmobile trail (ascending briefly) descends steadily through an attractive conifer forest for 1 mi to rejoin the Trout Pond Trail at its 0.1 mi point. This connector trail allows for a loop hike via Trout Pond and Mud Pond trails. (Turn R at this lower jct. to Russell Brook Rd. trailhead in 0.1 mi.)

The Mud Pond Trail (also blue-marked) turns R (W). At 2 mi, a spur path L leads to Mud Pond, passing a camping area. Continuing W past the spur path, the trail ascends gradually to a jct. at 2.3 mi. The marked trail turns sharply L; a snowmobile trail continues W (straight).

Heading S, the trail stays on mostly level terrain some distance from Mud Pond. As the route swings SE, the long descent to Russell Brook Rd. begins. Approaching the outlet brook from Mud Pond, the route again heads due S on attractive terrain high above the brook. The trail unexpectedly ascends before the final descent to a trail register at 3.9 mi; the trailhead is 100 yd farther. This Russell Brook Rd. trailhead is 1.4 mi S of the Trout Pond Trail parking area.

🐾 Distances: To height of land on Cherry Ridge, 0.8 mi; to jct. near Mud Pond, 1.9 mi (turning L at jct. leads to Trout Pond Trail, 2.9 mi total); to R, spur path to Mud Pond, 2 mi; to snowmobile trail, 2.3 mi; to trail register at Russell Brook Rd., 3.9 mi (6.2 km).

Beaver Kill Range from Graham Mt. Tony Versandi

Beaver Kill–Willowemoc Creek Section

Here are the waters for which the great trout fisherman Theodore Gordon invented the dry fly.

✳ Trails in winter: These trails are somewhat isolated and thus not as utilized in winter as they might be otherwise. The trails of the Beech Mountain Nature Preserve, the Mongaup Pond, and Frick Pond region, and the Willowemoc Wild Forest adjacent to them are especially good for skiing.

Below is a list of suggested hikes in this region.

SHORT HIKE
Frick Pond Loop: 2.15 mi (3.4 km). Though mostly away from the pond, the loop combines three trails to offer several bridges, a boardwalk, a magnificent conifer forest, mossy wetland, and meadows. (Retrace at Times Square to avoid wet ground on last leg; 2.3 mi round-trip.)

MODERATE HIKES
Quick Lake Trail to Junkyard Jct. to Flynn Trail, to return: 6.5 mi (10.4 km).

HARDER HIKES
Mongaup Pond Loop: 9.8 mi (15.7 km). From Mongaup Pond State Campground, combine three trails up Mongaup Mt. and Beaver Kill Ridge, down the Long Pond–Beaver Kill Ridge Trail and back via the Mongaup-Willowemoc Trail to the pond, for a strenuous but marvelous woods walk. No vistas, but a nice variety of trail experience.

Trail Described		*Total Miles (one way)*		*Page*
109	Long Pond–Beaver Kill Ridge Trail (Southern Section)	4.2	(6.7 km)	218
110	Long Pond–Beaver Kill Ridge Trail (Northern Section)	3.0	(4.8 km)	219
111	Neversink-Hardenburgh Trail	7.8	(12.5 km)	220
112	Mongaup-Hardenburgh Trail	7.3	(11.7 km)	222
113	Mongaup-Willowemoc Trail	3.2	(5.1 km)	224
	Frick Pond Region			225
114	Quick Lake Trail (via Frick Pond)	7.2	(11.5 km)	225
115	Flynn Trail	3.3	(5.3 km)	228
116	Big Rock Trail	1.6	(2.6 km)	229
117	Loggers Loop Trail	1.8	(2.9 km)	230

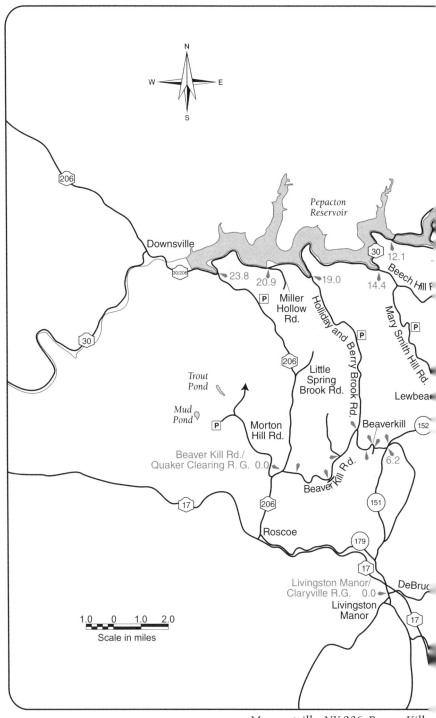

Margaretville–NY 206, Beaver Kill

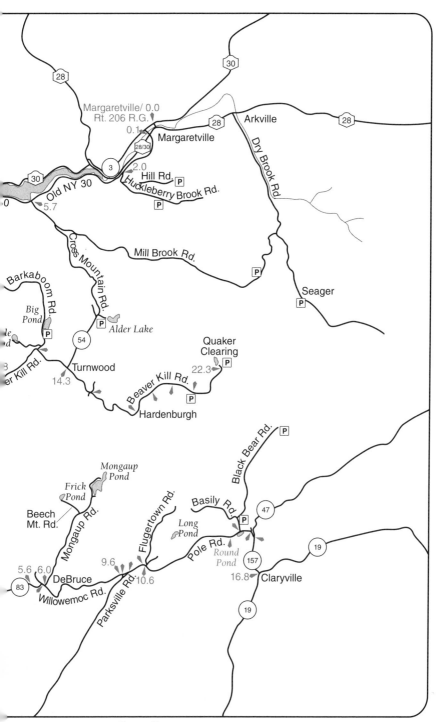

Livingston Manor to Claryville

Beaver Kill–Willowemoc Creek Section **217**

Route Guide for Livingston Manor to Claryville (see map pp. 216–217)

Mileage W to E	Description	Mileage E to W
0.0	Livingston Manor, jct. Old NY 17 (CR 179) and DeBruce Rd (CR 81) DeBruce Rd. runs NE under NY 17 and passes Willowemoc Motel.	16.8
2.4	Cross bridge; DeBruce Rd. is Sullivan CR 81/82.	14.4
5.6	Sign for DeBruce if driving E; CR 81/82 now Sullivan CR 83 if driving E.	11.2
6	Cross bridge.	10.8
6.05	Road N is Mongaup Rd.; Mongaup Pond Public Campgrounds 3.9 mi on this road. DeBruce Rd. is now Willowemoc Rd. if driving E.	10.75
9.6	Large bridge over Willowemoc Creek in hamlet of Willowemoc	7.2
9.7	Jct. road S to Parksville; continue E	7.1
10.5	Willowemoc Campsite	6.3
10.6	Bridge over Fir Brook; jct. at E end of bridge. If going to Long Pond–Beaver Kill Ridge Trail, turn N at jct. and immediately bear L again onto a second road. The second road is Flugertown Rd.; Willowemoc Rd. is now called Pole Rd.	6.2
14.2	Sullivan/Ulster County line	2.6
14.7	Round Pond on S side of road	2.1
14.9	Jct. Turn R onto Round Pond Rd. if driving E; turn L onto Pole Rd. if driving W.	1.9
15.5	Jct. Round Pond Rd. and West Branch Rd. (CR 47). Turn R if driving E; turn L if driving W. (Unmarked Round Pond Rd. makes a 180-degree turn uphill.) Ulster CR 47 becomes Sullivan CR 157 near Claryville.	1.3
16.8	Claryville bridge over E Branch of Neversink River; jct. CR 157 and CR 19 (Claryville Rd.)	0.0

109 Long Pond–Beaver Kill Ridge Trail
(Southern Section, Black Bear/Basily Rd. to Flugertown Rd.)

Trails Illustrated Map 755: E9 / Map 143, Southern Catskills: G8, trail LB

The entire Long Pond–Beaver Kill Ridge Trail runs 7.3 mi from the jct. of Black Bear Rd. and Basily Rd., near Round Pond, to a jct. with the Mongaup-Hardenburgh Trail (trail 112) on Beaver Kill Ridge. The description given below is the section from the Black Bear/Basily Rd. jct. to Flugertown Rd. (See Long Pond–Beaver Kill Ridge Trail [trail 110] for description from Flugertown Rd. to Beaver Kill Ridge.)

▶Trailhead: Trail access is off Round Pond Rd., accessed from the E from Ulster CR 47/Sullivan CR 157 on an unmarked hairpin turn to the N, easily missed coming from the N. It climbs to Round Pond. (This hairpin turn is just N of the Sullivan County–Ulster County line.) (See Route Guide, p. 218.) Bear R onto Black Bear Rd. at a fork 0.6 mi from CR 47, for 0.2 mi to the Black Bear/Basily Rd. jct. From Livingston Manor (see Route Guide, p. 218), at Round Pond turn L onto Black Bear Rd. for 0.2 mi to the jct., with a large parking area. ◀

Trail miles to Long Pond and Flugertown Rd. are calculated from the Black Bear/Basily Rd. jct. parking area (0.0 mi). Basily Rd. goes to a T-intersection at 2 mi; turn L to a final parking area at 2.4 mi—it is possible to drive this far, depending on your vehicle, road conditions, and weather.

At 2.4 mi, a barrier indicates private property. The red-marked trail SW follows a sometimes-wet old road to the Long Pond Lean-to spur trail at 3.1 mi. (It is 0.4 mi to the lean-to, and another 150 yd down steeply to the pond, which is not good for swimming.)

At 3.5 mi, the trail reaches the jct. of the old spur path to Long Pond. (The path leads L 0.25 mi to Long Pond, passing the former lean-to site. A snowmobile trail continues from that site.)

Continue on the red-marked trail, avoiding side paths. The trail descends quite steeply and at 4.1 mi reaches a bridge over a channel of the Willowemoc Creek. The trail then crosses a footbridge over the main creek and reaches Flugertown Rd. at 4.2 mi. To continue on the trail, turn R 0.05 mi to a DEC sign, L, before reaching a vehicular bridge.

(If hiking to Long Pond from Flugertown Rd., the only DEC sign visible at roadside is where the trail heads N toward Beaver Kill Ridge [trail 110]. The trail S to Long Pond [trail 109] is 0.05 mi S of that sign; it crosses Willowemoc Creek on a footbridge past a hemlock glade. If you have reached the vehicular bridge at about 2.5 mi on Flugertown Rd., you have passed both trailheads.)

𝍫 Distances: To Basily Rd. T-jct., 2 mi; to barrier and possible parking, 2.4 mi; to spur trail to Long Pond Lean-to, 3.1 mi; to old spur trail to Long Pond, 3.5 mi; to Flugertown Rd., 4.2 mi (6.7 km).

110 Long Pond–Beaver Kill Ridge Trail
(Northern Section, Flugertown Rd. to Beaver Kill Ridge)

Trails Illustrated Map 755: F8 / Map 143, Southern Catskills: F8, trail LB

This description begins at the 4.2 mi point of the Long Pond–Beaver Kill Ridge Trail (trail 109). It climbs to Beaver Kill Ridge, where it joins the Mongaup-Hardenburgh Trail (trail 112). It can be used in combination with other trails to make enjoyable backpack trips.

▶Trailhead: The trailhead is on the W side of Flugertown Rd., 2.5 mi N from Willowemoc Rd. (See Route Guide, p. 218.)◀

The trail leaves a DEC signpost (0.0 mi) and follows red foot trail markers as well as orange snowmobile trail markers up a gradual to moderate grade. The route levels at 0.2 mi, then resumes a moderate ascent at 0.25 mi, leveling as it approaches a jct. at 0.4 mi. Here, the Long Pond–Beaver Kill Ridge Trail turns N (R), leaving the snowmobile trail, still following red markers. (The L fork, with yellow markers, is the continuance of the Mongaup-Willowemoc Trail [trail 113].)

The level red-marked trail follows an old woods road, gradually ascending to 0.7 mi, where it begins a downgrade to 0.85 mi in a hemlock woods; avoid a woods road R. The almost flat, wide route swings NE and passes through attractive deciduous forest. Note the maidenhair fern.

The route becomes a footpath, reaching a wet area at 1.2 mi, beyond which the trail heads NW up a moderate grade through a rocky landscape. In a series of pitches, it ascends a spur of Beaver Kill Ridge, levels at 1.5 mi, and then steeply ascends a large ledge.

At 1.8 mi, the trail reaches the crest of the spur at 2754 ft elevation, turns N, and follows the spur crest to Beaver Kill Ridge. The grade eases considerably. At 2.2 mi the trail nears a large drop-off at a cliff edge a little way off-trail, L; rocks to sit on invite a break to enjoy views of the open woods below.

With only a few short pitches, the hiker can relax and enjoy this excellent forest. In several places, the trail is essentially flat. Partially blocked views can be seen off the E side of the ridge at 2.9 mi. At a T-jct. in a small clearing at 3 mi, the trail joins the Mongaup-Hardenburgh Trail (trail 112; Mongaup Pond is 3.7 mi W; Beaver Kill Rd. is 3.6 mi N). Ascent from Flugertown Rd. to this jct. is 1025 ft.

🥾 Distances: To Mongaup Pond–Willowemoc Trail jct., 0.4 mi; to wet area, 1.2 mi; to crest of spur, 1.8 mi; to Mongaup-Hardenburgh Trail, 3 mi (4.8 km).

111 Neversink-Hardenburgh Trail

Trails Illustrated Map 755: F10 / Map 143, Southern Catskills: G8, trail NH

This trail follows a good dirt road N near the West Branch of the Neversink, skirts the Beaver Kill Range to the E staying on contour at 2500–2600 ft, and then swings W into the valley of the Beaver Kill. It progresses from a drivable road for 3.1 mi, to one possibly too rough for the normal car, to a very pleasant woods road. How far one drives along it depends on the vehicle, the weather, and the judgment of the driver.

Trail descriptions are given from the DEC parking area on Black Bear Rd., since that is the farthest point at which one can legally park.

▶Trailhead: See trailhead description above (trail 109) to get to the Black Bear/Basily Rd. jct. where there is a large parking area, R. Black Bear Rd. bears R from this fork. There is an unmarked pullout on state land partway along the road on the R; beyond a hunting lodge pullout at 3.1 mi from Round Pond Rd., the road enters state land and becomes a narrow Seasonal Limited-Use route (0.0 mi).◄

Continuing N along Black Bear Rd., following yellow DEC trail markers, there is a final parking area on the R in 0.3 mi. The route reenters private land, passing the edge of a clearing that has a large camp L at 0.5 mi. The road returns to the forest at the far side of the clearing, at an elevation near 2575 ft. Soon back on state land, the absence of vehicles results in a very nice woods road for hiking.

The trail makes a sharp horseshoe turn, crossing an attractive tributary of Fall Brook at 0.7 mi. The way is enjoyable, with gradual grades. It crosses another small brook at 1.6 mi, ascends briefly, and reaches Fall Brook Lean-to L, at 1.85 mi.

This lean-to and privy are in excellent condition. A good spring at 2 mi provides water. Here, 40 ft L of the trail, a pipe emerges from the ground and gives a steady flow across the trail. The trail is nearly level as it leaves the Neversink watershed and drops into the Beaver Kill valley at 2.3 mi. A bench mark indicates that the elevation is 2653 ft. Several drainages can make this a wet section; trailwork with large flat rock is evident.

The route becomes more a path, having been a woods road to this point, skirts a wet area, and then at 2.65 mi reaches a beaver pond with a grassy beaver lodge and dam. Across the water are views of Doubletop Mt. NE and Graham Mt. N. Skirting the W side of the pond in a muddy section, the path continues through a narrow valley. At 2.8 mi, signs show the border of Big Indian Wilderness Area coming into Balsam Lake Mt. Wild Forest.

The upper Beaver Kill is a rippling brook that grows in size as the trail descends to the lowlands; there is a small island. The hiker must cross to the N bank on wet and slippery rock at 2.95 mi. This section is picturesque, with small ripplets of water singing out and green mossy boulders providing a feast for the eyes.

At 3.2 mi, an old wooden bridge goes L over the stream to private property; the trail continues straight through a small clearing on a high-clearance vehicle road. At 3.3 mi, a designated campsite is indicated, some 200 ft off to the R, with a brook at its back edge. This is an ideal location for camping away from the trail. Another designated camping area is at 3.8 mi at L by the stream.

The woods road is now wider, but still pleasant to walk. It crosses Tunis

Neversink River. Moonray Schepart

Pond outlet bridge at 3.9 mi and soon thereafter, at 4 mi, the relocated section of trail turns R (N) from the woods road. It crosses a brook on rocks and then winds with ups and downs through hemlock. Vly Pond Outlet is crossed on stepping stones S of Vly Pond, but this crossing is not precarious. The route crosses a woods road at 4.6 mi and then passes over the new Gulf of Mexico Brook footbridge at 4.7 mi.

A gradual ascent begins at 4.75 mi up a low ridge. Large trees are prominent in this section. Topping the ridge at 5.25 mi, the trail turns and descends to 5.75 mi amid hemlock, where it crosses Black Brook on a good bridge. The route ascends a woods road, passes a trail register, and reaches the Balsam Lake Mt. trailhead parking area at 6.2 mi. This is located at the end of Beaver Kill Rd. The trail officially continues SE along Beaver Kill Rd. to the Hardenburgh trailhead parking area on the N side of the road at 7.8 mi.

🐾 Distances: To crossing of tributary, 0.7 mi; to Fall Brook Lean-to, 1.85 mi; to watershed divide, 2.3 mi; to Beaver Kill crossing, 2.95 mi; to split from woods road, 4 mi; to Gulf of Mexico Brook bridge, 4.7 mi; to Black Brook bridge, 5.8 mi; to Balsam Lake Mt. parking area, 6.2 mi (9.9 km). To Mongaup-Hardenburgh Trail parking area, 7.8 mi.

112 Mongaup-Hardenburgh Trail

Trails Illustrated Map 755: F8 / Map 143, Southern Catskills: F8, trail MH

The trail climbs Mongaup Mt. and then goes E and N along Beaver Kill Ridge before reaching Beaver Kill Rd. near Quaker Clearing. Few views reward the hiker until the leaves have fallen off the trees in autumn. However, as a woods ramble, it is "par excellence." Spotting vehicles requires extensive driving, so the hiker may wish to use just part of this trail for a loop hike, in conjunction with other trails.

▶Trailhead: Trail access is off DeBruce Rd. 6.05 mi E of Livingston Manor. (See Route Guide, p. 218.) Turn N on Mongaup Rd. and drive 2.8 mi to the jct. of Mongaup Pond Rd. Turn R here for 1.1 mi to the Mongaup Pond Public Campground tollbooth. Bear L from the tollbooth for another 1.1 mi to a T-jct. at Areas G–F. Turn L into Area G.

The trailhead is on the N side of the paved G Loop Rd. Travel about 0.3 mi into Area G to the new parking area, R, up a slope. Walk back along the road to the trailhead at the barrier rocks (0.0 mi)◀.

Follow blue hiking trail markers and red snowmobile markers to a pond in 80 yd. The grassy perimeter road swings L along the shoreline of Mongaup Pond, reaching a jct. at 0.3 mi at a DEC sign. The trail heads L away from the pond; the snowmobile trail continues straight. The route is near a small brook for a short distance before turning L again at an unmarked jct. at 0.45 mi.

The blue-marked trail climbs gradual grades with short moderate pitches through a beech-birch forest to 1.2 mi, where an extensive section of blowdown, caused by Hurricane Floyd, changed the character of the trail. Berry bushes abound on the now-sunny hillside.

The trail enters a hemlock woods and the pitches become steeper. The path reaches the wooded middle summit (2980 ft) of Mongaup Mt. at 1.8 mi, having ascended 800 ft from Mongaup Pond.

The footpath turns E and shortly reaches large ledges to the L, where the route begins a series of moderate and steep downgrades to a small col at 2.3 mi. Gradual grades ascend to scenic mossy ledges at 2.4 mi, where the route pitches up, passing a deep cleft between sections of ledge and an overhang.

Varying gradual and moderate grades reach the flat E summit of 2928 ft Mongaup Mt. at 3 mi, then long pleasant downgrades lead to the next low spot of the ridge at 3.3 mi in an area filled with huge ferns. At 3.4 mi, the trail ascends gradually and then very steeply, easing just before a jct. at 3.7 mi near the W high point on Beaver Kill Ridge (3062 ft). Ascent from the col is 380 ft.

The red-marked Long Pond–Beaver Kill Ridge Trail (trail 110) enters from the R at the jct. clearing. (This trail runs 3 mi to Flugertown Rd.) The blue-marked Mongaup-Hardenburgh Trail continues ENE; the trail ascends to the high point (3062 ft) at 3.7 mi, and then descends steeply to 3.8 mi. A good view E can be seen from a ledge at 4 mi. Descent continues and the route becomes indistinct as it goes through a rocky area, so care is required to follow trail markers.

A col in the ridgeline is reached at 4.4 mi and ascent from this low point begins at 4.7 mi, steepening to the middle high point of Beaver Kill Ridge, a flat summit (3224 ft), from 5.2 mi to 5.3 mi. The trail descends to a narrow ridge and then climbs to a broad, flat section at 5.4 mi, where a spring sometimes flows. Caves, boulders, and mossy ledges provide scenery at 5.8 mi.

A moderately steep grade reaches a high point at 6.2 mi. Ledges off the trail offer views. The trail turns NE and descends slightly before following a nearly flat ridge from 6.4 mi to 6.5 mi, then steeply descends to another level section at 6.7 mi. Then the steep descent continues until the trail swings R, becoming level at 6.9 mi. At 7.1 mi, large rocks and ledges adorn the trailside.

Private property signs mark the Balsam Lake Angler's Club at 7.2 mi. The 150-ft-wide Beaver Kill corridor is privately owned. Fishing is strictly prohibited. A long suspension bridge at 7.25 mi crosses the Beaver Kill and the trail returns to state land. A short upgrade brings the trail to the DEC signpost and parking area at Beaver Kill Rd. at 7.3 mi. (The Balsam Lake Mt. [Quaker Clearing] parking area is 1.6 mi E; Little Pond Public Campground is 7.6 mi W.)

🥾 Distances: To jct. at end of Mongaup Pond, 0.3 mi; to middle summit of Mongaup Mt., 1.8 mi; to Mongaup Mt. E summit, 3 mi; to Long Pond–Beaver Kill Ridge Trail jct., 3.7 mi; to middle high point, 5.2 mi; to E high point, 6.2 mi; to Beaver Kill suspension bridge, 7.25 mi; to Beaver Kill Rd., 7.3 mi (11.7 km). It is 1.6 mi. to end of Beaver Kill Rd.

113 Mongaup-Willowemoc Trail

Trails Illustrated Map 755: F8 / Map 144, Western Catskills: F8, trail MW and Map 143, Southern Catskills: F8, trail MW

This trail runs from the Mongaup Pond Public Campground to the Long Pond–Beaver Kill Ridge Trail (trail 110/109). It can be combined with that trail and the Neversink-Hardenburgh Trail (trail 111) or Mongaup-Hardenburgh Trail (trail 112), and from them, access can be obtained to the Balsam Lake Mt. and Mill Brook Ridge Trails to the Delaware Ridge Trail system to make multiday backpack trips.

▶Trailhead: Access is via Mongaup Pond Public Campground. (See Route Guide, p. 218.) From the campground tollbooth, bear R toward Area B and almost immediately turn L into the parking lot for the beach and picnic area. Park here.

Hike 0.2 mi to Area B, turn R at site 38, and follow the red-marked snowmobile trail from the rear of site 38. When this connector trail reaches the camp perimeter snowmobile trail at a T-jct., turn L. Follow the snowmobile trail N approximately 0.8 mi to the Mongaup-Willowemoc Trail jct.◀

The Mongaup-Willowemoc Trail, R, follows yellow trail markers E (0.0 mi). A steady, gradual incline ascends to 0.6 mi, where the terrain nearly levels to 0.8 mi, as the trail passes through the low point of a N-S ridge. A moderate downgrade descends to a small bridge at 1.2 mi and reaches Butternut Jct. at 1.3 mi. (The Wild Azalea Trail heads S.) The route levels and then traverses rolling terrain before crossing a large wooden bridge over Butternut Brook at 1.7 mi.

Across the bridge, the route immediately turns R at a T-jct. This is an attractive section, with the rippling brook, mosses, and rocks holding the hiker's attention as the trail follows the top of a high bank above the brook.

Swinging L, the path continues through an interesting hemlock grove and then ascends gradually to cross another small bridge at 2.3 mi. Gradual climbing resumes and the trail crosses a wide woods road at 2.5 mi. (It runs from Flugertown Rd. N to Sand Pond, which is privately owned.)

Soon heading N on level ground, the trail comes to the Long Pond–Beaver Kill Ridge Trail (trail 110/109) jct. at 2.8 mi. Here, the Mongaup-Willowemoc Trail and the Long Pond–Beaver Kill Ridge Trail merge, following both yellow and red trail markers. Bear R and head E. (The Long Pond–Beaver Kill Ridge Trail runs L 2.6 mi N to join the Mongaup-Hardenburgh Trail [trail 112] for a nice loop back to Mongaup Pond.)

The level trail soon descends moderately, then climbs gradually to 3 mi. From here the route descends on varying grades to Flugertown Rd. at 3.2 mi. (The continuation of the Long Pond–Beaver Kill Ridge Trail [trail 109] is 90 yd SW [R] on Flugertown Rd.)

🐾 Distances: To ridge crossing, 0.6 mi; to Butternut Jct., 1.3 mi; to Butternut Brook, 1.7 mi; to woods road, 2.5 mi; to Long Pond–Beaver Kill Ridge Trail jct., 2.8 mi; to Flugertown Rd., 3.2 mi (5.1 km).

Fern woods near Mongaup Mt. Joanne Hihn

FRICK POND REGION

Trails Illustrated Map 755: F7 / Map 144, Western Catskills: E8

The Frick Pond trailhead provides access to a 13.8 mi network of trails in the Willowemoc Wild Forest. A series of old roads were seeded with grasses and now are wonderfully open routes for easy day trips, backpacking, and especially cross-country skiing. While there are few distant views, the ponds, flora, and open routes are enjoyable to travel.

Each of the trail descriptions in this network has additional information for skiing, provided in the "Trails in Winter" section. (Also see map, p. 226.)

▶Trailhead: Refer to the 6.05 mi (W-E) point in the Route Guide, p. 218. Turn N onto Mongaup Rd. and drive 2.7 mi to a road jct. where there is a Mongaup Public Campsite signpost. Turn L onto Beech Mountain Rd. and travel 0.4 mi to a double parking area at the Frick Pond trailhead. (Do not travel onto the posted private property beyond the parking area.) There are two trailheads (Flynn and Quick Lake) on opposite sides of this road, a trail register, and an exhibit board.◀

114 Quick Lake Trail *(via Frick Pond)*

Trails Illustrated Map 755: E7 / Map 144, Western Catskills: E8, trail QL

Quick Lake is a destination well suited for an overnight backpacking trip or as part of a long loop in conjunction with the Flynn Trail (trail 115). It follows old woods roads and has some challenging long grades past Junkyard Jct.

Frick Pond Region

226 *Catskill Trails*

▶Trailhead: Refer to the trailhead information under Frick Pond Region (see p. 225).◀

The Quick Lake Trail follows red DEC trail markers from the NW corner of the parking area (0.0 mi). After descending gradually, the route reaches a trail register at 0.15 mi on a wide woods road where the trail turns L. The nearly level roadway heads N through occasional wet spots, reaching a signpost at the first jct. with the Loggers Loop Trail (trail 117) at 0.45 mi. The Loggers Loop Trail bears R.

The Quick Lake Trail continues straight ahead along the S edge of a meadow and then drops down a moderate grade. There are good views of Frick Pond during the descent to the pond's shore at 0.5 mi. Here, the route turns L and crosses the pond outlet on a wide 50-ft-long bridge. It bears R, climbing a small grade some distance from the shore through attractive large trees, including tall white pines.

Just after a second small bridge, the route reaches the Big Rock Trail (trail 116) jct. at 0.7 mi. The Quick Lake Trail continues straight ahead to the NNW. The surrounding terrain is a fern-filled open woods; a pretty mossy drainage is L of the trail. The grade gradually ascends with occasional level stretches. The route enters a small hemlock grove at 0.9 mi, crosses a stream at 1.2 mi, and comes to a meadow at 1.3 mi.

The second jct. with Loggers Loop Trail (trail 117) is at 1.5 mi at Ironwheel Jct. The iron wheels and axle of an old wagon are found here. The trail leaves the jct. heading S, and assumes a moderate upgrade. Bear R at a jct. at 1.7 mi where an arrow sign indicates the way toward Junkyard Jct. (A snowmobile trail goes L to Quick Lake.)

The route has curved to the NW. Though the woods road changes direction often, its general direction is N on moderate and gradual grades to a height of land at 2.5 mi. The elevation is 2750 ft, a gain of 610 ft from the trailhead.

After a slight descent, the route bears R at an arrow sign at 2.55 mi and ascends gradually. It then slightly descends, passing a rock ledge shaped like a tank at 2.8 mi and reaching Junkyard Jct. at 3.2 mi. (The Flynn Trail [trail 115] enters this jct. from the E.)

From this jct., the Quick Lake Trail winds NW 150 ft to where the actual junkyard is found. A mostly level woods road leads to what is generally referred to as Western Vista at 4 mi. The distant view W, across the Shin Creek Valley and beyond, is particularly impressive in autumn, when multicolored leaves cover the distant ridge.

From here the trail loses about 800 ft in elevation before reaching Quick Lake. Gradual and moderate grades descend SSW. A four-way jct. with an arrow sign points the way to Quick Lake at 4.3 mi, where the trail turns R and descends to the W. Soon, the route bears R at another jct. and then passes straight through a third and fourth jct. Follow trail markers carefully. Finally, at 4.9 mi the route turns abruptly L at yet another jct., where a "Trail to Quick Lake" sign with directional arrow is found.

Following a level stretch over bare rock on the roadway at 5.3 mi, the trail swings N and NW. Then the roadway curves W and descends with moderate grades in a very widely cleared section at 5.6 mi. The trail makes a sweeping R turn NNW and continues descending with lessening steepness, finally leveling and turning W and SW with more gradual downgrades. Passing by a side road at the L at 6.8 mi, the trail continues a winding descent until it reaches Quick Lake.

At 7.1 mi, a side path L leads steeply down a slope to the shore of the lake, but the trail continues straight ahead, leveling at its closest point to Quick Lake at 7.15 mi. (The trail continues to a yellow barrier gate at 7.2 mi.)

Quick Lake is 125 ft off the trail and has a few fire rings, a picnic table, and new lean-to. Beavers have cut many trees around the shoreline.

❄ Trail in winter: Quick Lake Trail is excellent for intermediate skiing as far as Western Vista at 4 mi. From this point to Quick Lake requires expert skills and good stamina.

🐾 Distances: To first Loggers Loop Trail jct., 0.45 mi; to Big Rock Trail jct., 0.7 mi; to Ironwheel Jct., 1.5 mi; to height of land, 2.5 mi; to Junkyard Jct., 3.2 mi; to Western Vista, 4 mi; to wide downgrade, 5.6 mi; to barrier gate, 7.2 mi (11.5 km).

115 Flynn Trail

Trails Illustrated Map 755: F7 / Map 144, Western Catskills: E8, trail FY

This trail gradually increases in vertical ascent until 610 ft of elevation has been gained over its 3.3 mi of distance to the Quick Lake Trail (trail 114) at Junkyard Jct. In part, it follows a wide gravel road to Hodge Pond in the Beech Mt. Nature Preserve and then a more grassy woods roads to Junkyard Jct.

▶Trailhead: Refer to the trailhead information under Frick Pond Region (see p. 225).◀

Mark Schaefer

The Flynn Trail leaves the E edge of the road (0.0 mi) opposite the parking area, following blue DEC trail markers. It skirts the E side of a private home through woods and then rejoins the road, which is now state land, at 0.1 mi. There is a barrier at L.

The trail turns R (N) and runs up a steady grassy road grade. The route levels at 0.4 mi, but soon resumes climbing. The road curves NNE and views are seen to the NW at 0.7 mi. Large ledges and an overhang are interesting at 0.9 mi. The trail levels briefly at 1 mi and 1.1 mi. (Avoid side roads.) The Big Rock

Trail (trail 116) jct. at 1.7 mi is in another level zone. (The Big Rock Trail drops off steeply to the L.) The snowmobile trail to Mongaup Pond is to the R.

The level stretch curves W. The trail reaches another unmarked jct. at 2 mi, just after passing the boundary of Beech Mt. Nature Preserve. The trail turns L and descends steadily, entering a large meadow at the edge of Hodge Pond at 2.4 mi. (No camping is permitted in the preserve or at Hodge Pond. Public transit is granted only for use of the DEC trail and for fishing at Hodge Pond. Please do not disturb any scientific equipment you may see, since long-term studies are in progress.) Follow the road past the pond outlet and up a gradual slope. Hodge Pond can be seen very well 100 yd downslope R at 2.55 mi.

Continuing up the roadway, the route passes a series of small fields. At direction arrow signs at 2.7 mi, avoid the grassy lane that forks R. Follow the L side of the fork uphill, where it soon curves L (NW) at 2.8 mi.

Increasing grades lead to another jct. and the trail swings L again with arrow signs at 2.9 mi. The route continues on generally level terrain, sometimes on flat rock, until Junkyard Jct. at 3.3 mi. Here, the Quick Lake Trail (trail 114) enters from Frick Pond to the SW and leaves for Quick Lake to the NW.

❃ Trail in winter: This is an excellent intermediate ski trail that can be combined with other trails to make a very nice outing.

❅ Distances: To barrier, 0.1 mi; to Big Rock Trail jct., 1.7 mi; to Hodge Pond, 2.4 mi; to first arrow jct., 2.7 mi; to Quick Lake Trail at Junkyard Jct., 3.3 mi (5.3 km).

116 Big Rock Trail

Trails Illustrated Map 755: F7 / Map 144, Western Catskills: E8, trail BR

This is a short, steep trail until it reaches Times Square jct. From there to the Quick Lake Trail (trail 114) jct., it becomes a flat walk in what is perhaps the most attractive part of the whole region. Most people will hike only this second part in conjunction with other trails, but a few stalwarts may combine it with sections of the Flynn Trail (trail 115) and Quick Lake Trail (trail 114) to make a larger loop.

▶Trailhead: Trailheads for this trail are at the 1.7 mi point of the Flynn Trail (trail 115) and the 0.7 mi point of the Quick Lake Trail (trail 114).◀

Following yellow trail markers, the Big Rock Trail leaves the Flynn Trail (trail 115) and quickly loses elevation to the W. Bear R at a pair of woods road forks at 0.05 mi and 0.1 mi as the trail turns NNW.

Moderate grades become steep at 0.3 mi and turn SSE. Only a few level zones break the pattern as the winding trail descends through deciduous forest. A big swing W occurs at 1 mi, before the woods road levels off at a four-way jct. with the Loggers Loop Trail (trail 117) called Times Square, at 1.1 mi. There has been a loss of 600 ft in elevation in this 1.1 mi distance.

From here, the character of the terrain changes radically and the walk becomes a flat stroll through exceptional woodland. Leaving Times Square, the trail heads SW through deciduous forest, then enters a magnificent hemlock grove at 1.25 mi. Ferns, mosses, and other vegetation will occupy your curiosity. Two attractive bridges cross over inlets of Frick Pond before a 285-ft-long raised boardwalk at 1.45 mi traverses a small wetland area. The trail ends at the Quick Lake Trail (trail 114) at 1.6 mi.

❄ Trail in winter: Only very skilled skiers should attempt the section of trail from the Flynn Trail to Times Square. The route here is quite wide but becomes progressively steeper over its course. The section from Times Square to the Quick Lake Trail is suitable for nearly all skiers and can be combined with other trails to make a delightful loop.

🚶 Distances: To steep zone, 0.3 mi; to Times Square, 1.1 mi; to raised boardwalk, 1.45 mi; to Quick Lake Trail jct., 1.6 mi (2.6 km).

117 Loggers Loop Trail

Trails Illustrated Map 755: F7 / Map 144, Western Catskills: E8, trail LL

This generally flat trail has a few easy grades and the route can be combined with the Quick Lake Trail (trail 114) to make what is sometimes called the Loggers Loop.

▶Trailhead: This trail may be accessed at jcts. along the Quick Lake Trail (trail 114) at 0.5 mi and 1.5 mi.◀

The trail bears R from the 0.5 mi point on the Quick Lake Trail, climbing a small grade. It then crosses an open field. Yellow trail markers guide you up a gradual grade at 0.1 mi on a wide woods road. The way levels and Frick Pond can be partially seen in the distance L through trees.

The trail passes through Times Square jct. (where it intersects the Big Rock Trail [trail 116]) at 0.55 mi without turning. The route is now a somewhat more narrow woods road that curves N as it climbs a moderate grade. Height of land is at 0.8 mi amongst black cherry and yellow birch.

At 1.3 mi, the route bends NW and eventually W. At a woods road fork at 1.4 mi, the trail continues L (SW). (The R fork leads to a low shelf in an open field. A brook flows past the far edge of the clearing, making this a nice camping spot for backpackers.)

The L fork passes beneath the low shelf and gradually descends. There is an interesting sedimentary rock outcrop at 1.7 mi. At Ironwheel Jct., at 1.8 mi, the trail rejoins the Quick Lake Trail.

❄ Trail in winter: This trail is suitable for skiers of nearly all levels of ability and can be combined with other trails to make interesting loop routes.

🚶 Distances: To Times Square, 0.55 mi; to height of land, 0.8 mi; to Quick Lake Trail jct., 1.8 mi (2.9 km). 🍃

Extended and Challenging Opportunities

Fine opportunities for both extended and challenging outings exist in the Catskills. Extended trips in particular are often overlooked, because the extensive road network of the Catskills makes day trips possible in almost any section. This guidebook is designed to describe trips found within the same local road network. Consequently, trips that overlap chapters can be difficult to discern.

One of the purposes of this chapter is to provide complete sequencing of extended outings for the hiker. Where an extended outing overlaps more than one guidebook chapter, the sections are listed with mileages. The hiker should refer to each separate chapter for a description of the specific trail section.

Different types of challenges require different skills, degrees of physical stamina, and experience. Enjoyment, appreciation, aesthetics, and self-renewal are fundamental parts of the "recreating" involved in recreation. These are best obtained when the outing is commensurate with the hiker's abilities. Sometimes, adding a day to the length of a trip or knowing when to quit a bushwhack can make the difference between a marvelous experience and a bad memory. Good planning makes good trips.

LONG AND EXTENDED OUTINGS

Backpacking in the Catskills can be enhanced if plans anticipate certain factors. Trails in the Catskills tend to start climbing almost immediately and then level off on ridgetops, where they become long enjoyable rambles. Take your time in the early stages of a hike with a heavy backpack until the terrain levels.

Carry plenty of water; little water is found on the ridges. It will often be necessary to drop down off a ridge to lower elevations to a lean-to for water. Remember that camping is not permitted above 3500 ft elevation, except in winter. Carry a light rope; occasionally you may wish to lower a heavy pack down a short vertical section, rather than descend with it on your back.

Although trails frequently cross roads, don't expect to find general stores for supplies or immediate help in emergencies on these roads. Rural roads are generally isolated and houses are far apart.

The Devil's Path

The Devil's Path offers some of the most challenging and interesting hiking in the Catskills. It extends 24.6 mi from Platte Clove in the E to Spruceton Rd. in the W. In the process, it keeps to ridgelines, going over Indian Head, Twin, Sugarloaf, Plateau, most of Hunter, and West Kill mts. Descents drop into Jimmy Dolan Notch, Pecoy Notch, Mink Hollow, Stony Clove, and Diamond Notch. These descents can be dangerous when wet or icy. It is split by NY 214 and is described in four sections in this book, with Plateau summit and Diamond Notch as other break points:

Trail Sections		Miles
Trail 30	Eastern Section, E-W	10.2
Trail 31	Eastern Section, W-E	3.0
	Subtotal	13.2
Trail 33	Western Section, E-W	4.3
Trail 39	Western Section, W-E and E-W	7.1
	Subtotal	11.4
TOTAL		24.6 (39.4 km)

The trails of the extreme E section date back to Colonial days, but they were not officially designated as hiking trails until 1930. The Hunter Mt. section was built in 1935 and the West Kill section was constructed in 1973–74.

Escarpment Trail

The Escarpment Trail can be completed in a single day by fast hikers, but it is usually done in sections. It makes a splendid three-day backpack trip. The long ridge trail runs S-N from North-South Lake Public Campground to NY 23, near Windham. First development as a trail began in 1932 with the work of A. T. Shorey around North Lake. The N section was completed in 1967. In 1987 a portion of the original trail, which climbed past Kaaterskill Falls from NY 23A, was deleted. The trail now starts from the DEC parking area at Schutt Rd., just outside the main gate to North-South Lake Public Campground. Most of the trail is also the Long Path.

Sections of Escarpment Trail		Miles
Trail 10	Southern Section, N-S Lake–Dutcher Notch	11.6
Trail 9	Northern Section, Dutcher Notch–NY 23	12.6
TOTAL		24.2 (38.8 km)

Delaware Ridge Trail *(See Delaware Wild Forest Section)*
The Finger Lakes Trail
The Finger Lakes Trail connects with the Delaware Ridge Trail from the W. Road sections are being decreased yearly. Write to Finger Lakes Trail Conference, Inc., P.O. Box 18048, Rochester, NY 14618-0048 for maps and information.

Mill Brook Ridge Trail
The Mill Brook Ridge Trail has connected the Delaware Ridge Trail to the Dry Brook Ridge Trail and that, in turn, links directly with the Neversink-Hardenburgh Trail and the network of trails from Long Pond to Mongaup Pond and Quick Lake.

The Long Path

The Long Path is a dream transformed only partially into reality. In the 1930s, members of the Mohawk Valley Hiking Club proposed a "long path" that would compare to Vermont's Long Trail. It would start at the George Washington Bridge in New York City and end in the Adirondacks. For many years the trail went only to NY 23, N of Windham Peak. Renewed interest extended the trail to John Boyd Thacher State Park near Albany (1995). From time to time, new sections of trail are opened and a little more of the dream becomes reality.

The Long Path follows established trails in the Catskills. The list below is only for the Catskill sections covered in this guidebook. Those interested in trail descriptions for the whole Long Path should see the Guide to the Long Path, published by the New York–New Jersey Trail Conference.

Long Path sections S-N, as covered in this guide   *Miles*
Proposed route through Sundown Wild Forest replaces Upper Cherrytown Rd. section. (Awaits Unit Management Plan.)

Trail 63	Long Path (Upper Cherrytown Rd.–Peekamoose Rd.)	9.6
East on Peekamoose Rd.		0.5
Trail 62	Peekamoose-Table Trail (from Peekamoose Rd. to summit of Table Mt.)	4.7
Trail 65	Table-Peekamoose Trail (from Table Mt. summit to Phoenicia–East Branch Trail)	3.7
Trail 68	Phoenicia–East Branch Trail (jct. Table-Peekamoose Trail to Curtis-Ormsbee Trail)	1.7
Trail 69	Curtis-Ormsbee Trail	1.7
Trail 70	Slide-Cornell-Wittenberg Trail (jct. of Curtis-Ormsbee Trail to Cornell summit)	3.0
Trail 49	Wittenberg-Cornell-Slide Trail (Cornell summit to Woodland Valley Campground)	4.7
Woodland Valley to Phoenicia via Woodland Vally Rd., NY 28, NY 214		5.75
Phoenicia to Tremper Mt. trailhead via CR 40		2.0
Trail 51	Phoenicia Trail to Tremper Mt. summit	3.1
Trail 53	Warner Creek Trail from Tremper Mt. to Silver Hollow Notch (0.9 mi from Stony Clove via Notch Inn Rd.)	8.4
Trail 32	Daley Ridge Trail from Silver Hollow Notch to Plateau Mt. (0.4 mi from E [true] summit)	3.0
Trail 30	Devil's Path (Plateau Mt./Daley Ridge trail jct. to Overlook Trail)	8.4
Trail 24	Overlook Trail/Platte Clove Preserve Trail to Platte Clove Rd.	1.0
Platte Clove Rd. to Kaaterskill High Peak Trail		0.2
Trail 22	Kaaterskill High Peak Trail to Long Path jct.	3.3
Trail 19	Long Path Jct. to Malden Ave.	5.4

Malden Ave. to NY 23A		0.35
NY 23A E to Harding Rd. Trail		0.3
Trail 18	Harding Rd. Trail	2.7
Trail 17	Sleepy Hollow Trail (Harding Rd. Trail to Escarpment Trail)	0.15
Trail 10	Escarpment Trail (S Section)	8.9
Trail 9	Escarpment Trail (N Section)	12.6
TOTAL		95.15 (152 km)

Dry Brook Ridge Trail

The Dry Brook Ridge Trail runs from Margaretville to the Beaverkill Valley. This long trail has relatively easy hiking once Pakatakan Mt. ridge is reached. It is 13.7 mi (22 km) long. It connects with the Delaware Ridge Trail network via the Balsam Lake Mt. Trail. From its southern terminus, it connects via either the Neversink-Hardenburgh Trail or the Mongaup-Hardenburgh Trail with the network of trails from Long Pond to Mongaup Pond and Quick Lake.

Appendix I
Glossary of Terms

azimuth: A clockwise compass bearing swung from N.

bivouac: Camping in the open with improvised shelter or no shelter.

bushwhack: An off-trail hike, usually requiring compass and map.

cairn: A pile of stones that marks a summit or route.

chimney: A steep, narrow cleft or gully in the face of a mountain, usually by which the mountain may be ascended.

clove: A narrow valley.

cobble: A small stony peak on the side of a mountain.

col: A pass between adjacent peaks in a mountain chain or a low spot in a ridge.

corduroy: Logs laid side by side across a trail to assist travel in wet areas.

cripplebush: Thick, stunted growth at higher elevations.

dike: A band of different-colored rock, usually with straight, well-defined sides, formed when igneous rock is intruded into the existing rock. Dikes can manifest themselves either as gullies, if the dike rock is softer (as in the Colden Trap Dike), or as ridges.

duff: Partly decayed plant matter on the forest floor. Duff's ability to burn easily has started many forest fires.

fire ring: A circle of stones used as a site in which to build small fires.

herd path: An unmarked, unmaintained path created by hikers.

hollow: A small valley.

kill: A Dutch word for waterway, creek, or river.

lean-to: A three-sided shelter with an overhanging roof and one open side.

logging or lumber road: A crude road used to haul logs after lumbering.

notch: A narrow pass.

summit: The top of a mountain.

tote road: A better road constructed in connection with logging operations and used for hauling supplies. Often built with corduroy, many of these roads are still evident after eighty years and are often used as the route for present-day trails.

vlei (vly): A Dutch word for swamp or marsh (pronounced vly).

woods road: An old road, logging road, or tote road.

Appendix II
Catskill 100 Highest Peaks

This list of mountains suggests many possibilities for interesting climbs and explorations in the Catskill Forest Preserve and beyond. Some peaks are open to the public, while others are on or surrounded by private property. Always obtain permission from landowners before hiking these lands.

The thirty-five peaks exceeding 3500 feet in elevation are those that must be climbed for membership in the Catskill 3500 Club. (Winter climbs of four peaks are also required for membership, noted with a "W.") The club determined the criteria for a "peak": to be considered a separate summit, there must be at least a 250-foot drop between peaks or the peak must be at least one-half mile away from another.

The Catskill 67: A Hiker's Guide to the Catskill 100 Highest Peaks under 3500' by Alan Via complements this guidebook, offering route suggestions and information about additional Catskill peaks. As Via notes, the original list of ninety-eight peaks was determined by Father Ray Donahue; Mark Schaefer added the other four while verifying the accuracy of the first ninety-eight, and looking for numbers ninety-nine and one hundred.

An asterisk indicates a footnote, the number corresponding to the roster number. A "+" means the peak name is unofficial and not listed on U.S.G.S. maps. "Tr" indicates a marked, maintained trail to the summit. "C" means a canister is on an untrailed summit. An extra "T" indicates a summit fire tower. Five Catskill towers have been renovated within the Blue Line and most have summit stewards during summer months; 2740-foot Tremper Mt. is the unlisted fire tower peak.

No.	Name	Elev. (ft.)	Remarks	U.S.G.S. Topographic Map
1	Slide	4180	TrW	Peekamoose Mt.
2	Hunter	4040	TrT	Hunter
3	Black Dome	3980	Tr	Freehold
4	Blackhead	3940	TrW	Freehold
5	Thomas Cole	3940	Tr	Hensonville
6	West Kill	3880	Tr	Lexington
*7	Graham	3868		Seager
8	Cornell	3860	Tr	Phoenicia
9	Doubletop	3860	C	Seager
10	Table	3847	Tr	Peekamoose Mt.
11	Peekamoose	3843	Tr	Peekamoose Mt.
12	Plateau	3840	Tr	Hunter
*13	Sugarloaf	3800	Tr	Hunter
14	Wittenberg	3780	Tr	Phoenicia

+15	SW Hunter	3740	C		Hunter
16	Lone	3721	C		Peekamoose Mt.
*17	Balsam Lake	3720	TrT		Seager
18	Panther	3720	TrW		Shandaken
19	Big Indian	3700	C		Shandaken
20	Friday	3694	C		West Shokan
21	Rusk	3680	C		Lexington
*22	Kaaterskill High Peak	3655			Kaaterskill
23	Twin	3640	Tr		Bearsville and Hunter
24	Balsam Cap	3623	C		West Shokan
25	Fir	3620	C		Shandaken
26	North Dome	3610	C		Lexington
27	Balsam	3600	TrW		Shandaken
*28	Bearpen	3600			Prattsville
29	Eagle	3600	Tr		Seager
30	Indian Head	3573	Tr		Woodstock
31	Sherrill	3540	C		Lexington
32	Vly	3529	C		West Kill
33	Windham High Peak	3524	Tr		Hensonville
34	Halcott	3520	C		West Kill
35	Rocky	3508	C		West Shokan
36	Mill Brook Ridge	3480	Tr		Arena
37	Dry Brook Ridge	3460	Tr		Seager
38	Woodpecker Ridge	3460			Seager
39	Olderbark	3440			Bearsville
40	Roundtop	3440			Kaaterskill
41	Roundtop	3440			Prattsville
42	Huntersfield	3423	Tr		Ashland
*43	Belleayre	3420	Tr		Fleischmanns
+44	St. Anne's Peak	3420	Tr		Lexington
45	Stoppel Point	3420	Tr		Kaaterskill
+46	South Bearpen	3410			West Kill
+47	NE Halcott	3408			West Kill
48	Spruce	3380			Shandaken
49	Beaver Kill Range	3377			Claryville
50	South Vly	3360			West Kill
51	Pisgah	3345			Margaretville
+52	East Wildcat	3340			Peekamoose Mt.
+53	North Plattekill	3340			Hobart
54	Shultice	3280			Roxbury
55	South Plattekill	3260			Hobart
+*56	Winnisook Lake	3260			Shandaken
57	NW Moresville Range	3240			Roxbury
+*58	Willowemoc	3224	Tr		Willowemoc

+*59	Narrow Notch	3220			Roxbury
60	Onteora	3220			Hunter
61	Richmond	3220			Ashland
62	Utsayantha	3214	T		Stamford
+*63	High Falls Ridge	3211			Claryville
64	Van Wyck	3206			Peekamoose Mt.
65	Giant Ledge	3200	Tr		Shandaken
66	Burnt Knob	3180	Tr		Freehold
67	Mongaup	3177			Willowemoc
68	Cradle Rock Ridge	3160			Arena
69	West Wildcat	3160			Peekamoose Mt.
70	East Jewett Range	3140			Hunter
71	Overlook	3140	TrT		Woodstock
+72	Pine Island	3140			Lexington
73	White Man	3140			Roxbury
74	Acra Point	3100	Tr		Freehold
75	Barkaboom	3100			Arena
76	Cave	3100			Hensonville
77	Cowan	3100			Hobart
+78	Packsaddle	3100			Lexington
79	Plattekill	3100			Woodstock
+*80	Red Kill Ridge	3100			Fleischmanns
81	West Stoppel Point	3100			Kaaterskill
82	Rose	3090			West Kill
83	Ashokan High Point	3080	Tr		West Shokan
+*84	Sand Pond	3062			Willowemoc
85	Churchill	3060			Stamford
86	Irish	3060			Roxbury
87	Round Top	3060			Hobart
88	Denman	3053			Claryville
+*89	Montgomery Hollow	3040			Roxbury
+90	SW Moresville Range	3040			Roxbury
91	West Cave	3040			Ashland
92	Woodhull	3040			Peekamoose Mt.
+*93	Little Pisgah	3020			Margaretville
+94	Southeast Warren	3020			Hobart
95	Little Rocky	3015			West Shokan
+*96	Hubbell Hill	3000			Margaretville
*97	Old Clump	3000			Roxbury
+98	Silver Hollow	3000	Tr		Bearsville
+99	Hodge Pond	2985			Willowemoc
+100	East Gray Hill	2980			Roxbury
+101	Meeker Hollow	2980			Hobart
102	Red Hill	2980	TrT		Claryville

Appendix II **239**

*7   An old woods road leads to an unmarked, unmaintained path to its summit. (It is on private property and permission should be sought.)
*13 Formerly called Mink Mt.
*17 Formerly known as Balsam Roundtop.
*22 Summit is reached by the informal Twilight Park Trail from a snowmobile trail.
*28 From Ski Run Rd. near Prattsville, an old woods road runs to the E summit and a path off the woods road goes to the W summit. Bearpen was recently acquired by New York State.
*43 Summit is on NW end of mountain, not at old fire tower site.
*56 Located W of Winnisook Lake.
*58 E of Mongaup Mt. at headwaters of Willowemoc Creek.
*59 Located E of Narrow Notch.
*63 Located NW of High Falls.
*80 Also known as Butternut Mt.
*84 Located N of Sand Pond.
*89 Located S of Montgomery Hollow.
*93 Located SE of Pisgah.
*96 Located N of Hubbell Hill Hollow.
*97 Located NW of Roxbury; USGS gives another peak this name on Hobart Quadrangle.

Appendix III

State Campgrounds and Day-Use Areas in the Catskill Park

Public campgrounds have been established by the DEC at many attractive spots throughout the state. Listed below are those that might be useful as bases of operations for hiking in the Catskill Park. DEC publishes individual campground brochures and a complete list of all campgrounds is contained in a brochure of New York State Forest Preserve public campgrounds. These brochures are available from DEC, 625 Broadway, Albany, NY 12233, 518-457-2500, www.dec-campgrounds.com.

Beaver Kill. Off NY 17, 7 mi NW of Livingston Manor. (See Route Guide for Beaver Kill Rd.–Quaker Clearing.)

Mongaup Pond. Off NY 17, 3 mi N of DeBruce. (See Route Guide for Livingston Manor to Claryville.)

Kenneth L. Wilson Public Campground. Off NY 28 near Boiceville.

Woodland Valley. Woodland Valley Rd., off NY 28 near Phoenicia. (See Route Guide for Woodstock-Shandaken.)

Little Pond. Off NY 17, 14 mi NW of Livingston Manor. (See Route Guide for Beaver Kill Rd.–Quaker Clearing.)

Bear Spring Mountain. Off NY 206, 5 mi SE of Walton.

Devil's Tombstone. Off NY 214, 4 mi S of Hunter.

North-South Lake. Off NY 23A, 3 mi NE of Haines Falls. (See Route Guide for Palenville, North-South Lake.)

Belleayre Mountain Day-Use Area. Off NY 28, just SE of Pine Hill, Ulster County. Includes Pine Hill Lake, a six-acre man-made lake with a swimming area, fishing, and picnic facilities.

Day-Use Area. Off NY 28, 1 mi N of Boiceville, Ulster County (site of the future Catskill Interpretive Center). Includes two short interpretive foot trails and information kiosk.

About the Editors

Residents of central New York, Carol Stone White and David Scott White hike extensively in the Catskills, Adirondacks, New England, and the Finger Lakes region. They write hiking columns for the *Poughkeepsie Journal's* "My Valley" and the magazine *Catskill Mountain Region Guide*, and their articles have appeared in ADK's *Adirondac* magazine and the *Adirondack Explorer*. Carol edited *Catskill Peak Experiences* and *Adirondack Peak Experiences*, completing the trilogy in 2012 with *Peak Experiences: Danger, Death, and Daring in the Mountains of the Northeast*, published by University Press of New England.

In 1994, Carol and David became members of the winter Catskill 3500 Club, those who climb all thirty-five peaks exceeding 3500 feet. The Whites went on to become Winter Forty-Sixers in 1997, and Carol compiled *Women with Altitude*, which chronicles the lives and adventures of the first thirty-three women to climb the forty-six high peaks in winter; she was #20. The couple completed winter climbs of the forty-eight peaks over 4000 feet in the White Mountains, and have climbed eight of Colorado's 14,000-footers.

In addition to editing *Catskill Trails*, the Whites wrote *Catskill Day Hikes for All Seasons*, also published by the Adirondack Mountain Club. From 2001 to 2003, they hiked 350 miles, using a surveyor's wheel, to fine-tune trail measurements throughout the Catskill Forest Preserve. They also assisted in the production of the National Geographic Trails Illustrated Map #755, Catskill Park, coordinated with *Catskill Trails* and published in partnership with the Adirondack Mountain Club.

The Whites participate in trail maintenance, lead hikes, restore lean-tos, and have taught three four-week hiking classes. They have served in various volunteer leadership positions for ADK, the Adirondack Forty-Sixers, and the Catskill 3500 Club, for which David is today membership chair and Carol conservation committee chair. Carol received the Susan B. Anthony Legacy Award in 2007 with long-distance swimmer Lynne Cox and polar explorer Ann Bancroft.

Dave is former president of Clinton Computer Systems, and Carol former village trustee and chair of the Clinton Planning Board.

Join us!

30,000 members count on us, and so can you

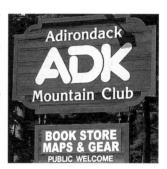

- We produce the most-trusted, com- prehensive trail maps and books
- Our outdoor activities take you all around the world
- Our advocacy team concentrates issues that affect the wild lands and waters important to our members and chapters throughout the state
- Our professional and volunteer crews construct and maintain trails
- Our wilderness lodges and information centers give you shelter and direction

Benefits of Membership include:

- Fun outdoor recreation opportunities for all levels
- *Adirondac* magazine (bimonthly)
- Special rates for ADK education and skill-building programs, lodging, parking, publications, and logo merchandise
- Rewarding volunteer opportunities
- Supporting ADK's mission and thereby ensuring protection of the wild lands and waters of New York State

Lodges and Campground

- Adirondak Loj, on the shores of Heart Lake, near Lake Placid, offers year-round accommodations in private and family rooms, a coed loft, and cabins. It is accessible by car, and parking is available.
- The Adirondak Loj Wilderness Campground, located on ADK's Heart Lake property, offers thirty-two campsites and sixteen Adirondack lean-tos.
- Johns Brook Lodge (JBL), located near Keene Valley, is a backcountry facility accessible only on foot and open on a seasonal basis. Facilities include coed bunkrooms or small family rooms. Cabins near JBL are available year-round. Both lodges offer home-cooked meals and trail lunches. Member discounts are available at all lodges and the campground. Visit us!

ADK centers in Lake George and on our Heart Lake property near Lake Placid offer ADK publications and other merchandise for sale, as well as backcountry and general Adirondack information, educational displays, outdoor equipment, and snacks.

ADK Publications

FOREST PRESERVE SERIES
1 Adirondack Mountain Club High Peaks Trails
2 Adirondack Mountain Club Eastern Trails
3 Adirondack Mountain Club Central Trails
4 Adirondack Mountain Club Western Trails
5 Adirondack Mountain Club Northville–Placid Trail
6 Adirondack Mountain Club Catskill Trails

OTHER TITLES
Adirondack Alpine Summits: An Ecological Field Guide
Adirondack Birding: 60 Great Places to Find Birds
Adirondack Canoe Waters: North Flow
Adirondack Mountain Club Canoe and Kayak Guide: East-Central New York State
Adirondack Mountain Club Canoe Guide to Western & Central New York State
Adirondack Paddling: 60 Great Flatwater Adventures
An Adirondack Sampler I: Day Hikes for All Seasons
Catskill Day Hikes for All Seasons
Forests and Trees of the Adirondack High Peaks Region
Kids on the Trail! Hiking with Children in the Adirondacks
No Place I'd Rather Be: Wit and Wisdom from Adirondack Lean-to Journals
Ski and Snowshoe Trails in the Adirondacks
The Adirondack Reader
The Catskill 67: A Hiker's Guide to the Catskill 100 Highest Peaks under 3500'
Views from on High: Fire Tower Trails in the Adirondacks and Catskills
Winterwise: A Backpacker's Guide

MAPS
Trails of the Adirondack High Peaks Region
Northville-Placid Trail
Trails Illustrated Map 742: Lake Placid/High Peaks
Trails Illustrated Map 743: Lake George/Great Sacandaga
Trails Illustrated Map 744: Northville/Raquette Lake
Trails Illustrated Map 745: Old Forge/Oswegatchie
Trails Illustrated Map 746: Saranac/Paul Smiths
Trails Illustrated Map 755: Catskill Park

ADIRONDACK MOUNTAIN CLUB CALENDAR

Price list available upon request, or see www.adk.org

INDEX

Note: Locations are indexed by proper name with Mount *or* Mountain *following.*

A

abbreviations and conventions, in guidebooks, 15
Acra Point, 28
 via Northern Escarpment Trail, N-S, 38–42
  via Acra Point/Burnt Knob Access Trail, 34
 via Northern Escarpment Trail, S-N, 42–43
  via Batavia Kill Trail, 34–35
Adirondack Mountain Club, 4, 11, 243–244. *See also* Forest Preserve Series guides
Alder Lake, 194, 196
 via Alder Lake Loop, 198–199
 to Big Pond, section of Touchmenot Trail, 199–200
Arkville to Seager Section, 177–191
 introduction, 177–179
 Balsam Lake Mt. Trail, 188–190
 Doubletop Mt. bushwhack, 183
 Dry Brook Ridge Trail, 183–186
 German Hollow Trail, 186–187
 Graham Mt. unmaintained trail, 183
 Huckleberry Loop Trail, 187–188
 Kelly Hollow Ski Trail, 190–191
 Mine Hollow Trail, 181
 Rider Hollow Trail, 180–181
 Seager Trail, 181–182
Artists Rock, 46
 via Escarpment Trail, 49–53, 55
Ashley Falls, 46
 via Mary's Glen Trail, 57–58
Ashokan High Point, 132
 via Ashokan High Point Trail, 137–138

B

Balsam Cap, 131
 Balsam Cap bushwhack, 135–136, 152

Balsam Lake Mt., 183, 185, 194
 Balsam Lake Mt. Trail, 188–190
  via Dry Brook Ridge Trail, 183–186
  via Mill Brook Ridge Trail, 196–198
Balsam Mt., 177
 Pine Hill–West Branch Trail, 160–162
  via McKinley Hollow Trail, 163–164
  via Mine Hollow Trail, 181
  via Rider Hollow Trail, 180–181
Batavia Kill Trail, 34–35
Bearpen Mt., 169, 171–172
bears
 bear canisters, 25, 26
 hunting season for, 24
 safety precautions, 25–26
beaver fever *(Giardia lamblia),* 24
Beaver Kill Ridge, 215
 Beaver Kill Ridge Trail, northern section, 219–220
 Beaver Kill Ridge Trail, southern section, 218–219
 Mongaup-Hardenburgh Trail, 222–223
Beaver Kill–Willowemoc Creek Section, 215–230
 introduction, 215–218
 Frick Pond Region, 225–230
 Long Pond–Beaver Kill Ridge Trail, northern section, 219–220
 Long Pond–Beaver Kill Ridge Trail, southern section, 218–219
 Mongaup-Hardenburgh Trail, 222–223
 Mongaup-Willowemoc Trail, 224
 Neversink-Hardenburgh Trail, 220–222
Becker Hollow Connector Trail, 98
Becker Hollow Trail, 97–98
Beech Mountain Nature Preserve, 215
Belleayre Mt.
 via Belleayre Mt. Trail, 162, 165–166
 via Belleayre Ridge Trail, 166–167

Belleayre Mt. continued
   via Cathedral Glen Trail, 167–168
   via Lost Clove Trail, 164
   via Pine Hill–West Branch Trail, 160–162
Belleayre Ridge Trail, 166–167
Belleayre Ski Area, 166–168, 177
Big Indian Mt.
   bushwhack, 163
   via Pine Hill–West Branch Trail, 160–162, 183
Big Indian–Pine Hill to Denning Section, 145–168
   introduction, 145–149
   Belleayre Mt. Trail (Pine Hill–West Branch Trail), 165–166
   Belleayre Ridge Trail, 166–167
   Big Indian Mt. bushwhack, 163
   Cathedral Glen Trail, 167–168
   Curtis-Ormsbee Trail, 155–156
   Fir Mt. bushwhack, 162–163
   Giant Ledge–Panther Mt. Trail, Southern Section, 158–160
   Lone Mt. bushwhack, 151–152
   Lost Clove Trail, 164
   McKinley Hollow Trail, 163–164
   Peekamoose-Table Trail (from Phoenicia–East Branch Trail), 150–151
   Phoenicia–East Branch Trail, 152–154
   Pine Hill–West Branch Trail (Biscuit Brook–Pine Hill Trail), 160–162
   Red Hill Trail, 149–150
   Rochester Hollow Trail, 165
   Rocky Mt. bushwhack, 152
   Slide-Cornell-Wittenberg Trail to Cornell, 156–158
   Winnisook Easement, 155
Big Pond to Beech Hill Rd. Section of Touchmenot Trail, 201–202
Big Rock Trail, 229–230
Biscuit Brook–Pine Hill Trail, 146, 160–162.
   See also Pine Hill–West Branch Trail
Black Dome Mt.
   via Black Dome Mt. Trail, 29, 31
   via Black Dome Range Trail, 31–32
Black Dome Valley–Northern Escarpment Section, 27–43
   introduction, 27–29, 30
   Acra Point/Burnt Knob Access Trail, 34
   Batavia Kill Trail, 34–35
   Black Dome Mt. Trail, 29, 31
   Black Dome Range Trail, 31–32
   Blackhead Mt. Spur Trail, 31
   Colgate Lake Trail to Dutcher Notch, 36–37
   Dutcher Notch Trail, 35
   Elm Ridge Trail, 33
   Northern Escarpment Trail, Dutcher Notch to NY 23, 42–43
   Northern Escarpment Trail, NY 23 to Dutcher Notch, 38–42
Blackhead Mt.
   via Blackhead Mt. Spur Trail, 31
   via Black Dome Mt. Trail, 29, 31
   via Northern Escarpment Trail, N-S, 38–42
   via Batavia Kill Trail, 34–35
   via Northern Escarpment Trail, S-N, 42–43
   via Colgate Lake Trail to Dutcher Notch, 36–37
   via Dutcher Notch Trail, 35
boat rental, at North-South Lake Public Campground, 49
Brock Mt., 208–210
Burnt Knob, 27
   via Acra Point/Burnt Knob Access Trail, 34
Burroughs, John, 12, 145, 169
   memorial at Rochester Hollow, 146, 165
   memorial plaque at Slide Mt., 122, 157
   Memorial State Historic Site, 174–175
   Woodchuck Lodge, 174–175
Burroughs Range, 115, 145, 146, 175
   Slide-Cornell-Wittenberg Trail to Cornell, 156–158
      via Curtis-Ormsbee Trail, 155–156
      via Phoenicia–East Branch Trail, 152–154
   Wittenberg-Cornell-Slide Trail to Cornell, 120–122

bushwhacks, 17–18
Buttermilk Falls
   in Kaaterskill High Peak area, 47, 50, 64–65
   in Peekamoose area, 131, 138

C

Cabot Mt.
   via Touchmenot Trail, 201–202
   via Campground Trail, 202
   via Little Pond Trail, 203
Camel's Hump, via Black Dome Range Trail, 31–32
Campbell Mt. Trail, 208–210
campfires
   Leave No Trace principles, 16
   regulations, 21
Campground Trail from Little Pond, 202
campgrounds, list of state campgrounds, 241
camping sites
   permit requirements, 21, 22
   regulations, 21
   wilderness camping, 20–21
   see also campgrounds *and* lean-tos
canisters
   bear resistant, 25, 26
   on trailless peaks, 18
Cathedral Glen Trail, 167–168
Catskill 100 Highest Peaks, 237–240
Catskill 3500 Club, 18, 108, 110–111, 169, 237
Catskill Center for Conservation and Development, 14, 67, 149, 169, 177
Catskill Mountain House site, 45, 46, 51, 55
Catskill Park, 7, 14
Catskills area, history of settlement of, 11–14
cellular phone cautions, 18
clothing
   insect-borne diseases and, 26
   for winter hiking, 19–20
Cole, Thomas, 13, 32, 45, 52
Colgate Lake, 36, 37
   Colgate Lake Trail to Dutcher Notch, 36–37

Colonel's Chair Trail, 101–102, 109–110
compass use, 15, 17, 18–19, 23
Cooper, James Fenimore, 45
Cornell Mt., 116
   via Slide-Cornell-Wittenberg Trail, 156–158
   via Curtis-Ormsbee Trail, 155–156
   via Phoenicia–East Branch Trail, 152–154
   via Wittenberg-Cornell-Slide Trail, 120–122
Coykendall Lodge remains, 194, 198
crampons, 19–20
Curtis, William, 153, 155
Curtis-Ormsbee Trail, 155–156

D

Daley Ridge Trail to Plateau Mt., 93–94
deer
   deer ticks and, 26
   hunting season for, 24
DEET, 26
Delaware Ridge Trail system, 193, 204, 224, 232
Delaware Wild Forest Section, 193–213
   introduction, 193–196
   Alder Lake Loop, 198–199
   Alder Lake to Big Pond Section of Touchmenot Trail, 199–200
   Big Pond to Beech Hill Rd. Section of Touchmenot Trail, 201–202
   Campbell Mt. Trail, 208–210
   Campground Trail from Little Pond Campground to Big Pond Jct., 202
   Huggins Lake Trail (unmaintained), 206
   Little Pond Trail, 203
   Little Spring Brook Trail, 210–211
   Mary Smith Hill Trail, 204–205
   Middle Mt. Trail, 204
   Mill Brook Ridge Trail, 196–198
   Mud Pond Trail, 213
   Pelnor Hollow Trail, 206–208
   Trout Pond Trail, 211–213
Denning–Woodland Valley Trail. *See* Phoenicia–East Branch Trail

Department of Environmental Conservation (DEC), of New York State, 14, 15, 18, 20, 21, 22, 23, 24
   emergency telephone numbers for, 23
Department of Environmental Protection (DEP), of New York City, 15
Devil's Path, 231–232
   Eastern Section, Indian Head to Plateau, 81–85
   Eastern Section, Plateau Mt. from NY 214, 89, 91–93
   West Kill Mt. Traverse, E-W, 105–106
   West Kill Mt. Traverse, W-E, 106–107
   Western Section, Diamond Notch Falls from NY 214, 94–96
Devil's Tombstone Campground, 87, 89, 95
Diamond Notch, 88
   via Diamond Notch Trail, 98–99
Diamond Notch Falls, 101
   via Devil's Path, West Kill Mt. Traverse, 106–107
   via Diamond Notch Trail, 98–99
   via Devil's Path from NY 214, 94–96
   from Spruceton Rd., 103, 105
distance and time, on trails, 19
Doubletop Mt. bushwhack, 183
drinking water safety, 24
Dry Brook Ridge Trail, 177, 179, 183–186, 234
Dutcher Notch
   via Colgate Lake Trail, 36–37
   via Dutcher Notch Trail, 35
   Escarpment Trail, Schutt Rd. to, 49–53, 55
   Northern Escarpment Trail, NY 23 to, 38–42
   Northern Escarpment Trail, Dutcher Notch to NY 23, 42–43

E

Eagle Mt.
   via Pine Hill–West Branch Trail, 160–162
      via McKinley Hollow Trail, 163–164
      via Rider Hollow Trail, 180–181
      via Seager Trail, 181–182

Eastern hemlock (*Tsuga canadensis*), 13
Echo Lake Trail, 76–77
   via Overlook Trail, 73–74, 76
Elm Ridge Trail, 33
emergencies
   cellular phone cautions, 18
   procedures and contacts, 23
   see also safety issues
Escarpment Trail, 232
   Dutcher Notch to NY 23, northern section, 42–43
   NY 23 to Dutcher Notch, northern section, 38–42
   Schutt Rd. to Dutcher Notch, 49–53, 55
Esopus Creek, 145
extended and challenging opportunities, 231–234
   Delaware Ridge Trail, 193, 224, 232
   Dry Brook Ridge Trail, 183–186, 234
   Escarpment Trail, 49–53, 55, 232
   Long Path, 64–65, 140–143, 233–234
   see also Devil's Path

F

falls. *See* waterfalls
Finger Lakes Trail, 232
Fir Mt. bushwhack, 160, 162–163
fire towers, 237
   Balsam Lake Mt., 188, 189, 194, 197
   Hunter Mt., 87, 96–97, 98, 102, 108–109
   Overlook Mt., 76, 115, 127, 128
   Red Hill, 146, 149–150
   Tremper Mt., 115, 124, 125, 237
Flynn Trail, 228–229
Forest Preserve
   creation of, 13–14
   regulations of, 21
Forest Preserve Series guides, 11
   abbreviations and conventions, 15
   guidebook basics, 14
   maps used, 15, 17
forest rangers, contacting of, 22

Frick Pond Region, 215, 225–230
  Big Rock Trail, 229–230
  Flynn Trail, 228–229
  Loggers Loop Trail, 230
  Quick Lake Trail, 225, 227–228
Friday Mt., 131
  bushwhack, 135–136
Friends Nature Trail.
  See Huckleberry Point Trail

G

German Hollow Trail, 186–187
Giant Ledge, 146
  via Giant Ledge–Panther Mt. Trail,
    Southern Section, 158–160
      via Phoenicia–East Branch Trail
        152–154
      via Woodland Valley Trail, 119–120
  via Fox Hollow–Panther Trail, 117, 119
Giardia lamblia (beaver fever), 24
Graham Mt., 185
  unmaintained trail to, 183
Great Wall of Manitou, 12, 45, 145
  and Mitchie Manitou (evil spirit), 12
group camping permits, 21, 22
Guyot, Arnold, 87, 110, 145, 162

H

Halcott Mt. bushwhack, 113
Harding Rd. Trail and Spur Trail, 63–64
Haynes Mt., Pine Hill–West Branch Trail
  to, 160–162
Hotel Kaaterskill, 45, 55, 58–59, 63
Huckleberry Loop Trail, 177, 179, 187–188
  via Dry Brook Ridge Trail, 183–186
Huckleberry Point Trail, 69, 72–73
  via Long Path to Kaaterskill High Peak,
    70–71
Hudson, Hendrick (Henry), 11
  ghost of crew members, in Irving story,
    60, 63
Hudson River School of landscape
  painting, 13, 32, 45, 52
Huggins Lake Trail (unmaintained), 206

Hunter Mt., 87, 88, 101, 102
  via Becker Hollow Trail, 97–98
  via Colonel's Chair Trail, 109–110
  via Hunter Mt. Trail, 96–97
  via Devil's Path, 94–96, 105–107
  via Spruceton Trail, 108–109
hunting seasons, 24, 25
  archery (bow) season, 24
  big game seasons, 24, 25
  muzzle-loading season, 24
  turkey season, 24

I

Indian Head Mt., 67, 69
  Devil's Path, Eastern Section, 81–85
    via Overlook Trail, 73–74, 76
    via Jimmy Dolan Notch Trail, 77
insect-borne diseases, 26
Irving, Washington, 13

J

Jimmy Dolan Notch
  Devil's Path, Eastern Section , 81–85
    via Jimmy Dolan Notch Trail, 77
Jockey Hill trails, 129
John Burroughs Memorial State Historic
  Site. *See* Burroughs, John

K

Kaaterskill Falls, 46, 59–60
  via Kaaterskill Falls Trail, 59–60
Kaaterskill High Peak, 69
  Long Path to, from Platte Clove, 71–72
  Long Path to Kaaterskill High Peak
    snowmobile trail, 64–65
  from Long Path via N, 70–71
Kanape Brook, 131, 137
Kelly Hollow, 177
Kelly Hollow Ski Trail, 190–191

L

Laurel House Hotel, 45, 55, 59
lean-tos
  availability and regulations, 20–22

Index **249**

lean-tos continued

Baldwin Memorial (Tremper Mt.), 124
Balsam Lake Mt., 189, 198
Batavia Kill, 34, 39, 43
Beaver Meadow (Mill Brook Ridge Trail), 196, 197
Belleayre Mt., 162, 166
Biscuit Brook, 160, 162
Bouton Memorial (Table Mt.), 140, 151
Campbell Mt., 209
Devil's Acre (Hunter Mt.), 96, 105
Devil's Kitchen (Overlook Trail), 67, 69, 74, 82, 93
Diamond Notch, 88, 96, 99
Dry Brook Ridge, 185
Echo Lake, 76
Elm Ridge, 39, 43
Fall Brook (Neversink-Hardenburgh Trail), 221
Fox Hollow, 117
Hirschland (Belleayre Mt.), 166
John Robb (Hunter Mt.), 108
Kelly Hollow, 177, 190
Long Pond, 219
McKinley Hollow, 161, 164
Mink Hollow, 80, 84, 91, 126
Pelnor Hollow, 206, 207
Quick Lake, 228
Rider Hollow, 180
Rochester Hollow, 146, 165
Shandaken (Seager Trail), 182
Terrace Mt., 123
Tremper Mt., 124, 125
Leave No Trace principles, 16
Lexington to Shandaken Section, 101–113
  introduction, 101–103, 104
  Colonel's Chair Trail, 109–110
  Devil's Path, E-W, 105–106
  Devil's Path, W-E, 106–107
  Diamond Notch Falls from Spruceton Rd., 103, 105
  Halcott Mt. bushwhack, 113
  North Dome Mt. bushwhack, 111–112
  Rusk Mt. bushwhack, 110
  Sherrill (Mt.) bushwhack, 112–113
  Southwest Hunter Mt. bushwhack, 110–111
  Spruceton Trail, 108–109
Little Pond, 194
Little Pond Trail, 203
Little Pond State Campground, 201, 202–203
  Campground Trail from Little Pond, 202
Little Pond Trail, 203
Little Spring Brook Trail, 194, 210–211
Loggers Loop Trail, 230
Lone Mt., 146
  bushwhack to, 151–152
Long Path, 233–234
  to Kaaterskill High Peak from Platte Clove, 71–72
  to Kaaterskill High Peak snowmobile trail from Palenville, 64–65
  Upper Cherrytown Rd. to Peekamoose Rd., 140–143
Long Pond–Beaver Kill Ridge Trail
  northern section, 219–220
  southern section, 218–219
Lost Clove Trail, 164
Lyme disease, 26

M

maps, 6, 15, 17
  compass skills and, 15, 17, 18–19, 23
  markers and signs, on trails, 18–19
Mary Smith Hill Trail, 204–205
Mary's Glen Trail, 57–58
McKinley Hollow Trail, 163–164
Middle Mt. Trail, 204
Mill Brook Ridge Trail, 196–198, 232
Milt's Lookout, 35, 53
Mine Hollow Trail, 181
Mink Hollow (Eastern Devil's Path)
  Devil's Path, Eastern Section, 81–85
  from Elka Park, 81
  from Lake Hill, 126
  from Roaring Kill trailhead, 79–80

Mink Hollow (Western Devil's Path)
Devil's Path, West Kill Mt. Traverse,
106–107
Mitchie Manitou (evil spirit), 12
Mongaup Mt., 215
via Mongaup-Hardenburgh Trail,
222–223
Mongaup-Willowemoc Trail, 224
Mongaup Pond Public Campground, 214,
222, 224
mosquitos, West Nile virus and, 26
Mud Pond Trail, 194, 213

N

National Geographic Trails Illustrated
maps, 6, 9, 15, 17
Neversink River, 145, 150, 152, 153, 220
Neversink-Hardenburgh Trail, 220–222
New York State Police, emergency
telephone numbers for, 23
New York–New Jersey Trail Conference, 149
Catskill Trails maps of, 6, 15, 17
North Dome Mt. bushwhack, 111–112
North Point, 46
Escarpment Trail, Schutt Rd. to Dutcher
Notch, 49–53, 55
Mary's Glen Trail, 57–58
Rock Shelter Trail, 58
Northern Escarpment Trail
Dutcher Notch to NY 23, 42–43
NY 23 to Dutcher Notch, 38–42
North-South Lake, 46
North-South Lake Loop, 56
North-South Lake Public Campground,
45–46, 49, 52, 54, 56, 232
Notch Inn Rd. Connector Trail, 94
Notch Lake, 85, 87, 88, 89, 105

O

Oliverea-Mapledale Trail, 161, 163, 180
Onteora Lake, 115, 128–129
Ormsbee, Allan, 153, 155
Otis Railroad Line, 55, 62

Overlook Mountain House, 115
ruins of, 76, 115, 127
Overlook Mt., 115
via Overlook Mt. Trail, 127–128
via Overlook Trail, 73–74, 76

P

Pakatakan Mt., 177, 183–186
Palenville, North-South Lake Section, 45–65
introduction, 45–49
Catskill Mountain House site, 55
Escarpment Trail, Schutt Rd. to Dutcher
Notch, 49–53, 55
Harding Rd. Trail and Spur Trail, 63–64
Kaaterskill Falls Trail, 59–60
Long Path to Kaaterskill High Peak
snowmobile trail from Palenville, 64–65
Mary's Glen Trail, 57–58
North-South Lake Loop, 56
Poet's Ledge Trail, 65
Rock Shelter Trail, 58
Schutt Rd. Trail, 58–59
Sleepy Hollow Horse Trail, 60–62
Panther Mt., 115, 116
Giant Ledge–Panther Mt. Trail, Southern
Section, 158–160
via Phoenecia–East Branch Trail
from CR 47, 153–154
via Woodland Valley Trail, 119–120
Panther Mt. Trail, 117, 119
Pecoy Notch
Devil's Path, Eastern Section, 81–85
via Pecoy Notch Trail, 77–78
Peekamoose Mt., 131, 132
via Peekamoose-Table Trail from
Peekamoose Rd., 138–140
via Peekamoose-Table Trail from
Phoenicia–East Branch Trail, 150–151
Peekamoose Section, 131–143
introduction, 131–133, 134
Ashokan High Point Trail, 137–138
Balsam Cap bushwhack, 135–136, 152
Friday Mt. bushwhack, 135–136
Long Path (Upper Cherrytown Rd. to
Peekamoose Rd.), 140–143

Index **251**

Peekamoose Section continued

  Peekamoose-Table Trail, 138–140
  Samuels Point bushwhack, 133, 135
Pelnor Hollow Trail, 194, 206–208
permits, for camping, 21, 22
Phoenicia–East Branch Trail, 152–154
  Woodland Valley Trail (segment of), 119–120
Phoenicia Trail to Tremper Mt., 123–124
Pine Hill–West Branch Trail, 146, 160–162, 165–166
Plateau Mt.
  Devil's Path, Eastern Section, 81–85
    via Mink Hollow from Elka Park, 81
    via Mink Hollow from Lake Hill, 126
    via Mink Hollow from Roaring Kill, 79–80
  Devil's Path from NY 214, 89, 91–93
    via Daley Ridge Trail, 88, 93–94
Platte Clove Preserve, 67, 74, 82
Platte Clove Section, 67–85
  introduction, 67–70
  Devil's Path, Eastern Section, 81–85
  Echo Lake Trail, 76–77
  Huckleberry Point Trail, 72–73
  Jimmy Dolan Notch Trail, 77
  Kaaterskill High Peak from Long Path via N, 70–71
  Long Path to Kaaterskill High Peak from Platte Clove, 71–72
  Mink Hollow Trail from Elka Park, 81
  Mink Hollow Trail, Northern Section, 79–80
  Overlook Trail, 73–74, 76
  Pecoy Notch Trail, 77–78
  Roaring Kill Connector Trail, 79
Plattekill Falls, 67
Plattekill Mt. (on Overlook Trail), 73–74, 76
Poet's Ledge Trail, 65
  via Long Path from Palenville, 70–71
Pople Hill, via Long Path, 140–143
"posted" signs, on private property, 19
Pratt, Zadock, 13, 169, 173–174

Pratt Rock Park, 169, 173–174
Prattsville, 173–174
Prattsville to Arkville Section, 169–175
  introduction, 169–171
  Bearpen Mt., 171–172
  John Burroughs Memorial State Historic Site and Woodchuck Lodge, 174–175
  Pratt Rock Park, 173–174
  Vly Mt. bushwhack, 172–173
private property, "posted" signs on, 19
Pulpit Rock, 82, 92

Q

quarries
  Codfish Point (Overlook Trail), 74
  Dibbles Quarry (Pecoy Notch Trail), 67, 77–78
Quick Lake Trail, 215, 225, 227–228

R

rabies, 26
Red Hill, 146
  Red Hill Trail, 149–150
reservoirs, 15
Rider Hollow, 177
  Rider Hollow Trail, 180–181
Rip Van Winkle (fictional character), 13, 45, 60, 63
Roaring Kill Connector Trail, 79
Rochester Hollow, 146
  Rochester Hollow Trail, 165
Rock Shelter Trail, 58
Rocky Mt., 146
  bushwhack, 150, 151, 152
Roundtop Mt. (Bearpen Mt. area), 171–172
Roundtop Mt. (Kaaterskill High Peak area),
  Kaaterskill High Peak from Long Path, 70–71
  Long Path to Kaaterskill High Peak snowmobile trail from Palenville, 64–65
  Long Path to Kaaterskill High Peak from Platte Clove, 71–72
Rusk Mt. bushwhack, 110

S

safety issues
  bears, 25–26
  cellular phone cautions, 18
  drinking water, 24
  emergency contacts and procedures, 23
  on extended trails, 231
  during hunting seasons, 24, 25
  insect-borne diseases, 26
  rabies, 26
  trailless peaks, 17–18
  when camping, 20–21
  in winter, 19–20, 23
Samuels Point bushwhack, 133, 135
Schutt Rd.
  Escarpment Trail, to Dutcher Notch, 49–53, 55
Schutt Rd. Trail, 58–59
Seager Trail, 181–182
Sherrill (Mt.) bushwhack, 112–113
signs and markers, on trails, 18–19, 20
Ski Run Rd. (Bearpen Mt.), 171–172
Sleepy Hollow Horse Trail, 60–62
Slide Mt., 116, 145, 146
  via Slide-Cornell-Wittenberg Trail, 156–158
  via Curtis-Ormsbee Trail, 155–156
  via Phoenicia–East Branch Trail, 152–154
  via Wittenberg-Cornell-Slide Trail, 120–122
snowshoeing
  equipment rentals, 109
  safety precautions, 20, 23
Southwest Hunter Mt. bushwhack, 103, 110–111
Spruceton Rd. to Diamond Notch Falls, 103, 105
Spruceton Trail (to Hunter Mt.), 108–109
St. Anne's Peak, 105–106, 106–107
Stony Clove, 87
Stony Clove Section, 87–99
  introduction, 87–89, 90
  Becker Hollow Trail and connector, 97–98
  Daley Ridge Trail to Plateau Mt., 93–94
  Devil's Path, Eastern Section, 89, 91–93
  Devil's Path, Western Section, 94–96
  Diamond Notch Trail, 98–99
  Hunter Mt. Trail, 96–97
  Notch Inn Rd. Connector Trail, 94
Stoppel Point, Escarpment Trail to, 49–53, 55
Sugarloaf Mt., 67, 69
  Devil's Path, Eastern Section, 81–85
  via Mink Hollow from Elka Park, 81
  via Mink Hollow from Lake Hill, 126
  via Mink Hollow from Roaring Kill, 79–80
  via Pecoy Notch from Roaring Kill, 77–78
SW Hunter Mt. bushwhack, 103, 105, 110–111

T

Table Mt., 131, 132, 146
  via Peekamoose-Table Trail from Peekamoose Rd., 138–140
  via Peekamoose-Table Trail from Phoenicia–East Branch Trail, 150–151
tanneries, 13, 169, 173–174
Terrace Mt. Trail, 122–123
Thomas Cole Mt., via Black Dome Range Trail, 31–32
ticks, Lyme disease and, 26
Touchmenot Mt., 194, 202–203
Touchmenot Trail
  Alder Lake to Big Pond Section of, 199–200
  Big Pond to Beech Hill Rd. Section of, 201–202
trailless peaks, 17–18
trails, generally
  day hiking and wilderness camping on, 20–21
  distance and time on, 19
  lean-tos on, 21–22
  signs and markers on, 18–19, 20
  trailless peaks, 17–18
  in winter, 19–20

Index **253**

Tremper Mt.
   via Phoenicia Trail, 115, 123–124
   via Warner Creek Trail, 125–126
   via Willow Trail, 124–125
Trout Pond Trail, 194, 211–213
Tsuga canadensis (Eastern hemlock), 13
Twilight Park Trail, 70–71
Twin Mt., 67, 69
   Devil's Path, Eastern Section, 81–85
   via Jimmy Dolan Notch Trail, 77
   via Pecoy Notch Trail, 77–78

U
unmaintained trails
   bushwhacks, 17–18
   Graham Mt., 183
   Huggins Lake Trail, 206
   Twilight Park Trail, 67, 70¬–71

V
Vernooy Falls, 132
   via Long Path, 140–143
Vly Mt. bushwhack, 172–173

W
Warner Creek Trail–Long Path, 125–126
waste disposal, 16, 21, 24
water, purifying for drinking, 24
waterfalls
   formation of, 12
   Ashley Falls, 46, 57–58
   Bastion Falls, 60
   Buttermilk Falls, in Kaaterskill High Peak area, 47, 50, 64–65
   Buttermilk Falls, in Peekamoose area, 131, 138
   on Colgate Lake Trail to Dutcher Notch, 37
   Diamond Notch Falls, 94, 103, 105, 107
   Kaaterskill Falls, 46, 59–60
   Kelly Hollow, 177
   Plattekill Falls, 67
   on Seager Trail, 182
   Vernooy Falls, 132, 140, 142
   Wildcat Falls, 64–65

West Kill Mt., 102
   West Kill Mt. Traverse, E-W, 105–106
   via Diamond Notch Falls from Spruceton Rd., 103, 104
   West Kill Mt. Traverse, W-E, 106–107
West Nile virus, 26
Wildcat Falls, 64–65
Willow Trail, 124–125
Willowemoc Wild Forest, 225
Windham High Peak, 27, 28
   Northern Escarpment Trail, N-S, 38–42
   via Elm Ridge Trail, 33
   Northern Escarpment Trail, S-N, 42–43
   via Acra Point/Burnt Knob Access Trail, 34
Winnisook Club, 153, 155
winter hiking cautions, 19–20, 23
Winterwise: A Backpacker's Guide (Dunn), 20, 23
Wittenberg Mt., 116
   via Wittenberg-Cornell-Slide Trail, 120–122
   via Slide-Cornell-Wittenberg Trail, 156–158
Woodchuck Lodge, 174–175
Woodland Valley State Campground, 116, 119–120, 122, 154, 158
Woodland Valley Trail to Giant Ledge–Panther Trail, 119–120
Woodstock-Shandaken Section, 115–129
   introduction, 115–117, 118
   Jockey Hill, 129
   Mink Hollow Trail, 126
   Onteora Lake, 128–129
   Overlook Mt. Trail, 127–128
   Panther Mt. Trail, 117, 119
   Phoenicia Trail to Tremper Mt., 123–124
   Terrace Mt. Trail, 122–123
   Warner Creek Trail–Long Path, 125–126
   Willow Trail, 124–125
   Wittenberg-Cornell-Slide Trail, 120–122
   Woodland Valley Trail to Giant Ledge–Panther Mt. Trail, 119–120

Notes: